"This book is electric! Hübner goes about [
with the skills available only to someone [
apologetics-oriented, take-no-prisoners, Calvinist-Piperian-Brownian
conservative evangelical subculture. Brilliant. Learned. Passionate.
Creative. Angry. Hopeful? Maybe. You must read it for yourself and find
out. I will be studying this book for a long time to come."

— DAVID GUSHEE
Past President, American Academy of Religion
Distinguished University Professor of Ethics, Mercer University
Author of **After Evangelicalism**

"This book is special: at once incendiary and charming, you are invited
into the world of Christian fundamentalism, in all of its glory and
complexities and traumatic realities. This world is a crazy place, filled
with all of the political zealotry, casual sex(ism), and apocalyptic young-
earth creationism one could desire. Hübner's story is a dynamic,
sobering testament to that reality. From the depths of his days as an
Internet apologist to his interdisciplinary career as a professor, we see
the impact of religious fundamentalism on heart, mind, and body. For
those who have walked through the valley of the shadow of fear, may
you be filled with curiosity and joy at the sight of another theologian on
the journey. From one sojourner to another, I am happy to commend to
you the work of my colleague and dear friend."

— NICHOLAS RUDOLPH QUIENT
Associate Pastor, The First Baptist Church of Redlands
Co-Host of the Sinnergists Podcast

"Many of Jamin's experiences mirror my own, and I am grateful we were
friends while surviving as faculty at evangelical "liberal arts colleges."
Reading this book has once again encouraged me, and given me a
hopeful way forward, as he always has as a friend. His theological
nuance and understanding highlights why evangelicalism is, in many
ways, so superficial, and it will encourage anyone that their own
deconstruction can lead to a stronger, more robust, and more inclusive
faith in God. I will be passing along his book to my friends who come to
me for help as they struggle with asking questions of who God really is."

— KRISTY WHALEY
PhD Theology (Candidate), University of Glasgow
Former Theology Faculty, Colorado Christian University

"I had the pleasure of taking classes from Dr. Hübner and doing my BA thesis under his mentorship. He played a key role in my own deconstruction experience, and I could not recommend a more suitable person to walk alongside. This book emulates much of his personality: funny, well thought-through, and sharp when needed. Highly recommended for questioning, conservative evangelicals—especially those who are tired of all the trite answers of lamestream apologetics."

— ROBERT WARD
Graduate Student, McMaster Divinity College

"If you're one of those members of Generation X, Y or God help you, a millennial, and find yourself navigating the chartless doldrums of the political and moral Bermuda Triangle, having become separated from the evangelical armada in Hurricane 2016 or any number of earlier existential tropical depressions, this book will help guide you home. Or, at the very least, it will make being lost at sea a little easier to take."

— NATHAN CARPENTER
UPS Driver, Malcontent

"This book is damnably dangerous. Pastors, parents and patriots of conservative evangelicalism should snatch this book from whatever naughty hands or liberal library it has found its way into and burn it along with Rachel Held Evans and the rest of these post-evangelical heretics. It has the potential to undue all the certainty, conformity and comfortableness that it has cultivated in the compost of American fundamentalist religion. So if your intention is to remain in evangelicalism and have your theology nicely pampered, coddled, and sheltered from a world of different ideas and possibilities, *do not under any circumstances read this book.* If, on the other hand, you maintain that it is *possible* for there to be some Christians out there that have a different take on things, and you are curious as to what their ideas are, then *Deconstructing Evangelicalism* might just open up a whole new world to you."

— JONNY BRAUCHLI
FedEx Driver, An Angel of Light

DECONSTRUCTING EVANGELICALISM

A LETTER TO A FRIEND
AND A PROFESSOR'S GUIDE TO
ESCAPING FUNDAMENTALIST CHRISTIANITY

JAMIN ANDREAS HÜBNER

Hills Publishing Group • Rapid City, South Dakota

Printed in the United States of America with chlorine-free, acid-free ink on 55# paper made from 30% post-consumer waste recycled material
Cover photo by Jamin Andreas Hübner, taken in Rapid City, South Dakota

ISBN-13: 978-0-9905943-6-9
ISBN-10: 0-9905943-6-X

Typeset in Palatino Linotype, inspired by Giambattista Palatino (1515-1575), designed by Hermann Zapf (1918-2015) and originally produced by the Stempel foundry (1895-1986) in Frankfurt, Germany.

Reprinted with Permission: Jamin Andreas Hübner, review of John Piper, *A Peculiar Kind of Glory: How the Christian Scriptures Reveal Their Complete Truthfulness* (Wheaton: Crossway, 2016) for *The Canadian American Theological Review* 5:1 (2016):91-95.

BISAC Subject Headings:
    REL012000 RELIGION / Christian Living / General
    REL078000 RELIGION / Fundamentalism

About the Author

Dr. Jamin Andreas Hübner (BA Theology; MA Religion; MS Applied Economics; ThD Systematic Theology) is a professor of economics at Western Dakota Technical Institute, the University of the People, and a Research Fellow for the Center of Faith and Human Flourishing at LCC International University (Klaipėda, Lithuania). He formerly served as an Associate Professor of Christian Studies, Dean, and Director of Institutional Effectiveness at John Witherspoon College. Hübner's writing and research has been published by Wiley-Blackwell, Palgrave MacMillan, University of Toronto Press, the American Academy of Religion, Eisenbrauns, and other scholarly venues. He has also served on the Executive Board of the Canadian American Theological Association, on the regional program committee for the Society of Biblical Literature and the American Academy of Religion, and as a referee and editor for several academic journals. He and his wife Jessica run several small businesses in the Black Hills of South Dakota with their two rescue dogs, Shosta and ζωή, and two tarantulas, Qoheleth and Hevel.

CONTENTS

APPENDICES

For the people of Rojava,

To the hundreds who fell,
The thousands of children who now mourn,
The hundreds of thousands who now wander without homes,
This month of October, 2019.
For too long you've bore the ultimate price under the great and false
gods of our species: Power, Greed, and Religious Authoritarianism.

https://www.facebook.com/30
9517367730/posts/10157083606
877731/

ACKNOWLEDGEMENTS

"You need to publish this."

"I know it's personal, but have you ever considered maybe publishing this?"

"Can I send this to a couple of my relatives? Say, you could even publish this…"

I would like to blame this book on my friends. (You know who you are.) As a person with an overcommitment problem, I've learned how to say "no"—especially to popular projects that "my people" (grumpy arrogant professors) might look down upon. But, fine, you win this one.

Special thanks to Ruth Ryder, an intellectual colleague who somehow finds time to both proofread and offer constructive criticism of my unorthodox writing projects. But being an unorthodox orthodox heterodox Christian herself makes it all the more fun. Anyway, I take responsibility for any errors in the book.

Special thanks also to Jessica who somehow manages to tolerate intolerable hours of her friend, roommate, and husband typing out endless sentences that no one actually reads. "Our lot in life." (And thanks for reading through the manuscript last-minute—which came at the fair price of one pumpkin pie by 6pm that evening.)

JAH
Rapid City, South Dakota
Reformation Day, 2019

ORIENTATION

This book is divided into three parts.

The first part, "Scaffolding," attempts to sketch out the mechanics of "evangelical deconstruction." It tries to explain the hows and whats behind the increasing numbers of post-evangelicals of the conservative, American variety. While not exactly a "fun" discussion, it seeks to be acutely honest and forthright about the experience and facts of the situation. I also explain my particular role in this larger movement.

The second part, "A Letter to a Friend," is the centerpiece of the book, which is a personal, autobiographical account of my de- and re-construction experience in the form of a letter sent to my friend "Hans."

The third part consists of appendices—reference material aimed at re-orienting those who are skeptical and those who aren't sure where to go next in re-building their intellectual and spiritual lives as Christians. Much of my published work involves criticism, but I think it is unfair and unhelpful to point people away from something without also pointing them *towards* something better, positive, and hopeful.[1] I include a number of academic resources from my own teaching career since they were included in the original letter to Hans and have proven useful to other audiences in a similar context. As appendices, the bulk of this material are "extras." But for some, they will fill-in important details that may have remained undiscovered. (I wish someone did this for me years ago.)

---

[1] But if you really want to get depressed, see Chrissy Stroop and Lauren O'Neal, eds., *Empty the Pews: Stories of Leaving the Church* (Indianapolis: Epiphany Publishing, 2019).

SCAFFOLDING

The times, they are a-changin.
— BOB DYLAN

6,500 people who identify as "Christian" stop identifying as such every 24 hours. Over 3,000 churches close their doors every year. The largest and fastest growing religious group in the United States is "non-religious."[1] The bulk of this whole movement is in North America, and it mainly applies to the two dominant strands of institutional Christianity—Roman Catholicism and conservative evangelicalism.[2] A recent article for the *Washington Post* noted that "About 26 percent of Americans 65 and older identify as white evangelical Protestants. Among those ages 18 to 29, the figure is 8 percent…evangelical leaders are tidying up the kitchen while the house burns down around them."[3] Wheaton College, or "evangelical Harvard," is having to hunt for students for the first time in decades.[4]

There is now a trove of collected data that specifically explain why all of this is happening.[5] I'm not here to review that topic, much less

---

[1] See Charles Farhadian, *Introducing World Religions: A Christian Engagement* (Grand Rapids: Baker Academic, 2015); David Crary, "Poll: Church membership in US plummets over past 20 years," *Associated Press* (April 18, 2019); Thomas Rainer, "Hope For Dying Churches," *Facts and Trends* (January 16, 2018).

[2] This shift is part of a larger social, blues composition themed "The end of the West." I groove to some parts of it, but not many—especially since there are other songs playing in other rooms with more hopeful melodies.

[3] Michael Gerson, "Why White Evangelicals Should Panic," *The Washington Post* (September 2, 2019).

[4] Not long ago Wheaton's acceptance rate was around 50%. It currently stands at 85%.

[5] Surveys of the "nones" plainly identify the three main reasons: "I question a lot of religious teachings," "I don't like religious organizations," and "I don't like the positions churches take on social/political issues." Becka Alper, "Why America's 'Nones' Don't Identify With a Religion," *Pew Research* (August 8, 2018). Cf. Valerie Tarico, "Right-wing evangelicals are driving Americans to atheism using these 8 simple techniques." *Rawstory*

sound the alarms.[6] I'm here to offer my own (partial) account of leaving conservative evangelicalism[7] in hopes of (a) providing shared discourse, encouragement, and signposts for those who have undergone similar experiences and religious trauma, and (b) unfolding some of the inner mechanics of "deconstruction" from the trenches of academia.[8]

Because of these statistical realities, it is no surprise that this kind of book is now extremely common. It's merely the latest in the subgenre alongside Diana Butler Bass's *Strength for the Journey: A Pilgrimage of Faith in Community*, Rachel Held Evans's *Faith Unraveled: How a Girl Who Knew All the Answers Learned to Ask Questions*, David Gushee's *Still Christian: Following Jesus Out of Evangelicalism*, Nadia Bolz-Weber's *Pastrix*, Lyz Lenz's *God Land: A Story of Faith, and Renewal in Middle America*,[9] and the many writings of other renowned post-conservative[10] Christians like Stanley Grenz, Sarah Bessey, Peter Enns, Rob Bell, Jen Hatmaker, Marcus Borg, Philip Clayton, Lauren Winner, Dianne Anderson, Jonathan Merritt, Keith Giles, et al.[11] In that sense, my story is anything but new.

(April 29, 2019).

[6] I don't necessarily see these shifts as "bad" or "alarming," at least any more than any other socio-religious shift. And in some sense, there is much dead wood needing to be burned.

[7] There's no single, strict definition of "conservative evangelicalism." Although unwieldy, this book's title would have been more accurate as "Deconstructing American Conservative Evangelicalism." I use "American evangelicalism" synonymously with "conservative evangelicalism," "evangelical fundamentalism," and "fundamentalist evangelicalism." I realize there are potentially further delineations between "conservative evangelicalism" and "neoevangelicalism," but they are generally insignificant for the purposes of this work.

[8] Thirdly, my apologetics podcast and blog fans from over a decade ago are wondering what on earth happened to me. (Though, I don't think this book will make them happy…)

[9] Cf. similar faith journeys, but with somewhat different endings, like Austin Fischer, *Faith in the Shadows* (Downers Grove: InterVarsity Press, 2018); Barbara Brown Taylor, *Leaving Church: A Memoir of Faith* (New York: HarperOne, 2006); Chrissy Stroop and Lauren O'Neal, eds., *Empty the Pews: Stories of Leaving the Church* (Indianapolis: Epiphany Publishing, 2019); Deirdre Sugiuchi, *Unreformed* (forthcoming).

[10] "Post-conservative" here is a supercategory of "post-evangelical," because it also includes mainline Protestants (Episcopalians, Lutherans, etc.) who usually aren't associated with the "evangelical" label.

[11] At a conference on evangelicalism at Northeastern Seminary a few years ago, I asked my colleague Richard Mouw (the keynote speaker) during a Q&A session about a "post-evangelical" identifier. He apparently hated it so much he spent the next year writing a book defending the label "evangelical" (see *Restless Faith: Holding Evangelical Beliefs in a World of Contested Labels* [Grand Rapids: Brazos Press, 2019]. Cf. Mark Labberton, ed., *Still*

In fact, it's basically a biographical blend of Gushee, Enns, and Evans. My conscious commitment to both (a) the life and teachings of Christ, and (b) to sound scholarship, resulted in (among other things) my termination as an Associate Professor of Christian Studies at a conservative evangelical college, and my abandoning of that identity entirely.

Like Gushee, I was pressured by forces emerging from the largest Protestant denomination in the U.S. (Southern Baptist Convention) about my published views of gender.[12] In fall of 2018, just after being promoted to Chief Academic Officer, the College President (the former President of Criswell College and Dean of Chapel at Union University) walked me into his office. He expressed dismay at my publications affirming women in ministry (and at the "tone" of those publications that critiqued female subordinationist views), and then said that it was my last semester.[13] Like Enns, I was in "confessional Reformed" circles (e.g., an alum of Dordt University and Reformed Theological Seminary) and pushed out because of my views on the literary and historic origins of the Bible. I regularly taught "Introduction to the Bible," where I presented a variety of academic perspectives just as any good professor at a liberal arts college would do. But this wasn't up to some students' expectations, so I underwent a number of doctrinal interrogations on inerrancy carried out by the college President.[14] Finally, like Evans, I was

---

Evangelical?: Insiders Reconsider Political, Social, and Theological Meaning [Downers Grove: IVP, 2018]). While I sympathize with some of his concerns, I'm not sure how important an "evangelical" identity is for either Kingdom work (i.e., redemptive transformation) or the survival of Christian faith in North America. In any case, a summary of more reasonable evangelicalisms can be found in John Stackhouse Jr., "Evangelical Theology Should be Evangelical," ed. John Stackhouse Jr., *Evangelical Futures* (Grand Rapids: Baker, 2000), 40-41. I also remain on the Executive Board of the Canadian-American Theological Association, the only ecumenical, Christian theological academic society in North America, and has a "broadly evangelical" orientation.

[12] I realize for Gushee it was largely the "gay issue" and not as much women in ministry. In any case, these publications are (partially) listed in Appendix A.

[13] Admittingly, my doctoral dissertation was entitled "A New Case for Female Elders: An Analytical Reformed-Evangelical Approach" (2014). This didn't exactly keep me off the radar of the doctrine police! (I should also note that the unofficial reason for my termination was whistle-blowing the board about an impending financial crisis and failed capital campaign that left the college without a campus. But that's another book for another time.)

entrenched in young earth creationism and the popular apologetic movement of the 1980s-2000s.[15] Eventually, I just couldn't reconcile all the internal incoherencies, hypocrisies, and high-school level arguments.

Having come into this world in 1987, I'm also writing as one of those godless millennials that are taking over the planet by storm. I haven't the slightest clue why anyone would use fabric softener, want to "flip through the channels," or try to dignify American politics. I don't usually have a beard—though I do wear skinny jeans and enjoy a good local craft beer.[16] What difference this makes is something only you can decide.

More importantly, this book centers around a letter I wrote to a friend this past year (which I'll talk about more in a minute). This unique format should make for a more interesting read.[17]

This book will hit home for the "young, restless, and reformed," or graduates of Southern Baptist Theological Seminary, Liberty University, Westminster Seminary, or similar schools. Most of all, it will speak to those who have been part of the American-evangelical-industrial-complex of Wayne Grudem's *Systematic Theology*, John Piper/Desiring God Ministries, John MacArthur/Grace to You Ministries, The Gospel Coalition, Acts 29 Network, Sovereign Grace Ministries, the countless one-man show "apologetics ministries," Founders Ministries, Focus on the Family, Lifeway Christian Resources and Crossway publishers, denominations like the SBC, EFCA, and PCA, the "faith-family-freedom-guns-n-hawtdawgs-Trump-2020" spirit, and even obscure topics like N. T. Wright and "the New Perspective heresy." Whatever your story or situation, hopefully you'll find something worth thinking about in the pages ahead.

---

[14] I find it ironic that institutions in America worried about religious persecution and discrimination are frequently those most skilled at performing it.

[15] The main figures here were Francis Schaeffer, Josh McDowell, David Noebel, and Chuck Colson, and later Frank Turek, Norman Geisler, Ravi Zacharias, Lee Strobel, J. P. Moreland, Greg Koukl, Nancy Pearcey, et al. Kent Hovind (Creation Science Evangelism) and Ken Ham (Answers in Genesis) were the main figures in YEC. Today Jason Lisle (Creation Ministries International) and some in the Intelligent Design movement are carrying that torch.

[16] In my case, those excellent local breweries are Hay Camp and Lost Cabin.

[17] Cf. Greg Boyd's *Letters from a Skeptic* (Colorado Springs: David C. Cook, 2008, orig. 1994).

ON "DECONSTRUCTION"

So what's up with this word "deconstruction"? Why is it in this book's title, and what does it really mean?

The phenomenon of "deconstruction"—a term usually (originally?) employed in 20th century philosophy for post-modern literary analysis[18]— is now more or less synonymous with intellectual, spiritual, and social change after modernity. The term has gained considerable currency amongst post/non-evangelical groups dedicated to it—such as The Deconstructionists and The Liturgists,[19] as well as among social media venues of "progressive Christianity" and "progressive evangelicalism," Christian mysticism,[20] and popular podcasts like *The Bible For Normal People*.[21] The reason for this connection between "deconstruction" and post-evangelicals is possibly due to the fact that "Bible-believing Christians" have always been "in the world of the text" (as "people of the book"), and that is the area of human experience in which philosophical and literary deconstruction was originally focused.[22]

---

[18] The seminal work here is Jacques Derrida, *Of Grammatology*, trans. Gayatri Chakravorty Spivak (Baltimore: John Hopkins University Press, 2016, orig. 1967). David W. Odell-Scott, "Deconstruction," in *The Handbook of Postmodern Biblical Interpretation*, ed. A. K. M. Adam (St. Louis: Chalic Press, 2000), 55, remarks that deconstruction is "an un-con-structuring, un-doing, de-composing, un-settling, de-stabilizing. Components and their relations are put into a play that is not an obliteration." For a concise and honest introduction to "postmodern" thought (by a Christian no less), it is still hard to beat the clarity and conciseness of Stanley Grenz, *A Primer on Postmodernism* (Grand Rapids: Eerdmans, 1996), and more effectively, in conjunction with Joseph Natoli and Linda Hutcheon, eds. *A Postmodern Reader* (Albany: State of University New York Press, 1993). Cf. Carl Raschke, *Postmodern Theology* (Eugene: Cascade, 2017) and *The Coming Reformation: Why Evangelicals Must Embrace Postmodernity* (Grand Rapids: Baker Academic, 2004).

[19] A podcast and community born out of the experience of Michael Gungor (a former evangelical musical artist) and his friends (www.theliturgists.com).

[20] E.g., Richard Rohr's Center for Action and Contemplation, and various projects exploring the intersection of Medieval Christian or eastern thought and Christianity (e.g., theosophy, the perennial tradition, etc.)

[21] Cf. *The Robcast* and *Exvangelical Podcast*.

[22] "Because at its functional level all language is a system of differences, says Derrida, all language, even when spoken, is writing, and this truth is suppressed when meaning is taken as an origin, present and complete unto itself. Texts that take meaning or being as their theme are therefore particularly susceptible to deconstruction, as are all other texts insofar as they are conjoined with these. For Derrida, written marks or signifiers do not

Words accomplish amazing things—whether building, destroying, or just changing history. Regardless, in this new religious context, deconstruction simply refers to the process of questioning one's own beliefs (that were once considered unquestionable) due to new experiences, reading widely, engaging in conversations with "the other,"[23] and interacting in a world that is now more connected and exposed to religious diversity than ever before.[24]

From a traditional perspective, of course, this is all just a nice way of talking about "people who are committing apostasy." To completely rethink one's faith is to commit the sin of doubt and play with the fires of hell and heresy.[25] The faith experience of your Sunday school days should generally be same faith experience of your retirement days. If there are any major shifts in this period between cradle and grave, they don't indicate growing up; they indicate instability, or "falling away."

Whether or not the term "deconstruction" is being used in a "philosophically-correct" manner, it remains appropriate over "destruction" because it highlights the *constructed* (i.e., contingent, impermanent) nature of reality—or at least what we think we know of it. Our ideas, metaphors, language, customs, and ethical rules are constructed elements of life that can be modified, remodeled, or abandoned as much as a physical house. Humans are capable of reshaping our world in any number of ways. This late-modern/post-

---

arrange themselves within natural limits, but form chains of signification that radiate in all directions. As Derrida famously remarks, 'there is no outside-text' (Derrida 1974 [1967], 158), that is, the text includes the difference between any 'inside' or 'outside.'" Gary Aylesworth, "Postmodernism," *The Stanford Encyclopedia of Philosophy* (Spring 2015 Edition), Edward N. Zalta (ed.). https://plato.stanford.edu/archives/spr2015/entries/postmodernism.

[23] I.e., marginalized groups and/or "outsiders."

[24] Note, for example, Tyler Huckabee, "How to Deconstruct Your Faith Without Losing It: Sarah Bessey, Mike McHargue and Father Richard Rohr on why real faith begins with doubt," *Relevant Magazine* (October, 2017). The theme of doubt and uncertainty has played no little role in this discussion. See, for instance, Peter Enns, *The Sin of Certainty* (New York: HarperOne, 2016); Gregory Boyd, *The Benefit of the Doubt: Breaking the Idol of Certainty* (Grand Rapids: Baker Books, 2013); Sarah Bessey, *Out of Sorts: Making Peace with an Evolving Faith* (New York: Howard Books, 2015); Daniel Taylor, *The Myth of Certainty* (Downers Grove: InterVarsity Press, 1999); William James, *The Varieties of Religious Experience* (New York: Oxford University Press, 2012), 256.

[25] Note that "heresy" comes from Greek αἱρετίζω, to "choose" or "decide for oneself."

modern[26] perspective contrasts to the creation myth/epic of classical western theism, which is primarily ruled by God's unchanging nature and laws; humans exist to re-enforce those laws upon all who fail to worship the one true King. Human history is told not as constructing conduits for meaning or even searching for God, but as a story of hopeless rebellion against what has been uniquely revealed. As such, the permanent, decreed ideas of conservative evangelicalism and western intellectual thought should not (or *can't* be) "messed with." To do so invites demons to the door.

This "can't be messed with" attitude has become a particular site of deconstructive transformation. For example, one hears evangelicals say a married lesbian couple "aren't actually married," or "a woman's preaching isn't real preaching," or "biblical scholars who don't believe the Bible is the Word of God aren't doing real scholarship," or "Kelly isn't a 'real man' because of y and z." But, in the view of post-conservatives and those deconstructing, the existence and daily experience of such persons suggests otherwise. If we can't trust what our eyes are seeing and ears are hearing, what can we trust? (Who's the relativist now?) This line of thinking raises the question as to who has the right to define what is "real," and what that even means. The perfect marriage, the perfect Bible, the perfect family, the perfect politic, the perfect church, the perfect "gender role," is something we don't have; what *we have* is what we have. Why is that not "real"? (And this focus on achieving God's "perfect design" seems a lot more Greek than Hebrew or Christian in the first place.)[27] Furthermore, this "can't be messed with" attitude seems to neglect the reality of constant cultural and evolutionary

---

[26] Anthony Giddens, *The Consequences of Modernity* (Stanford: Stanford University Press, 1990) argues that we are not yet really in a "post-modern" world.

[27] Cf. Brian McLaren, *A New Kind of Christianity* (New York: HarperOne, 2010), 41-42: "...the Greco-Roman mind transforms the Garden of Eden from its original earthy stuff into a transcendent Platonic ideal. It is no longer a *good* Jewish garden; it is a *perfect* Platonic, Greco-Roman garden. In this Platonic Garden, nothing ever changes, because in perfection change can only mean for the worst. This changelessness means that the Platonic Eden is a *state*, not a *story*....Every time we use terms like 'the Fall' and 'original sin,' I believe, many of us are unknowingly importing more or less of this package of Greco-Roman, non-Jewish, and therefore nonbiblical concepts like smugglers bringing foreign currency into the biblical economy..."

change. (Especially for the Christian: cannot the "unclean" be made "clean"? And isn't such movement and innovation "good news"?) In short, traditional and conservative Christians look at what's happening in the world and keep saying "you can't do that; God said..." while the rest of world keeps saying "we already are doing it; you're not the only ones listening to God..."

Many leave all forms of religious expression and identity after deconstruction,[28] while many others do not. Some describe their story like an unexpected home remodel, while others use less welcoming metaphors like war, escape, or abuse. Indeed, new knowledge of abuse within the (un)holy confines of evangelical establishments (e.g., #metoo), along with the fall of major leaders[29] and failed ideologies,[30] have further catalyzed evangelical deconstruction in the 21st century.

Evangelical apologetics and other standard preventive measures have also compounded the problem. Sociologists concur that the problem is, indeed, from the *inside*:

> Bradley Wright *et al.* (2011) also recently report from a study of the online narratives of 50 former Christians that 85% of their respondents named interactions with other Christians and disintegrated social bonds as highly significant bonds in their deconversion. It was not those *outside* the church that helped bring about their deconversion, but those

---

[28] These cases—such as Joshua Harris (author of *I Kissed Dating Goodbye*), Marty Sampson (writer for Hillsong and Delirious) and others who now identify as atheist or agnostic, are habitually scapegoated by conservative evangelicals as ammunition/proof for their own cause, as opposed to being a reason to question it. They imagine that such defectors "were never real evangelical Christians," despite all the evidence to the contrary. It is extremely difficult to question the "invisible/visible church" dogma of Protestantism, and generally break out of the "told you so" echo-chamber. See the "Death Spiral" graphic below.

[29] E.g., Mark Driscoll (Mars Hill), Paige Patterson (SWBTS), Bill Hybels (Willow Creek), Bill Gothard (Institute in Basic Life Principles), Doug Philips (Quiverful Patriarch), Perry Noble (NewSpring), Andy Savage (HighPoint Church), Tullian Tchividjian (New City Church), C. J. Mahaney (Sovereign Grace Church), James MacDonald (Harvest Bible Chapel), John Crist (comedian), et. al.

[30] E.g., "inerrancy of the autographs," purity culture, and "complementarianism," where (for example) John Piper advised during a Q&A interview that wives should endure abuse from their husbands "for a season." (The video was pulled by Desiring God Ministries, but remains available on the internet). Or, where Wayne Grudem re-wrote the historic doctrine of the Trinity to support female subordinationism.

inside. In other words, the push factors from church interactions were more significant than the pull factors from outsiders. This finding has also been explored by Robert Marriott (2015) who found that being hurt by other Christians played a major contributing role in the deconversion of his research participants.[31]

A recent study also showed "that students at CCCU schools are more likely to face a religious crisis than their secular counterparts."[32] This is the polar opposite of what the evangelical establishment has always asserted about Christian education. Christians are supposed to question their faith at *secular* universities, not at Christian colleges.

This research presents what business researchers call "disruptive innovation" and "the innovator's dilemma."[33] The same means that made the established institution or firm successful are what is now causing it to fail (thereby opening up a vulnerability that can be exploited by disruptive innovators).[34] Whether that's weekly church services, pulpits and expository sermons, altar-calls, popcorn prayers, weekly Bible studies, apologetics debate clubs, or whatever, these *were* the means of success, but are now the reason for failure. "Established firms have a good thing going and see little reason to jeopardize it," and they "assume that they already have the knowledge and expertise about what will work and need only apply it in new situations."[35]

This accurately describes the attitudes within American evangelicalism. The answers to problems (e.g., celebrities bailing, low enrollment, mass abuse and coverups, etc.) are the always same: do what should have worked before. Circle the wagons. That is what it *means* to "conserve." And when that (predictably) doesn't work yet again, the

---

[31] Josie McSkimming, *Leaving Christian Fundamentalism and the Reconstruction of Identity* (New York: Routledge, 2017), 32.

[32] Daniel Silliman, "Lose Your Faith at an Evangelical College? That's Part of the Process," *Christianity Today* (August 30, 2019).

[33] Clayton Christensen, *The Innovator's Dilemma* (New York: HarperBusiness, 1997).

[34] See Jamin Hübner, "Obstacles to Change: Overcoming the Hurdles of the State Apparatus in Higher Education," *The Journal of Religious Leadership* 15:1 (2017):16-56, at 26-27.

[35] Ibid., quoting Dwight Zscheile, "Disruptive Innovations and the Deinstitutionalization of Religion," *The Journal of Religious Leadership* 14:2 (2015):16-56, at 5.

leadership does something worse: it *increases the intensity* of these same strategies. This only amplifies the damage coming from the self-destructive cycle.

Evangelicals Defect

"Church sucks."
"Your arguments suck."
"You're not actually loving
  people."

Evangelicalism is Vindicated by Defection

"That's what happens when
  you don't go to our church
  and don't speak the truth..."
"That's what happens when
  you read *other* scholars..."
"That's what happens when
  you love *everyone*..."

The Death Spiral of Conservative Evangelicalism

Such Galvinizations Cause More Evangelicals to Defect

"But you're not *listening*..."
"But no one buys your
  arguments but *yourselves*..."
"But your *actions* don't
  correspond to your
  teachings..."

Evangelicals Galvanized in Their Rightness

"Our church *is* awesome..."
"We have *great* arguments..."
"We *do* love people..."

Recent Examples of the Evangelical Vindication and Galvanization Phase from the Evangelical-Industrial-Complex		
Source	Sample (Construction)	Subtext (Deconstruction)
Joe Carter, *The Gospel Coalition* (August 24, 2019)	"American churches don't just have a deficit of men—they have a shortage of unmarried young men. This trend makes it harder for young women to find mates who are spiritually compatible."	*God commands everyone to procreate and make more people (and make more evangelical Christians); these stats should spur us to enforce traditional values even more than before.*
Greg Morse, *Desiring God Ministries* (February 5, 2019)	"Play the Man You Are": "…effeminacy falls under the category of *abomination* and, if not repented of, threatens entrance into eternal life….Am I questioning wearing floral shirts and tight jeans? Perhaps."	*Failing to live up to evangelical gender roles—as virtually everyone today now does—may put you on the path to eternal damnation.* *We know what it really means to be a man or a woman.*
Brett McCracken and Becket Cook, *The Gospel Coalition* (August 23, 2019)	"From Gay to Gospel": McCracken: "Is there a way to reconcile following Jesus with having a gay identity?" Cook: "They are irreconcilable."	*It is morally wrong to identify as non-heterosexual and Christian.*
The Statement on Social Justice and the Gospel (MacArthur et al.) (September 4, 2018)	"We reject 'gay Christian' as a legitimate biblical category."	*Christianity isn't for non-heterosexuals.* *Non-heterosexuals are a mistake.*
Rosaria Butterfield, Twitter (October, 2019)	"Gay Christianity is a different religion. I'm not standing in the same forest with Greg Johnson and Wes Hill and Nate Collins looking at different angles of the trees, I'm in a different forest altogether."	*Get back in the closet or get out of the church.*
Mark Galli, *Christianity Today* (June 12, 2019)	"The Church Does Not Exist for the Sake of the World"; "the purpose of the church—the family of God—is not to make the world a better place, but to invite the world into the better place, the place called church."	*Evangelicalism isn't actually a failure because as long as we have our ducks in a row on our own territory, we still win.* *We shouldn't expect the church to make the world a better place (so why bother trying?)*
Ray Ortlund, *The Gospel Coalition* (January 2, 2019)	"Quit apologizing": "Quit apologizing for serving the Lord. Go boldly into 2019. Paint onto its canvas what the gospel demands. It awaits your strokes."	*Despite what you've heard, evangelicals have done nothing wrong on recent controversial issues. We'll keep doing what we're doing; no need to listen.*
John Piper, *Desiring God Ministries* (April 19, 2017)	"Is Male Headship a Lost Cause?": "…complementarianism will endure…[it] is not going to go away—[because] no matter how	*Evangelical views about men and women are eternal and inerrant. Proof of this is loyalty to our own ideas.*

	great opposition to Christianity becomes, there will always be a remnant of complementarians willing to die for the truth, and they will be the kind of people who will give their lives rather than conform to a nonbiblical culture."	*"Non-evangelical culture"* = *"nonbiblical culture."* *"Nonbiblical culture"* = *"culture against God and lacks God's voice; we can safely ignore and combat it for that reason."*
The Statement on Social Justice and the Gospel	"WE DENY that political or social activism should be viewed as integral components of the gospel or primary to the mission of the church."	*Social activism—protesting war, exposing racism, sexism and other prejudices in society, feeding the poor, supporting governance that promotes justice, challenging oppressive empires— have little to do with Christianity.*
John MacArthur, sermon (November, 2019)	"Let me tell you something: If children are in charge, we're in trouble. If women are in charge, we're in trouble…When women take over a culture, men become weak. When men become weak, they can be conquered, when all the men have been slaughtered, you [women] can sit there with all your jewelry and junk. You've been conquered, because you overpowered your protector."	*Men should fear sharing their power.* *Men should fear women, especially those seeking not to be subordinate.* *Women must be actively, intentionally, and consciously kept under control.* *Women are either inferior to men, or if not, they should at least be forced to behave as if they are.*
Andrea Palpant Dilley, *Christianity Today* (August 19, 2019)	"Celebrate Sexual Ethics. Don't Apologize For Them"; "Over the last five years, an increasing number of believers have changed their stance on sexual ethics and slipped from the grounded banks of orthodoxy into the current of the times."	*Our sexual-marital ethic has terminated in divorce rates, abuse, and sexual problems as bad as the secular world, but regardless of these concrete realities, we should still celebrate our theories on sexuality and marriage—because they're right.*
James R. White, twitter (June 22, 2019)	"Which is more likely to be the central cause for the fact that black women are 3.5x more likely to kill their unborn children? 1) Fundamentally rebellious sexual ethics; 2) Slavery from 160 years ago[?]"	*All cases of abortion are equally immoral, regardless of situation. Something about being black and female inclines them to be more sexually rebellious than not. Generational trauma can safely be ignored when dealing with social and structural societal problems.*

Andy Olsen, *Christianity Today* (August 19, 2019)	"Our September Issue: Go West, Young Scholar": "How could many-centuries-dead white men continue shaping the West? Can moderns or progressives still study Western civilization and all its colonist, slaveholding, promiscuous baggage?"	*Whatever is wrong with Western Civilization and Christendom, it isn't as significant as non-evangelicals are saying; we know we can be proud to be western; the "West is [still] the Best."*
John Piper, *Desiring God Ministries* (August 25, 2019)	"Christians care about all suffering, especially eternal suffering...Christians care about all injustice, especially injustice against God...Every human is guilty of an injustice, namely against God, that is infinitely worse than all the injustices against man put together."	*Despite recent criticism, our priorities are right, because we call people towards evangelical faith and away from hell, and towards a God who is legitimately narcissistic. Injustices against people are not our chief injustices against God; so we can prioritize the doctrinal over the social.*
Justin Taylor, *The Gospel Coalition* (May 8, 2019)	"Stop Saying the Ancient Israelites Believed the Sky Was a Big Solid Dome with a Heavenly Sea Above It"	*We're still going to try to give credibility to a scientifically-accurate reading of Genesis, the tenets of creationism, and deny that the biblical authors wrote down ideas that are a product of their time.*
Albert Mohler, *Albert Mohler* (August 16, 2010)	"The rejection of the Bible's inerrancy will please the evangelical revisionists, but it will rob the church of its secure knowledge that the Bible is indeed true, trustworthy and fully authoritative....The rejection of biblical inerrancy is bound up with a view of God that is, in the end, fatal for Christian orthodoxy."	*Secure knowledge about the full authority and truthfulness of the Bible is required for a Christian's faith; anything non-absolutist will result in total collapse. Anything that rejects biblical inerrancy (or the SBC version of it) is non-Christian; there is no room for a plurality of perspectives in bibliology.*
Mark Galli, *Christianity Today* (June 21, 2019)	"True Doctrine Doesn't Wait: Without good theology, you can't have Christlike love and compassion."	*Without evangelicalism, no one has the right to say they are loving like Christ (even when they are doing just that).*
Jerry Falwell Jr., Fox News (May, 2017)	"I think evangelicals have found their dream president."	*There is no degree of moral compromise (or love of money) that can dissuade our political loyalties and supersede the (greater) evil of permitting our political opponents to win office.*
Rick Perry, Fox News (November, 2015, 2019)	"You [Trump] are the chosen one."	

There's a saying in the business world: *"Past performance is no guarantee of future success."* Established firms, denominations, religions, and organizations tend to turn this proverb on its head: Past performance is *always* a guarantee of future success.

Why do the means of success become the means of failure for an established group? That's easy: *because the world never stops changing, so an asset today is often a liability tomorrow.* Any concrete embodiment or religious expression is going to take place in the space-time continuum, not in an abstract, timeless, theoretical world. That means such expressions will necessarily be subject to the *passing* of time. If time were frozen, if the world weren't a dynamic, moving story, if languages and perceptions didn't change, then things would be different. There would never be a need for new Bible translations, religious expressions, theologies, doctrinal formulations, prayers, hymns, confessions, rituals, routines, calendars, ethical rules, symbols, and so on.[36]

Honest theologians and public intellectuals are facing the music:

> ...our inherited symbolism no longer fits the overall cast of life as it is lived, understood, and experienced in today's world. So it must change, and change in decisive ways, if it is to continue to function properly— that is, if it is not to die out. Change in matters as deeply important to human life as religious symbolism is often difficult and painful; yet it happens all the time, as the history of every religion makes clear. The proper question to put with respect to Christian patterns of religious meaning, then, is not, *Will (or should) change occur in the present modes of symbolization and praxis of the churches?* But rather, *Are the churches willing and able to support the kind of moves that will enable Christian rituals and symbolism to continue their life-giving functions?*[37]

To put it differently, our religious and ideological constructs are exactly

---

[36] There would never be a need for *life,* or even God. Cf. Jürgen Moltmann, *The Living God and the Fullness of Life* (Louisville: Westminster John Knox, 2015), 36: "It is impossible to consider God as being unchangeable and immovable without declaring God to be dead."

[37] Gordan Kaufman, *In Face of Mystery: A Constructive Theology* (Cambridge: Harvard University Press, 1993), 437.

that: *constructs*. As such, they can be (and must be) carefully and regularly subjected to *deconstruction* for the same reason an old house must eventually undergo renovation.[38]

Conservative evangelicals are sort of like that grumpy old homeowner who placates his kids by painting a few things and changing the lightbulbs, but absolutely refuses to get new kitchen cabinets, remove that dysfunctional wall, or fix the roof that's been sagging and leaking for years. *"I like having just two plugs." "I got along with it for all these years. Why do I gotta change the sink now?" "Newer isn't always better (...these damn millennials think they know everything...)"* The old man sometimes dreams of having a host of guests over, but there's just no room for them, and the whole feel of the home is stale and lifeless. *"Oh well,"* he thinks. *"I don't like the way they dress anyway; some of them should just go back to the wherever they came from. They just don't fit."*

While it is not "new," the "deconstruction" experience is somewhat modern.[39] Around the 1700s, global trade, immigrations, and new discoveries about religion, history, and the Bible combined to raise questions about various orthodoxies. Perhaps the quintessential example of this after-modernity deconstruction comes from the letters of Friedrich Schleiermacher (1768–1834) to his father.

Friedrich was encountering this brave new world of science and modernity and found it difficult to reconcile with his dad's reformed orthodoxy. Young Schleiermacher complained that the world of Christianity is isolated, not taking new discoveries seriously, but should not fear:

> ...what we see in the scientific periodicals, we learn nothing about the objections, arguments, and discussions raised in the present day in regard to exegesis and dogmatics. Even in the lectures delivered to us

---

[38] For an excellent elaboration on this, see Laurel Schneider and Stephen G. Ray Jr., *Awake the Moment: An Introduction to Theology* (Louisville: Westminster John Knox, 2016), 1-67.

[39] On the "phases" of one's faith experience, see James Fowler, *Stages of Faith: The Psychology of Human Development and the Quest for Meaning* (New York: HarperOne, 1995, orig. 1981) and Janet Hagberg and Robert Guelich, *The Critical Journey, Stages in the Life of Faith* (Salem: Sheffield Publishing Company, 2004). It is no coincidence that evangelical deconstruction seems to happen most frequently in one's 20s-30s.

sufficient mention is not made of these matters, and yet knowledge of them is absolutely necessary for a future theologian. The fact that they fear to lay them before us, awakens in many minds a suspicion that the objections of the innovators must approve themselves to the intellect and be difficult to refute. I do not, however, share this opinion; and upon the whole, the small amount of discontent I feel in regard to this subject does not as yet disturb my tranquility, and you are the only person to whom I have mentioned it.[40]

His father responded by encouraging him to have faith, to read the Bible more, and to "Keep out of the way of this tree of knowledge, and of that dangerous love of profundity which would lure you towards it."[41] Predictably, this did not help Friedrich's budding faith crisis—nor address his specific concerns. He later went on to write one of the most influential theological works of the last two centuries[42] as "the Father of liberal theology," or "Father of modern theology."[43]

What's interesting is how little has changed since the 1780s. Every week, for example, one can personally witness a similar interchange between parents and their young-adult children at the dinner table, on various forums, or in the Progressive Christians, Former Fundamentalists, Exvangelical, and Liturgists Facebook groups. Same struggles. Same arguments. Largely the same results. The experience might be sketched like this:

> *Phase 1*: You deviate from the religious-theological norm one way or another, and slowly express doubts from inside the "orthodox" group.
> *Phase 2*: In response, the group encourages you to read the Bible more, pray more, and not ask any more tough questions.
> *Phase 3*: You take another step towards hell by reading a book by a non-

---

[40] Friedrich Schleiermacher, in *The Life of Friedrich Schleiermacher: As Unfolded in His Autobiography and Letters*, trans. Frederica Rowan (London: Smith, Elder, and Co., 1860), 46ff.

[41] Ibid.

[42] Friedrich Schleiermacher, *The Christian Faith* (two vols), trans. by Terrence Tice, Katherine Kelsey, and Edwina Lawler (Louisville: Westminster John Knox Press, 2016, orig. 1821).

[43] This ambiguity results in part because of the changing meaning of "liberal," and the perceptions of the speaker involved. (For example, evangelicals generally prefer calling him "liberal" in the more denigrating way.)

conservative author, or listening to a university lecture on the literary origins of the Bible.

Phase 4: Things escalate to a discussion with one of the group's authority figures who has a graduate degree, who then re-draws the same boundaries of doctrinal and moral purity, only with more serious language of consequences, eternal and otherwise.

Phase 5: You reveal that you have friends who aren't heterosexual (or worse, that *you* aren't heterosexual). You also reveal that you didn't vote in the last election—all of which basically announces to the whole world that you're shamelessly diving headlong into the lake of fire.

Phase 6: You enter the phase where friends and family have given up and only say "I'm praying for you."

Phase 7: Radio-silence until the next holiday or run-in at the grocery store.

The difference today is the *prevalence* of this kind of experience: it occurs continually—so much, in fact, that I could probably entitle this book "Deconstruction" and most onlookers would already know what I mean: *leaving religious fundamentalism.*

TAKING THE "FUN" OUT OF FUNDAMENTALISM

That's really what this book is about—not just the ideas embedded within a certain brand of American Protestantism, but a *culture*. An ethos. A consuming world-and-life view that's inherently militant, self-protective, and authoritarian.

One of the best terms for this culture and religious ethos is "fundamentalism." However, in some influential circles, this word is habitually derided as little more than a negative and unnecessary label. For example, in his seminal monograph *Warranted Christian Belief*, the reformed analytic philosopher Alvin Plantinga remarked:

On the most common contemporary academic use of the term ['fundamentalist'], it is a term of abuse or disapprobation, rather like 'son of a bitch', more exactly 'sonovabitch'...Still, there is a bit more to the meaning of 'fundamentalist' (in this widely current use): it isn't simply a term of abuse. In addition to its emotive force, it does have some cognitive content, and ordinarily denotes relatively conservative theological views. That makes it more like 'stupid sumbitch' (or maybe 'fascist sumbitch'?) than 'sumbitch' simpliciter....The explanation is that the term has a certain indexical element: its cognitive content is given by the phrase 'considerably to the right, theologically speaking, of me and my enlightened friends.' The full meaning of the term, therefore (in this use), can be given by something like 'stupid sumbitch whose theological opinions are considerably to the right of mine'.[44]

Witty as it is, Plantinga is mistaken. This is *not* "the most common contemporary academic use of the term" (though I have some guesses why he feels that way). Fundamentalism and its participants is a sociological phenomenon studied by historians, religious scholars and social scientists. Today, just like "racism"/"racists," "sexism"/"sexists," "white supremacy"/"white supremacists," and "terrorism"/"terrorists," "fundamentalism"/"fundamentalists" is a subject in its own right, stretching across cultures, religions, and epochs of history.[45] In fact, from 1987-1994, the American Academy of Arts and Sciences held "The Fundamentalism Project," which yielded no less than five volumes of original research.[46] That's quite an undertaking about little more than "stupid sumbitches whose theological opinions are considerably to the right of mine"![47]

---

[44] Alvin Plantinga, *Warranted Christian Belief* (New York: Oxford University Press: 2000), 245.

[45] See McSkimming, *Leaving Christian Fundamentalism and the Reconstruction of Identity*; Sathianathan Clarke, *Competing Fundamentalisms: Violent Extremism in Christianity, Islam, and Hinduism* (Louisville: Westminster John Knox, 2017); Joel Carpenter, *Revive Us Again: The Reawakening of American Fundamentalism* (New York: Oxford University Press, 1999); George Marsden, *Fundamentalism and American Culture* (New York: Oxford University Press, 2006); James Barr, ed. John Barton, *The Collected Essays of James Barr* (New York: Oxford University Press, 2014), volume 2 Part V, "Fundamentalism"; Luca Ozzano "Religious fundamentalism," in *Routledge Handbook of Religion and Politics*, ed. Jeffrey Haynes (Abingdon: Routledge 2016); Harriet Harris, "Fundamentalism," in *The Routledge Companion to Modern Christian Thought*, ed. Chad Meister and James Beilby (Abingdon: Routledge, 2013); Markku Ruotsila, *Carl McIntire and the Politicization of American Fundamentalism* (New York: Oxford University Press, 2016).

[46] All five volumes are edited by Martin Marty and Scott Appleby, and published by University of Chicago Press.

[47] Even the classification systems of modern libraries, such as BISAC, contains entries like

Here's an idea: What if we allowed scholars of fundamentalism to define and/or describe fundamentalism? (And what if we listened?)

...fundamentalism refers to a discernible pattern of religious militancy by which self-styled 'true believers' attempt to arrest the erosion of religious identity, fortify the borders of the religious community and create viable alternatives to secular institutions and behaviors.[48]

Religious fundamentalism is a communal mind-set [separatism, in/out dynamics] *steeped in a revealed Word-vision* [biblicism, Qu'ranism, literal interpretation, fixed textual foundation], *corroborated by a definitive ethical system of world-ways for human living* [includes patriarchalism, practical dos and don'ts in contrast to godless world], *and calibrated by an aggressive movement* [statism, nationalism, militancy] *that labors toward the goal that such a global order will govern the social, political, economic, cultural, and religious lives of all human beings* [universal in scope; colonization/proselytization].[49]

Christian fundamentalism may be understood as a totalizing and highly influential social movement, thoroughly adept in the acculturation of its participant members through embracing and promoting a defensive collective identity, suspicious of 'the other' but also committed to mission and evangelism. It is apparent that a guarded, fortressed and self-perpetuating inward focus (with requisite identity specifications) emerges.[50]

There's also the more objective *Encyclopædia Brittanica*:

Fundamentalism: a type of militantly conservative religious movement characterized by the advocacy of strict conformity to sacred texts. Once used exclusively to refer to American Protestants who insisted on the inerrancy of the Bible, the term *fundamentalism* was applied more broadly beginning in the late 20th century to a wide variety of religious

---

"REL078000 RELIGION / Fundamentalism."

[48] McSkimming, *Leaving Christian Fundamentalism*, 16, summarizing the research of the Fundamentalism Project.

[49] Clarke, *Competing Fundamentalisms*, 154.

[50] McSkimming, *Leaving Christian Fundamentalism*, 40.

movements. Indeed, in the broad sense of the term, many of the major religions of the world may be said to have fundamentalist movements.[51]

In my own research and experience, I describe fundamentalism as exhibiting many (though not necessarily all) of the following features:

1. *Groupthink* (the desire for unity hinders decision-making, responsibility, and creativity)
2. *Closed-mindedness* (there lacks an intentional, balanced presentation of other viewpoints; reading others' books and resources is only done to more effectively debate them—"ammo," not to genuinely understand)
3. *Pseudoscholarship* (regurgitations of secondary sources, anecdotes, universal statements and generalizations lacking qualifications, alternative schools frequently with phony degrees, etc.)
4. *Undeveloped binary thinking* (most or all issues are black and white, right or wrong, with no degrees or shades of uncertainty)
5. *Separatism* (social isolation, along with pride in exclusion and fear of inclusivity/diversity, especially of the 'other' [xenophobia])
6. *Cult-personalities* (one or two key figures monopolize the ideology, earn the group's trust, and drive the movement through public campaigns)
7. *Proselytism* (fear tactics of guilt/shame, triumphant claims of possessing truth, high emphasis on conversion)
8. *Self-legitimization* (persecution complex; criticism of dissenters is a constituent part of self-identity, while criticism *from* dissenters galvanizes the cause)
9. *Obsession with Certainty* (certainty is an indicator of truth; all doubt is a sign of moral or spiritual danger; all significant qualifications or exceptions are viewed as intolerable "compromises")[52]
10. *Biblicism and Bibliolatry* (unrealistic view of the Bible in terms of both historicity and literary features; no awareness of how language works and inability and unwillingness to separate one's views from the views of the deity)[53]

---

[51] Henry Munson, "Fundamentalism" (2019, accessed online).

[52] Ibid., 19: "'compromise and accommodation' are among the most dreaded words in the Fundamentalist vocabulary'," in referencing sociologist Nancy Ammerman. Alpha and Omega Ministries (James R. White) is a vivid case study, which literally sells "No Compromise" wrist-bands to adherents.

[53] Jamin Andreas Hübner, "Complementarianism and Biblical Truth," presented at the 2017

After researching and writing about these features, I came across a similar set of reflections by the renowned theologian Paul Tillich. The following quote comes from first three pages of his three-volume *Systematic Theology*:

> [Some theological systems] confuse eternal truth with a temporal expression of this truth....When fundamentalism is combined with an antitheological bias, as it is, for instance, in its biblicistic-evangelical form, the theological truth of yesterday is defended as an unchangeable message against the theological truth of today and tomorrow. Fundamentalism fails to make contact with the present situation, not because it speaks from beyond every situation, but because it speaks from a situation of the past. It elevates something finite and transitory to infinite and eternal validity. In this respect, fundamentalism has demonic traits. It destroys the humble honesty of the search for truth, it splits the conscience of its thoughtful adherents, and it makes them fanatical because they are forced to suppress elements of truth of which they are dimly aware.[54]

As early as the 1950s—and in the first pages of his seminal work no less, Tillich pulls no punches. This post-Scopes-Trial fundamentalism wasn't just bad news, it was profoundly anti-Christian. (It is no wonder that those inside the movement quickly distanced themselves from each other.[55])

Hence the similarly critical remarks of world religion scholar Huston Smith:

> Conservative Christians, commonly tagged as fundamentalists, incline

---

CBE National Conference in Orlando, Florida (July 23, 2017). For a more detailed look, see *idem*, "A Critical Review of The Nashville Statement," *Priscilla Papers* 33:1 (Winter 2019):19-30, first published in *Eyes to See and Ears to Hear Women: Sexual Assault as a Crisis of Evangelical Theology*, ed. Tim Krueger (Minneapolis: CBE International, 2018), pp. 83-113.

[54] Paul Tillich, *Systematic Theology* (Chicago: University of Chicago Press, 1967), 3.

[55] Hence Carl Henry's *The Uneasy Conscience of Modern Fundamentalism* (Grand Rapids: Eerdmans, 1947). Fuller seminary's "abandonment of inerrancy" under its second president was one of the most controversial icons of this struggle. See George Marsden, *Reforming Fundamentalism: Fuller Seminary and the New Evangelicalism* (Grand Rapids: Eerdmans, 1987).

toward a biblical literalism that is unworkable because it ignores the contexts that give words their meaning—different contexts, different meanings—and they are in constant danger of slipping into disastrous political agendas. Worse yet, they are untrue to Jesus. Jesus was invariably generous whereas fundamentalists tend to be narrowly dogmatic and chauvinistic.[56]

Fundamentalism engages in what Marcella Althaus-Reid calls "T-Theology." Capital T-Theology reveals the important, socio-economic aspect of this ethos:

> ...theology that wants to impose and keep in place a sexual-economic-religious system that does not have the capacity to wrestle with the complexity of people's lives—that, indeed, devalues such complexity. T-Theology is a grand imperial narrative of power. It seeks to classify all reality systematically [think Medieval scholasticism or reformed confessionalism]...it tries to provide holiness scripts for people's sexual and romantic lives [e.g., purity culture], and by identifying what is decent and God-willed, produces the indecent, that which (it pretends) is against God's will. T-Theology contributes religious stigmatization to economic and social oppression. It teaches people that there are values higher than the flourishing of people, and it then enforces those values violently and genocidally—Althaus-Reid is thinking here especially of the way colonial expansion in Latin America was justified by the need to bring Christianity to the indigenous inhabitants, who were stigmatized on the basis of their religious and sexual habits....T-Theology [teaches people]...how to justify...acts of brutality as, in a sense, acts of Christian love.[57]

Indeed—this is true not just for the Crusades, or religious wars of Europe, or for the colonial period, but for North America today. How many evangelicals habitually justify American wars? How many evangelical parents use physical violence ("spanking") to force their

---

[56] Huston Smith, *The Soul of Christianity* (New York: HarperOne, 2005), xx.
[57] Linn Marie Tonstad, *Queer Theology: Beyond Apologetics* (Eugene: Cascade Books, 2018), 85-86.

children into being "loving"?[58] How many times has the same evangelical T-mob accosted people of every kind and creed at Pride events, in front of abortion clinics, or from box-top street-preaching with megaphones, screaming, *"We're just 'speaking the truth in love'!"*[59] (How many thousands of likes have videos of these events amassed on YouTube?)

There's several reasons for this darkness in a supposedly loving religious community. One is fear. "Fear is the emotion that drives human beings to the most terrible deeds. The world that God loves is converted into a field of hatreds, a killing field."[60] Another (related) reason is xenophobia and "tribalism," two different words pointing to a larger social situation: We tend to trust ourselves more than others, so those outside our own group are trusted less. This facilitates the growth of fear for outsiders. This fear then facilitates the use of protective mechanisms—whether physical or intellectual weapons, or stories of self-justification, or theologies of divine favor.

This last mechanism is particularly potent and relevant to this chapter. Baked into fundamentalist religion is the dogma of a kind of social-special revelation: that one, chosen group on the planet has a monopoly on the truth, and are (a) thereby divinely-authorized to re-deposit it, and (b) granted immunity from outside criticism. "Any individuals or groups who believe they know what the absolute God requires," writes Gordon Kaufman, "feel themselves fully authorized to

---

[58] Cindy Wang Brandt, *Parenting Forward: How to Raise Children With Justice, Mercy, and Kindness* (Grand Rapids: Eerdmans, 2019), 24, 36: "Under this model, Scripture is used to justify spanking children into submission and physical coercing them into right behavior. This type of fundamentalism fails to create intrinsic motivations to do good and offers very little emotional validation because emotions are not trusted…Violence is violence. Not only does decades of research prove that spanking does not work, in that it is not effective in changing a child's behavior in the parent's favor, spanking also leads to plenty of undesired results, including increased aggression, antisocial behavior, physical injury, and mental health problems."

[59] It is unfortunate that it needs to be stated, but a large number of visitors of Planned Parenthood go in for a pap smear and STD tests and have no intention of seeking an abortion. Yet, in typical demonizing fashion, the mob frequently assumes that any women going into such venues must be "murderers" that "hate God's law" and need to "repent."

[60] Peter Hodgson, *The Christian Faith: A Brief Introduction* (Louisville: Westminster John Knox, 2001), 93.

carry out the divine will—at whatever cost to themselves and others."[61] This confidence and triumphalism (which further validates members of the group) frequently originates when the complexities of theology are forced into simplistic models—and then codified:

> In consequence of the highly complex character of the notion of God which we have inherited is often not clearly recognized; and the symbol 'God' is easily misused and may become quite dangerous. A nation or community or class or church, an entire people or a small elite group or sect, may come to believe God has authorized its particular practices, beliefs, and institutions; it is with *divine* authority, then, that certain activities and ideologies are enforced—both within the group and without—as right and true, others being opposed as false, even demonic. In consequence oppressive, repressive, and imperialistic behaviors of all sorts become justified in the name of God, and powerful religious fundamentalism and fanaticisms develop.[62]

Indeed, we are sometimes left wondering with Anne Primavesi: "Does the word 'God' have to leave furrows of violence, traces of pain on the face of Nature, and on the faces of all living beings, including ourselves?"[63]

---

[61] Kaufman, *In Face of Mystery*, 77.

[62] Ibid., 439. This problem applies to Calvinist Baptists as much as to conservative Mormons or Jehovah's Witnesses. The mechanism of socio-theological validation is the same: *God revealed. We've perceived it. Others don't. Game. Set. Match.* The question is whether this is what God in Christ was really doing—or if Jesus was trying to undermine this kind of game from the start. Regardless, if it doesn't terminate in love for God and people on the "outside" (i.e., the strange, deviant, and vulnerable), we should question its truthfulness— especially if we pay attention to the life of Christ.

The cartoon comes from Pastor Saji George (https://twitter.com/S_A_J_I).

[63] Anne Primavesi, *Sacred Gaia* (New York: Routledge, 2000), 14.

What isn't a wonder is why Brian McLaren gives the following advice: "In an age of religious violence like ours, people care much less about what you believe, and much more about whether you will kill for what you believe. So if you haven't figured out what you're going to do with passages like Deuteronomy 7 and 1 Samuel 15 and Psalm 137:9, you still have some important work to do. If you haven't grappled with these passages and others like them, your Bible is like a loaded gun and your theology is like a license to kill. You have to find a way to disarm your faith as a potential instrument of hate and convert it into an instrument of love."[64]

In light of this foregoing discussion, it should be no surprise why leaving this kind of twisted, coercive environment is traumatic[65]—and

---

[64] Brian McLaren, *The Great Spiritual Migration* (New York: Convergent, 2016), 73.

[65] The vomitous reactions to Albert Mohler's inaugural meeting as the new President of SBC is, at least in its immediacy, a classic case. See Julie Ingersoll, *Evangelical Christian Women: War Stories in the Gender Battles* (Qualitative Studies in Religion) (New York: New York University Press, 2003), 57; cf. Nancy Ammerman, *Baptist Battles* (New Brunswick: Rutgers University Press, 1990). This isn't to trivialize the longer, more miserable forms of religious trauma. Cf. Stroop and O'Neal, *Empty the Pews* and Marlene Winnel, *Leaving the Fold: A Guide for Former Fundamentalists and Others Leaving Their Religion* (Oakland: New

why it is also conducive to the overcorrections of atheism, apathy, and anti-religious sentiment. (It is also no surprise why Jesus reserved his harshest criticisms for the Truth-telling, loud-and-proud, doctrine-police.)

When religion becomes oppressive, it is no longer functioning as it should. When Christianity becomes oppressive, it is no longer "Christian" at all.[66]

LIFE AFTER TRADITIONAL RELIGIOUS MODELS

Evangelicalism in its current form will vanish. I have no doubt about it.
—MATT CHANDLER
(SBC Pastor, President of the Acts 29 Network)

Given the dominant public narrative about Christianity—Franklin Graham treating President Donald Trump as God's Anointed, clergy abuse scandals in every major denomination, churches more concerned with self-preservation than the gospel—it's getting harder to argue that we should be continuing with life-sustaining measures. It may be time to concede it's time to call hospice.

But for those of us who still believe, against the odds, that loving God and our neighbor can transform our world, the current scene represents something of an existential crisis. What are we to do?

For me, the answer is clear: The time for herculean efforts to stave off institutional death is past. We're going to have to start living what we say we believe and welcoming new life in radical ways. [67]

Harbinger Press, 1993), who coined the term "Religious Trauma Syndrome."
[66] Cf. Hodgson, *Christian Faith,* 150-51: "'I cannot rank among my principles of action a fear of vengeance eternal, gratitude for predestined salvation, or a revelation of future glories as reward.' In writing this, [George Eliot] anticipated what the philosopher Paul Ricoeur has described as the 'rotten points' present in every religion—accusation and consolation, taboo and shelter, the fear of punishment and the desire for protection." Cf. James. *Varieties,* 260: "The baseness so commonly charged to religion's account are thus, almost all of them, not chargeable at all to religion proper, but rather to religion's wicked practical partner, the spirit of corporate dominion....Piety is the mask, the inner force is tribal instinct."
[67] Amy Butler, "Christianity as we know it is dying. Let's welcome the new life ahead." *Religious News Service* (October 29, 2019).

The toxic culture of religious authoritarianism, fundamentalism, and sectarianism is undoubtedly front and center of the deconstruction movement. But this is just one layer of the lasagna. There is much more going on around the kitchen table.

In one of her books, Diana Butler Bass frames this larger conflict between "Old Lights" and "New Lights":

> ...the schismatic movements in mainline churches, evangelical leaders charging innovative youth pastors with heresy, the Vatican investigating nuns and silencing theologians, the Taliban and their like closing girls' schools and blowing up Buddhas, Jews attacking Jews because of different views of Israel, violent jihadists terrorizing millions, religious dictators shutting down the Internet, West African fundamentalists killing gay people and torturing children as witches— contemporary history is full of fear-filled, backward-looking, violent believers. But these are not wars of religion versus religion, like Christianity versus Islam. Rather, a new inquisition has been unleashed, and some of the worst violence is directed within. The greatest pressure points in the religious world are between dogmatics and romantics, between Old Lights and New, between those who wish to shore up the old religions and those who embrace the new spiritual awakening.[68]

In a different framework, Harvey Cox divides the evolution of Christianity in three major phases: the Age of Faith (30s-300s; a way of life); the Age of Belief (400s-1900; a system of ideas); the Age of the Spirit (1900-present, noninstitutional, experiential Christianity). It traverses from faith *in* Christ, to faith *about* Christ, to the *experience of* Christ.[69]

Leaning on Mark Dyer, Phyllis Tickle similarly suggests that "about every five-hundred years the Church feels compelled to hold a giant

---

[68] Diana Butler Bass, *Christianity after Religion: The End of Church and the Birth of a New Spiritual Awakening* (New York: HarperOne, 2012), 249. Ibid., 110: "As Harvey Cox argues… 'Fundamentalisms, with their insistence on obligatory belief systems, their nostalgia for a mythical uncorrupted past, their claims to an exclusive grasp on truth…are turning out to be rearguard attempts to stem a more sweeping tidal change."

[69] Harvey Cox, *The Future of Faith: The Rise and Fall of Beliefs and the Coming Age of the Spirit* (San Francisco: HarperOne, 2009). I find this framework particularly interesting, and encouraging.

rummage sale."[70] It happened in the 500s after the collapse of the Roman Empire, around 1000 with the "Great Schism" between the East and the West, at the Reformation in the 1500s, and now it's happening again today. What does this mean?

> First, a new, more vital form of Christianity does indeed emerge. Second, the organized expression of Christianity that up until then had been the dominant one is reconstituted into a more pure and less ossified expression of its former self. As a result of this usually energetic but rarely benign process, the church actually ends up with two new creatures where once there had been only one. That is, in the course of birthing a brand-new expression of its faith and praxis, the church also gains a grand refurbishment of the older one.[71]

We might then ask: *what does this look like?* Or, what *should* this look like? That's a discussion beyond the scope of this project. (Hence Appendix C). But there are reasons for hope, I think:

> Many people...are now finding this kind of solidarity in think tanks, support groups, prayer groups, study groups, projects building houses for the poor, healing circles, or mission organizations. So perhaps without fully recognizing it, we are often heading in the right direction these days. We are creating many para-church organizations, and some new studies claim that if we look at the statistics, we will see that Christians are not leaving Christianity as much as realigning with groups that live Christian values in the world, instead of just gathering to again hear the readings, recite the creed, and sing songs on Sunday. In that sense, actual Christian behavior might just be growing more than we think.
> *Remember, it is not the brand name that matters.*
> *It is that God's heart be made available and active on this earth.*[72]

---

[70] Phyllis Tickle, *The Great Emergence: How Christianity is Changing and Why* (Grand Rapids: Baker Books, 2008), 16.

[71] Ibid., 16-17.

[72] Rohr, *The Universal Christ*, 201. Cf. Peter Hodgson, *Winds of the Spirit: A Constructive Christian Theology* (Louisville: Westminster John Knox, 1994), 108: "The church 'as we know it' is in any event only a veiled, fragmentary, ambiguous image of God's kingdom, the basileia vision of Jesus. What we call God's kingdom other religions call by other names.

The practical and existential question that many of us still face is not so much if we will revise the faith of our parents (as important as that is), but rather: *will we take a leap of faith and follow God's call into the brave new world of the future*—just as Abraham and Sarah, Jesus' disciples, the monastics, scholastics, and reformers did? Or will we absolutize one of these cultural forms as a "golden age"—just as the Orthodox do for the Patristic period, the Catholics for the Medieval, the Reformed for the Reformation, and our boomer parents for the glorious mid-century 1950s-1980s? Will we re-stock the house after the rummage sale and get to work in building and living with new roommates in the fresh remodel, or just sell the farm and watch reruns of *The Office* by ourselves until finally heading off to the graveyard?

Put it this way: apathy and isolation aren't likely to lead towards a better life, nor do they support the Golden Rule, the Greatest Commandment, or the Fruits of the Spirit—which outline an ethos and way of life that remains as desirable and compelling today as much as ever. And if history only goes one direction, then we might as well go full-on Christian and bet on the future and actively bring God's "kingdom" to earth.

It's at least an option.

So I concur with Hodgson again, and want to close the foregoing prefatory introduction with his wise advice:

> With the stakes heightened for peace or global annihilation in the new millennium and with the prospect of a totally secularized world in which people look to technology for meaning and hope, religions must make common cause on behalf of peace and the revitalizing of spiritual

---

The names, finally, are unimportant. What is important is the transformative power of God's redemptive presence in the world. This presence will continue to take shape in a plurality of religious forms, of which the Christian will remain one of the most important." I also find it is interesting, for example, how many of my friends have become Eastern Orthodox and Anglican in this grand shaking-out. It lends credibility to the thesis of Thomas Oden, *The Rebirth of Orthodoxy: Signs of New Life in Christianity* (New York: HarperSanFrancisco, 2003). I find myself drawn to churches with a pipe organ and traditional liturgies—then again, also to churches with a foot so far in the future that it seems altogether new. In any case, we can expect both continuity and discontinuity.

resources. Precisely where this will lead Christian faith and theology in the future no one knows, but we must have courage to embark on the journey. Abandoning the old posture of superiority and exclusivity, and opening ourselves to a cooperative sharing with other traditions, does not mean abandoning our deep commitment to the gospel of Jesus Christ.[73]

A LOT CAN HAPPEN IN TEN YEARS

Now, we can finally introduce this book!

This book is centered around a letter I wrote to a friend ("Hans") about my "deconstruction" experience (2012-2014) and reconstruction experience (2015-).[74] I wrote it as part of a large wedding gift—complete with stacks of color-coded, individually-wrapped books, selections from my own publications, and detailed instructions on how to go about opening this unusually cumbersome box of paper. I explain all of this in the letter itself, so there's no need to elaborate now.

But I should mention what's left out of this story—which is everything prior to around 2009 (when I first met Hans). This earlier period of my biography involves all of the typical features of an American evangelical upbringing—Bible camp, Sunday school at the Baptist church, purity culture, Awana, Bible drills, "Worldview Weekends" with Brannon Howse, calling up people on phones encouraging them to vote for Bush, trips to the Black Hills to see "Dr. Dino" (Kent Hovind), confrontations with my high school biology teacher about evolution and the age of the earth, drama in local and national church politics (inevitably involving pastors either molesting congregants or lying to them), listening to hours of Rush Limbaugh in the tractor followed by Adventures in Odyssey, playing instruments for the "praise team," making out with my girlfriend on the lawn of a Christian college campus after midnight,[75] converting to a Five-Point

---

[73] Hodgson, *The Christian Faith,* 31.

[74] "Hans" is a pseudonym.

[75] Beyond "open hours," girls weren't allowed in boys' dorms and vice versa, so "lawns" and fields were often the only place left to continue conversation (and God knows what else). Actually, the effects of these campus policies would make for a great study in

Calvinist (because of a different girlfriend out-of-state), experimenting with this new thing called "blogging" outside of class, and shooting thugs in new PC games before going to theology lectures.

In short, all the standard stuff.

But this period involved some more unique features—like writing a book defending Calvinism at age 18 (featured in *Upfront* magazine,[76] and also upsetting some of my theology professors), publishing two others on apologetics before entering graduate school,[77] and serving as the right-hand-man of a notorious Baptist minister from Phoenix, Arizona.

James R. White, it seemed, could mercilessly refute anyone in debates, anywhere, at any time, about anything—from double-predestination to gay marriage to textual criticism to baptism to…intersectionality (which is apparently "utterly incompatible with a belief in the sovereign kingship of God and His divine decree."[78]) As a

---

behavioral economics—for all those thousands of econ grad students who I'm sure are reading this…

[76] Elisabeth Freeman, "Thirst for Truth," *Upfront* (December, 2006), 28: "Jamin Hubner has a passion for theology and teaching…Jamin's experience at Dordt has been a great inspiration to him and has added to his quest for truth and knowledge." My book was also endorsed by James R. White (mentioned below).

[77] This included the self-published *Light Up the Darkness: Christianity, Calvinism, and Coherence in the Film "I Am Legend"* and *The Portable Presuppositionalist* (dedicated to James R. White and endorsed by James Anderson, K. Scott Oliphint, and Camden Bucey). The preface to the third edition of the latter was my post-evangelical "coming out." There, among other things, I apologized to William Lane Craig for unfairly criticizing his views on inerrancy in previous editions. (I later apologized to him in person at a national ETS Conference; he was hastily running to a flight with bags in his hands, sweating all over, and had no idea what this skinny kid was apologizing for. He promptly forgave me anyway; nice fellow.)

[78] Twitter post by "DrOakley1689" (March 6, 2019). Many other baffling tweets have been posted from this account in recent years, revealing every manner of racial, sexual, and gender prejudice under the guise of "ministry" and "proclaiming the gospel." Particular acrimony is reserved for transgender persons and non-white pastors/professors who criticize racism. Paranoia is also hard to miss ("Totalitarianism. All around us. We must fight it for the sake of our grandchildren" [04/15/19]; "Western civilization is finished. The hordes are at the gate" [04/16/19]; "Big Brother already exists. He's watching, and the left is ready to unleash him" [04/17/19]; "Revolution is upon us" [11/3/19]; "Buy flash drives. Buy huge 2TB+ drives. Download. Store. Get ready for the new reality coming like a runaway freight train" [12/11/19]; and the boomer-classic, "The communists are taking over" [11/11/19]). The fact that White would openly brag, over public airwaves no less, about his Rush Limbaugh tie collection, valedictorian status in high school, and phony doctoral dissertation should have been an early warning flag that something wasn't quite right.

teenager with a 'tude heading to Dordt University to study theology, watching another outspoken individual perform heresy-hunts was downright entertaining. So over the years, I attended a number of events, listened to dozens of debates, read books, hung out in the chat channel, and regularly wrote for the blog. But ultimately, my extensive involvement with White's "Alpha and Omega Ministries" (AOMin) proved to be another case of a young person getting caught up in the confidence and charisma of a religious leader who had all the answers. I eventually—and thankfully—left when I realized (among other things) that God, truth, and academic scholarship had nothing to do with anything. All that mattered in the end was sufficient loyalty to one man's personal competitiveness and insatiable need to win. (Such is the case with many one-man show "apologetics ministries.")

That's how I met Hans, my friend and recipient of this letter. Hans was another die-hard fan of White's doctrinal invulnerability.[79] We co-debated some of those pesky Arminians in a two-day showdown in Vegas.[80] I was there on White's behalf, and instead of temporary debate partners, Hans and I became friends. As I said, I later came to leave this life as a 20-something Baptist Calvinist apologist.[81] Hans, on the other hand, mostly steadied the course. This obviously created some distance over the years.

---

[79] Hans is mainly a MacArthurite, a committed follower of the radio preacher and pastor John MacArthur (Grace to You Ministries), which is more influential than the AOmin tribe.

[80] "Arminians" are named after Jacob Arminius (1560-1609) and oppose Calvinism.

[81] Jeff Durbin sort of "filled my shoes" in this sectarian space as an altogether more slick, spirited, and uniquely unqualified, young, Reformed Baptist apologetics celebrity. In fact, so successful was his own "Apologia Church" startup (Tempe, AZ) that White left the eldership of his longtime home church and joined it to become a pastor. Apologia Church is an extension of Durbin's "Apologia Studios" media platform and entertainment business, which was in operation years before the church plant, has over 210,000 YouTube subscribers, and is a premier fundamentalist venue for young evangelicals. White's daughter Summer, who wrote the preface to a first edition draft of *The Portable Presuppositionalist* (and whom I courted in 2009), is also in the same scene as a co-host of the Patreon-funded, Reformed Baptist, politically anti-liberal, and anti-feminist podcast, *Sheologians*. All of these metastasizations—including my own short-lived "apologetics ministry" *RealApologetics* (2009-2010) and others like those by Luis Dizon (eacanada.wordpress.com/) and Michael Burgos Jr. (biblicaltrinitarian.com)—derive(d) much or most of their inspiration from White at AOMin and the Reformed Baptist community.

The letter in this book, then, was an all-out attempt in explaining my transformation over the decade since this inaugural event—and to open up new discourses and forge a friendship that, perhaps, didn't depend on doctrinal loyalties. That was the idea, anyway.

So that's the juicy backstory.

FINAL DISCLAIMERS

As a personal letter, I must ask for your patience and grace as readers. If this had been written to any other individual on the planet, it would have been very, very different. The headings, humor, arrangement, and much of the content and recommendations would have been altered. There are also the general obstacles of interpretative distance. This letter wasn't written to anyone but its original recipient. Given what you now know about the contextual background, some of the details and gestures ought to make more sense. But some things will inevitably remain obscure. It might also fail to be interesting. (It is, after all, two young white American male Christians who have a history of debating fine theological points from centuries ago. Yep, triggering and gross. You've been warned.)

While I have made a few minor adjustments to the original manuscript(s) as appropriate, it largely remains the same and publicizes a chunk of "my heart," as it were.[82] That's what friends give to each other. I don't exactly enjoy being in a vulnerable position—or knowing that I will receive hate mail. This is especially true because, like many post-evangelicals, it's embarrassing just to talk about who I was. Frankly, I sort of feel like a ten year old ruminating about my former life as a toddler—how I used to cry about everything, throw punches at my siblings simply because they said something I didn't understand, and crap my pants twice a day.

The steps toward maturity, it seems, are always and necessarily

---

[82] I added a couple footnotes post-submission that I originally intended to include but forgot at the time. Most other revisions were to make the manuscript appropriate for "public consumption."

immature.[83]

Don't misunderstand this, however. American evangelicalism is a broken clock that's right twice a day. I have many friends and family members who have appreciated aspects of that orientation because it has served them well and, in some cases, pulled them out of worse situations. *I'm not trivializing or invalidating such positive experiences.* In fact, I'm glad to have grown up in a world of memorizing the Psalms and going to Bible camp instead of millions of other possible alternatives. In contrast to others, I have no problem saying this. I also love the scriptures![84] But I still contend that many of the positive experiences are largely byproducts (or "positive externalities") instead of inherent characteristics of that culture. The same religio-ethical world that inspires one person can deter another. Bible drills, homeschool apologetics debate tournaments, and Michael W. Smith concerts are also a product of their time. (They made their mark on history. It was fun. But can we move on now?)

Furthermore, my frustration in these pages is not just that me and my friends were systematically lied to about the Bible's origins, the meaning and embodiments of Christian faith, and countless other things over the years (which happened),[85] but that *we have been regularly threatened for even asking questions,* whether the (usually veiled) threat is "being sent to hell" or subtly being excluded from church and family. It's one thing to inculcate your theological and ethical opinions into a

---

[83] Richard Rohr, *The Universal Christ* (New York: Convergent Books, 2019), 97.

[84] Note Jamin Andreas Hübner, *A Concise Greek Grammar* (Rapid City: Hills Publishing Group, 2017), which I wrote so more students can more effectively learn the New Testament.

[85] Cf. Nadia Bolz-Weber, *Pastrix* (New York: Jericho Books, 2013), 43: "The church…had containers into which every person and idea and event was to be placed. These were sometimes labeled 'saved' and 'not saved'…or perhaps 'us' and 'not us' (same thing) or simply just 'good' and 'bad'…I began to question the Great Christian Sorting System. My gay friends in high school were kind and funny and loved me, so I suspected that my church had placed them in the wrong category. And dancing, it turns out, was fun. Swimming in the same pool with boys was normal (and fun), and in the end, people who weren't Christians, to me, just felt easier to be around. Injustices in the world needed to be addressed and not ignored. Christians weren't good; people who fought for peace and justice were good. I had been lied to…"

generation—and I realize kids sometimes have to be told something, and that we're all on a journey, and that we feel we don't have adequate resources (because we often don't). But it's another thing to do all of this with a continual spirit of certainty while weaponizing God and religious texts. Historian George Marsden, borrowing from Jerry Falwell, wrote that "a fundamentalist is an evangelical who is angry about something."[86] But many post-evangelicals are also angry—and they have every reason to be.

One theologian explains the situation well, and I couldn't agree more:

> The resurgence of conservative and evangelical Christianity in recent years [the 1980s to the Trump era] is symptomatic both of the magnitude of the experienced threat and of the deep desire to recover stable ethical and religious foundations in a topsy-turvy age. I do not intend to make light of evangelical religion as an authentic piety and vital conservative force. But its potential for idolatry and ideology must also be recognized, its tendency to over-belief in the face of the threats and insecurities of our time—a false security based on illusory absolutes. The predominant representations of religion in our culture have become anachronistic and anti-intellectual; what is offered too frequently is a fundamentalist embrace of traditional beliefs and values and an explicit refusal to enter into dialogue with modernity. Religion provides a convenient escape for those who lack the strength to cope with the threats of modernity; it does not often enough provide resources for those who wish to respond to its challenges.[87]

I'm also at a point in life where some things are too important to ignore anymore, and other things I thought were important really aren't. When I shared the letter with a few people who found it beneficial (who then shared it with others who gave a similar response), I realized that while the original effect may have failed,[88] it may have had a larger

---

[86] Marsden, *Fundamentalism and American Culture,* 235.

[87] Hodgson, *Winds of the Spirit,* 60.

[88] To my knowledge, Hans hasn't actually read the letter yet—though, from what communication I've heard back, he did slip past the "Open First" envelope at the top to go

purpose. Authoritarian religion—especially conservative American evangelicalism that obsesses over the *authority* of God, the *authority* of the Bible, the *authority* of the pastoral office, the *authority* of male persons, the *authority* of USA, and so on—is a cause for tremendous social, spiritual, and intellectual damage in the lives of individuals and social institutions. Here, there is no question. I've seen it in my life, in countless others, and a huge chunk of the 6,500 that leave Christianity every day have experienced it too. Fundamentalism also seems to be gaining traction in recent times. (It's no wonder, then, that the relevance of "church" or "religion" is dropping to all-time lows in *this* part of the world.) Isn't it time we talk about all this in an honest way, without worrying about what happens to "our team"? What if we fought today's battles in front of our faces instead of other people's battles from centuries ago?

Last, but not least, I've built up quite a bit of momentum in this introduction, and it is virtually certain that you will be let down. Let's take a *deep* breath and plan on it.

(In…out.)

Your dreams of using your time wisely in reading this book are a sham—as are any hopes of finding God, meaning in life, the truth, hope, new friends, looking beautiful, clarifying your muscle lines, re-growing missing hair, getting rid of hair you wish you never had, becoming wise like Gandalf, etc. You might as well give up now, fire-up the Joe Rogan Experience on your phone and eat some ice-cream for a few hours. As I said: nothing here is new.

I hope you'll at least appreciate the effort, find it interesting—or better, use this volume to kindle a really nice campfire. It is autumn, after all.

And there, the smells and sounds and feeling of change—from the piles of warm leaves casting shadows below the low hanging sun, to the synchronous symphony of crickets in the thicket—can be as refreshing and hopeful as the first spring dew.

---

unwrap the books. Sigh. Typical American consumer. (Someday Hans will have both patience *and* manners. We're all still praying for him…)

Season of mists and mellow fruitfulness,
Close bosom-friend of the maturing sun;
Conspiring with him how to load and bless
With fruit the vines that round the thatch-eves run;
To bend with apples the moss'd cottage-trees,
And fill all fruit with ripeness to the core;
To swell the gourd, and plump the hazel shells
With a sweet kernel; to set budding more,
And still more, later flowers for the bees,
Until they think warm days will never cease,
For summer has o'er-brimm'd their clammy cells.

Who hath not seen thee oft amid thy store?
Sometimes whoever seeks abroad may find
Thee sitting careless on a granary floor,
Thy hair soft-lifted by the winnowing wind;
Or on a half-reap'd furrow sound asleep,
Drows'd with the fume of poppies, while thy hook
Spares the next swath and all its twined flowers:
And sometimes like a gleaner thou dost keep
Steady thy laden head across a brook;
Or by a cyder-press, with patient look,
Thou watchest the last oozings hours by hours.

Where are the songs of spring? Ay, Where are they?
Think not of them, thou hast thy music too,—
While barred clouds bloom the soft-dying day,
And touch the stubble-plains with rosy hue;
Then in a wailful choir the small gnats mourn
Among the river sallows, borne aloft
Or sinking as the light wind lives or dies;
And full-grown lambs loud bleat from hilly bourn;
Hedge-crickets sing; and now with treble soft
The red-breast whistles from a garden-croft;
And gathering swallows twitter in the skies.

—JOHN KEATS
"TO AUTUMN"

Scaffolding

My story is not all that unusual. I grew up.
I passed from adolescence to adulthood—spiritually as well as physically,
emotionally, and intellectually.

—DIANA BUTLER BASS

Given their amazing comebacks, might it be time for people of good faith to allow
that God's map is vast, with room on it for both a center and an edge?
While the center may be the place where the stories of the faith are preserved,
the edge is the place where the best of them happened.

—BARBARA BROWN TAYLOR

Most simply and most profoundly, we have lost a sense of belonging in our
world and to the God who creates, nurtures, and redeems this world and all its
creatures, and we have lost the sense that we are part of a living, changing,
dynamic cosmos that has its being in and through God. We have lost this sense
of belonging and of life, not as an intellectual matter, an idea, but as our daily
sensibility that accompanies and qualifies all we do, the unquestioned milieu in
which we conduct our lives.

—SALLIE MCFAGUE

If Christian theology does not help us to figure out how to stand up for those
being hurt who are right around us and those far away,
then it is not worth doing or studying.

—LAUREL SCHNEIDER AND STEPHEN RAY JR.

We must therefore, I think, bid a definitive good-by to dogmatic theology. In all
sincerity our faith must do without that warrant.

—WILLIAM JAMES

Theology is not entirely welcome in either the church or the university.

—PETER C. HODGSON

Claims are often made, by both Catholic and Protestant theologians, that theological work must begin with Christian faith, that it is essential to accept the Bible as God's revelation in order to do Christian theology, that the church's fundamental affirmations must be regarded as authoritative for faith and life...

...I want to argue, however, that all such authoritarian moves actually express not the vitality of faith but its threatening breakdown. It is necessary to make an authoritarian demand of this sort only when a conceptual frame no longer makes sense of experience, and has thus begun to seem useless or meaningless. Appeals to divine revelation as the ultimate authority in theology, therefore, should be regarded as a warning flag: they are made when the theological conceptual frame is not working as well as it should....

If it is faltering today, therefore, that is neither a reason to abandon it nor simply to reaffirm it. It is, rather, a reason to search out how and why its fundamental categories have worked in the past, and to see whether reformulation of them in new ways today might enable them once again to become effective. If and as this occurs, their reality, significance, and independent power will once more become evident, as they give experience significant form and as life's meaning is apprehended in the terms they prescribe....

We are quite capable...of living in a world even while it is being reconstructed, and of ourselves participating in the reshaping of our concepts and categories at the very moment we are using them to order our experience and give it meaning.

This is a precarious and dangerous project, repairing and rebuilding the very boat which keeps us afloat. But of course it is even more dangerous simply to sit complacently in that boat as it sinks, or to oppose or otherwise obstruct those seeking to rebuild it. If it has gotten into waters which it cannot manage, something must be done.

—GORDON KAUFMAN

A LETTER TO A FRIEND
TEN YEARS LATER

Sir Lord Hans I,
Most Magnificent,
Most Generous,
Mostly,

Congratulations on your recent relationship developments—not your marriage, of course, but the event of getting to see my glorious nose for the first time in so many years. Count it a privilege (and yes, you're very welcome).

There is so much I want to say and include in this letter that I have hesitated writing it for the past several weeks, and indeed, hesitated writing it all. But if the last fifteen years have taught me anything, it is that good friendships are always worth the trouble. I hope you feel the same (because you have a lot of reading ahead of you, and it's too early to lose heart.)[1]

LOVE AT FIRST DEBATE

We first met in the highly unusual context of doing a partnered theological debate in Vegas, and since those glorious days of youthful ignorance, much has occurred. Your plans to exit the business world and enter seminary (and subsequently win the world to MacAr...I mean to Christ *through* channeling MacArthur) have been postponed indefinitely (if not permanently), and my plans of taking over the world via Calvinism as James White 2.0 radically changed to put me in quite a different space within Christianity—indeed, if not reversed many of the priorities of my theological, spiritual, and intellectual orientation altogether.

In the interim, our communication has been scarce but nevertheless present, and what we could "catch-up" on is inevitably challenging. You've been insanely busy for the last decade (as have I, I guess), and there has been little means by which we could fill-in the gaps in our

---

[1] It may not be either wise nor practical to read this letter in one session.

experiences, learning and reading, questions and thought processes, challenges and adventures, pains and pleasures, etc. In the brief conversations we have had, I've only been able to manage updating you with the latest heresies I've endorsed, while my own (dual-career) preoccupation with the economic/business world has led to most of our attention on the mechanics of your corporate schemas. And I have been gratified by all that I have (thus far) learned from you. (And I hope that continues—assuming neither of us get run over by a random ice-cream truck.) It really is amazing how in our brief conversations before your wedding day, we could so efficiently and easily connect, communicate and stay interested and move through conversation seamlessly as if years had not passed. (There are evidently practical/personality reasons we're still friends). In any case, while I may not join your Klan in the dirty south, I am with you in spirit and mind, and know that my book-learning in business/econ only goes so far (not far), and that your tails of treachery and triumph in the trenches of the corporate ladder[2] are a tried source of priceless wisdom, for me, and for everyone—and for a variety of contexts and settings. I look forward to the books you will write and the mentorships you'll develop in various spheres of society. (I don't know if I look forward to any children you might have; who knows, they might be ugly and—*ack!*—become mainline Presbyterians someday.[3] But let us not speak of these ghastly speculations any further, for now is all there is, and the future is not yet ours.)

Nevertheless, I feel a bit slacking in my own contributions, and potentially excluding you. It's not fair, for example, to simply say "yeah here's what I think about x in the domain of Christian thought; surprise!" and then skedaddle for a half-year until the next phone call, without explaining myself or really providing any kind of scaffolding for continued conversation in that arena.[4] Thus far, I've dedicated my whole

---

[2] Mixing metaphors is fun, isn't it?

[3] Credit to Pete Enns for this joke.

[4] And I don't know how much time you have to invest in the experience of others who are also moving around ideologically and theologically, to understand how those developments germinate; it's possible you might be curious, irritated, or just feeling out-of-touch.

adult life to figuring out what the heck Christianity is all about, why it is that I've been handed the beliefs and traditions I have been handed, what needs to change (or what doesn't), how I and we are to live life, and how one might go about constructing a sense of life's "meaning." Most people on the planet will not have the opportunity to do this—to earn three degrees, read and write masses of literature, teach full-time as a professor, and engage in the highest levels of academics in the realm of Christian studies. I am (both of us are) drowning in privilege— unspeakable privilege.[5] And I take that seriously, and feel a tremendous responsibility to my friends and family, local community, to the church and academy, to share some of what I've learned—and explain how my journey has undertaken the twists and turns that it has, and what that might mean for me and for others in a similar stead. If my path right now is to learn, discern, teach, and discover, then it cannot simply be for myself, and should be to the benefit of all (at least to the extent that this is possible).

Of course, that trajectory towards externalization is tremendously risky—risky in giving myself a bigger head than I need, of speaking prematurely, in obtaining trust/authority from others that may not be truly merited or of genuine concern for others, risky in misdirecting friendship away from other possibly more important things, risky in that many people frankly aren't interested (especially in risking *their* own comforts and preinclinations, by entertaining alternative perspectives), etc. And perhaps most importantly, in this realm of "religion," everything is utterly personal. This is America, and from our upbringing we have been sewn to the evangelical cloth. We wear our crosses publicly, carry our latest Study Bibles to Starbucks, and vote for...well whatever you want to call it—and argue endlessly about it on social media. Families, like churches, are abruptly split simply by talking about various theological and ethical issues. True: our city councils no longer light people on fire for questioning the canons of Chalcedon. This is

---

[5] E.g., While you were waking up for the first morning as a married man (happily I assume), I took your new $95,000 Range Rover out for coffee just blocks from your house in the burbs. (If this wasn't overkill, I'm not sure what would be.) I actually almost wrecked the thing making a left turn...just kidding :)

progress. But real dialog today is hard to come by—though I am quite thankful you're the kind of person both patient and willing enough to hear people out before anything else (though you do quite like to see your team win…). All of that is to say, grant me grace as you read things that you may well find disconcerting.

This journey has been super, super difficult for me, the nonconformist, know-it-all farm-boy from South Dakota. But it nevertheless remains the best thing that the world of academia has taught me so far: opening myself up to criticism in a genuine, vulnerable way, and diving into research without knowing where on earth I'm going to end up. Both of those things are scary as hell. (Repeat: Scary. As. Hell.) No one prepares you for thinking in a completely new way— especially in the kind of religious context of my/our upbringing.[6] The sheer anxiety of asking forbidden questions—from the accuracy of the Bible to the existence of (or meaning) of "God" to sexual ethics, and above all, the anxiety of risking my career, losing friends and alienating family, and making a public fool of myself after putting myself out there with such boldness, is greater than I could have imagined.

But what choice is there with that path I've chosen (or rather, that has chosen me)? My job—as I understand a professor's job—is to get up in front of a group of young strangers and carefully inform them about various views on a subject, cautiously explain their rationale, and rigorously train them with the tools of critical thinking to be on their own.[7] That's at least my understanding of "education." "Indoctrination," as I've *slowly* come to learn, is where I would try to convince others to be on "my team," and be forced to end up telling students the same stuff over and over again, refuse to genuinely answer their questions and let them know weaknesses and areas of unknowns, and ultimately create an artificial sense of security that *might* survive the real world, but will almost certainly collapse over time. That path would be infinitely easier, and I've sometimes envied that comfort in the walks of others. I would

---

[6] Everything is black and white in youth, it seems, and as one ages, more things tend to become shades of gray.

[7] And if no one gets unexpectedly shot or pregnant in this process, all the better.

never have to question my own beliefs, never have to inform myself of other beliefs, and thus never have to empathize or see things from a perspective other than my own, never speak at a national conference where I knew my views would be openly scrutinized, and so on and so forth. The blue pill is more pleasant-looking for good reasons. Likewise, the red pill is the color of blood for good reasons.

The bizarre thing I've learned in the crucible is that (a) the two (education-indoctrination) are conflated more often than one would think, and (b) the tension between these two is typical of the tradition in which I've (we've) been raised, and is generally unsustainable long term. In my story, it came to unravel with both my involvement with AOmin and White and with John Witherspoon College.

HOW MY TEAM LET ME DOWN (PART I)

In the former case, the motto was all about debate (as you well know); "the first to plead a case seems right until another comes and examines" (Prov 18:17). But after years of blogging against anyone who dissented from my views, engaging in various activities with or on James White's behalf, and being an all-around asshole in my twenties,[8] I eventually found myself reading most books and material from those I disagree with simply for debate ammunition. I wouldn't allow myself to honestly entertain the rationality of opposing views (how could I? That's not how debates work—and I also think being young can prey on a person's defensiveness). "Dialog" didn't mean real conversation (which I found boring); it meant entrenched warfare and determined antithesis (blog-worthy, and more clicks). Perhaps above all, it meant *public performance*.

This is an element that is rightly missing (in a sense) from formal publications and the traditional guilds of academia—precisely so that real education doesn't quickly pervert into either propaganda or raw

---

[8] It didn't help that during my first two years of college, I was good friends and colleagues with Joe Baker (wildlovestory.com), who was (and continues to be) obsessed with John Eldredge, patriarchy, and masculinity.

entertainment. (The Ergun Caners, James Whites, and Jeff Durbins of the world noticeably thrive in the entertainment industry of tough-guy one-up-manship.[9]) Not that pride and performance isn't a thing at the university, but it's often far worse for those convinced God is on their side who are desperate for public attention. So, being that there was a really big world of Christian (and non-Christian) thinkers out there that I had neither explored nor was familiar with, eventually I wondered: could I possibly be in a position to systematically, habitually, *and publicly* criticize them and those like them—especially as they were actually Christians of the same family?

On both aomin.org and realapologetics.org (now a porn site from what I understand; didn't anticipate that one either), I found myself criticizing mostly Christians, in anxious states throughout the day worrying about getting blog posts out before bedtime, and producing far more heat than light. Was this really the gold standard of defending the faith? Was *anyone* really called by God for this "ministry work"? I also felt that something was wrong when I was always right, and when those around me found it difficult to have conversations where there was any disagreement. (I didn't want to become *that person*—habitually "argumentative." I'd rather be easy going, and be able to make *at least* as many friends as enemies.) So I walked away from AOmin and the 1689ers around 2011-2012 not knowing if I'd return. But, regardless, I realized I needed more "time in the woodshed," and it was one of the best decisions I've ever made.[10]

In the latter case, something similar happened, but with a twist. At JWC, education was the *mission,* the very purpose both I and the institution were there (or so it was propounded). But as I taught, learned

---

[9] Cf. the Bill Nye and Ken Ham "debate" of 2014. It was clearly a media project for amusement purposes.

[10] It also ended up being wise simply because of how notoriously divisive (I later realized) the 1689ers are. In addition to White's dramatic falling out with countless Reformed Baptist colleagues, and also later resignation from PRBC to join Apologia Church, there is the recent splitting of ARBCA over divine impassibility (and covering up sexual abuse), the splitting of the Founders Ministries board, and so on. The situation is probably worse than larger denominations, which is amazing considering how small the particular Baptist community is. (But that's how and why such groups exist in the first place: to dispute doctrine. It's "in their DNA." And if there's nothing to argue about, they'll *find* something!)

and explored, I finally ran up against the walls hidden behind all the familiar trees and shrubs of American evangelical thought.[11] That is, the education we were explicitly promising to students was not compatible with the indoctrination we were *implicitly* promising to *parents* and *donors*.

This is apparently the way most conservative evangelical schools work: parents, who are both genuinely (and rightly) concerned about their kids and their minds, but also sometimes (often?) irrationally fearful, send their sons and daughters to such schools to perpetuate the same ideas, values, cultural customs, etc. as they themselves have come to be aligned with, and to hopefully isolate them from the questionable activities of the world (again, as *they* see it).[12] I'm not saying all parents are uncritical of their own beliefs, nor am I saying that real education doesn't take place on the campuses of Azuza Pacific, Wheaton, Calvin, Houston Baptist, Eastern U, Bethel, or otherwise.[13] But (in my view), evangelical "higher ed" is frequently clouded in a system of indoctrination that is hellbent on *un*change, and indeed, anti-intellectualism (more on this in a moment).[14]

---

[11] I delineate the basic ideas of "American evangelicalism" below. But I use this label mostly synonymously with "conservative evangelicalism," "Christian fundamentalism," etc. Oddly enough, when I travel to Canada I'm actually not terribly uncomfortable with the label "evangelical," as it has a very different ethos.

[12] Since over 80% of the students I taught were homeschooled, and this was Rapid City, South Dakota, this led to a number of...interesting situations with parents. During a preview day, I was teaching a world religions class and several parents with their sons/daughters attended, and they were quite disturbed that a Christian person was teaching about Islam (among other things) in a way that wasn't intentionally negative. The whole idea of teaching a subject simply for the sake of education (i.e., deliver an encyclopedic lecture) was foreign to many in the JWC constituency. So in that respect, the project was more or less doomed from the start; the liberal arts and conservative evangelicalism don't mix.

[13] But on the other hand, places like Liberty, Masters, Bob Jones, Pensacola Christian, well...(ack, I feel dirty just saying the names of these places. Forgive me.)

[14] A prime example is the following stricture of New Saint Andrews College's *Resident Student Handbook* (2018): "The College also warns students, for the protection of their souls and the peace of the College, to avoid false teaching and errant doctrine. The College expects students will neither embrace nor promote, formally or informally, historic or contemporary doctrinal errors, such as Arianism, Socinianism, Pelagianism, Skepticism, Feminism, Pantelism, the so-called Openness of God theology, etc., among their fellow students. If students do come to embrace such errant doctrines personally, they promise by

As you also know, the sacred cows that make up the ideological framework in both of the above establishments (and American evangelicalism as a whole) are things like (1) verbal plenary inspiration of the Bible[15]; (2) inerrancy of the Bible + literalistic interpretation; (3) anti-evolution[16]; (4) female subordinationism[17]; (5) dogged support of the Republican Party; and to some degree (6) Christian (dispensational) Zionism. Anyone who has read the Nicene Creed (or the Sermon on the Mount) should eventually have to ask: how on earth did this hodge-podge 3x5 card of allowable opinion[18] come to achieve a kind of religious orthodoxy in 20th-21stcentury America? It's a long, winding journey of course, with endless books answering this question that we fortunately don't have time (or need) to discuss.[19] In any case, my point is to say that this "theology" or system of belief is noticeably *peculiar*.

Something that also became apparent leading up to the, well let's call it, the "transition of 2013-2014" (where I finally stopped identifying as evangelical and started making efforts to distance myself from it), was my apparently narrow understanding of "theology" and "doctrine." There is, to begin with, a huge difference between the two (doctrine being what the church has believed, theology being discourse about God and creation). And there is also the difference between theology and "biblical studies" (reading and studying the Bible as an anthology of religious literature—as a struggle in and of itself to make sense of the world by human authors—not simply as an infallible source of information about God). The friction between the departments is renowned. As a prof I heard once say: "Biblical scholars look at the work of theologians and say, 'But you're taking everything out of context!' and theologians look at the work of biblical scholars and say, 'But that's

---

their signed pledge to inform the College administration immediately and honestly in a letter offering to withdraw from the College."

[15] Although "dictation theory" is denied, this is practically what the theory amounts to.

[16] Most scholars on this subject would say "anti-science," but that's not entirely fair.

[17] Along with all other "traditional" gender issues—heterosexual marriage only, anti-transgender, stereotypical masculine/feminine roles, children stereotypes, purity culture, etc.

[18] Credit to the Catholic libertarian Tom Woods for this phrase.

[19] The works of George Marsden and Mark Noll come to mind.

heresy!'" (And lest one think this difference is trivial, I still cannot be a full member of the Institute of Biblical Research—despite being published in major biblical studies journals—because my doctoral degree is in theology and not OT or NT, and their rules explicitly do not allow that. I guess they aren't so different from ETS afterall...)[20]

But ultimately, for us, the whole idea of theology was simple—and basically indistinguishable from the simplistic view of (say) Lord Grudem[21]:

1. The Bible is the written Word of God, verbally plenarily inspired and inerrant in the original text (of only the Protestant 66-book canon).[22] Although it didn't drop from heaven, we should really treat it as if it were.[23] And though we might pay lip service to other "sources" of theology, the Bible is the only one that really matters.[24]

2. "Theology," or at least "systematic" theology, is simply extracting true information (propositions) from the "enscripturated" divine text. Although studies of authorship, background, culture, history, archeology, etc. may be helpful, none of that really matters because (supposedly) "God's views"

---

[20] IBR is one of two offshoots of ETS (Evangelical Theological Society), and has been growing in considerable popularity in recent years. It has an unofficial brand of being less fundy than ETS and closer to center. (The other offshoot is CATA, the Canadian-American Theological Association, where I serve on the Executive Board as Book Review Editor. It's quite underrated as an org.) ETS (which requires that members confess to (a) inerrancy and (b) the Trinity, and have a doctoral degree) is where one will find people like Grudem, Blomberg, Denny Burke, Sam Storms, basically all the profs of major evangelical schools and big names of conservative evangelicalism. ETS is notorious for infighting, and hundreds of people have left for that reason alone, and instead publishing their material and presenting their papers with IBR, CATA, or AAR/SBL. Hence my remarks here.

[21] I won't include "MacArthur" (Peace Be Upon Him) at this point, for your sake, even though his view is identical.

[22] The original King James Bible and Luther's Bible both included the Apocrypha, so we should even qualify "Protestant canon."

[23] Note Jamin Andreas Hübner, "The Diversity of Contemporary Reformed Theology: A New Encyclopedic Introduction with a Case Study," *The Canadian-American Theological Review* 8:2 (2019):44-102, at 79 and 94.

[24] The confusion between such "sources" also became evident, because if we think about it, "scripture" *is* "tradition," and "reason" *is* "experience." Etc. I am *so* bored of discussions about the "sources of theology" in these stale terms and their uncritical place in this space.

and "the views of the biblical authors" are the same. And hey, we have the text, and the priesthood of all believers, etc., so we're good to go. (We can do "deeper study" *when we run into trouble*.)

It doesn't take reading many books from alternative perspectives to realize just how hopelessly naïve this perspective really is.[25] For me in 2011-2013, I became fixated on inerrancy—but not the question of potential errors, and not on what "error" means, and not even on the fact of not having the autographs. Rather my question was the *meaning* of "autographs."[26] We imagine the Bible was written like a roster of individual authors who sat down each time to write a letter, and after they're done, it's finished. Then it gets faithfully copied after that. The fact is, less than 20% of the Bible was written anything like this.[27] "The original text" is actually a fiction, since the text (especially Old Testament) had multiple versions (yes, even multiple, parallel originals) that evolved through many phases, kind of like the history of a (series of) Wikipedia article(s) would.[28] This created a dilemma: to what phase do we say *"now"* is the "Bible"? Who am I to say one particular version or phase of the Bible's creation was "the divine moment" of inspiration and another isn't? (And why?) Combined with the fact that the NT authors used the LXX (a collection of different translations) as their "Bible," and that Jesus and Paul combined readings from both the LXX(s) and Hebrew text(s) to form their own (unique) readings, it was not only

---

[25] As noted in my colleague's recent book, Kirk MacGregor, *Contemporary Theology* (Grand Rapids: Zondervan, 2019), ch 6 "Princeton Theology," this specific, recent platform was essentially forged by Hodge. Hodge said Christian theology "is a system of doctrine." (While I may have agreed to that in the past, I would contend now that this is precisely what it is *not*.)

[26] Why fixated on inerrancy? Because it was mentioned in the College's Statement of Beliefs that I had to physically sign in front of an audience every year at Convocation, and I just didn't get it. It is also a staple of evangelical orthodoxy, which views it as a litmus test just for identifying as Christian.

[27] And in some sense, little of it is, since it is almost entirely a collection of oral traditions (or what *were* oral traditions).

[28] Even letters, like Romans, likely had two different versions (a copy Paul kept, and another he sent with specific greetings at the end and/or other revisions.)

impossible to insist on the existence of a singular fixed autographic text, but also out of line with both Hebrew and Christian tradition. (If it was good enough for Jesus and Paul, why did evangelicals threaten those who thought that it was good enough for Jesus and Paul?)[29]

But the Santa Claus of the singular fixed "autographs" (and an absentee Santa Claus at that) is not even what really bothered me. What bothered me is that my fellow evangelicals intentionally refused to answer this question and pretended as if this problem didn't exist—even though it is one of the most commonly acknowledged realities of textual criticism and biblical origins.[30] You can't do textual criticism of either Testament without asking and answering this question, and yet no evangelical (whether White, Wallace, or otherwise) genuinely answered it. So my team just didn't have the answers. In fact, in researching, I learned that some signers of the Chicago Statement on Biblical Inerrancy said the original autographs didn't even matter, because what mattered was the "canonical text" (the text that the church actually had and currently has), while others (signers of the same statement) said this was heresy (!?).[31] And the whole time, no one was willing to admit that it was *our human decision* to determine both (a) the idea of a singular moment of inspiration and (b) when that theoretical moment was in history.[32]

---

[29] For a fully-cited elaboration on this, see the attached "Review of Piper's *Peculiar Glory*" and also my syllabus for "The Origin of the Bible."

[30] In particular, see Eldon J. Epp, "The Multivalence of the Term 'Original Text' in New Testament Textual Criticism," *Harvard Theological Review* 92:3 (1999):245-81 and Michael Holmes and Bart Ehrman, eds., *The Text of the New Testament in Contemporary Research* (Boston: Brill, 2014), esp Holmes' article "From 'Original Text' to 'Initial Text'." I spoke with Holmes about this at annual SBL/AAR meetings. Like many others, despite being tenured at an evangelical school (Bethel), he isn't a member of ETS for this reason and the others already mentioned.

[31] E.g., compare Peter Davids, "Authority, Hermeneutics, Criticism" in *Interpreting the New Testament*, David Black and David Dockery, eds. (Nashville: Broadman and Holman, 2001), 11, with Timothy Mitchell, "What are the NT Autographs?" *JETS* 59:2 (2016):287-308 and John Brogan, "Can I Have Your Autograph?" in Vincent Bacote, Laura Quay, Dennis Ockholm, eds., *Evangelicals and Scripture* (Downers Grove: InterVarsity Academic, 2004) and E. Richards, "Reading, Writing, and Manuscripts" in *The World of the New Testament*, ed. Lee Martin McDonald and Joel Green (Grand Rapids: Baker Academic, 2015), 362.

[32] So it kind of irks me when profs don't take responsibility for their decisions (or intentionally play dumb)—especially decisions that happen to be used for heresy hunts and firing dozens of wonderful pastors and professors each year.

There were also double standards that surfaced in the heat of debate.[33] When James White would critique/debate Bart Ehrman (for example) he (like Wallace and anyone else in that camp) would say "these variants don't matter because they don't affect a major belief/doctrine of Christianity." But, wait…that's relevant to a perspective that *doesn't* tie inspiration to a singular fixed text, not to a view that *does*.[34] The "liberals" are supposed to be the ones arguing for an inspired "message" and for "major doctrinal" issues, not "conservatives." If you're going to say that every word is divinely inspired and inerrant and rail on others about it, don't tell me all of a sudden (i.e., when it's apologetically convenient) that only "central Christian truths" are what matter most.

So if I couldn't trust my own team on this issue—which was an issue said to be the very *foundation* of the whole Christian religion (!)—could I trust them on other related matters? (And was it ever wise to put one's faith in the opinions of a small group on an issue that most Christians throughout history didn't even care about?) These were gnawing questions I couldn't ignore—*if* I was going to educate, and not indoctrinate. And each new semester brought fresh questions, especially when reading new authors (and not just 'my boys'), and I decided that I was going to handle these issues like an adult instead of just repeating what I heard at a worldview weekend or apologetics training camp as a teenager.

This was just the beginning.

With more study, bigger and bigger holes appeared in what was supposed to be a seamless fabric of unquestionable truths. I was taught and encouraged to teach students in "Intro to Bible" that the Apocrypha

---

[33] It is no surprise that 1689ers are split over autograph inerrancy vs. *Textus Receptus* inerrancy; both have to demand a textual stability, certainty, and form that doesn't exist. White's regular, key criticisms of 1689er TROnlyism (and King-James Onlyism) applies to his own position as an Autograph-Onlyist, but he does not recognize this. (It seems his notorious, obsessive preoccupation with others' "inconsistency" has served an apologetically-useful distraction from his own.) Regardless, in this game, it is clear that neither scripture nor the Confession is sufficient to keep even the most dogged Reformed Baptists from falling into one kind of heresy about the Bible or another.

[34] And I just thought that a singular fixed autographic text *was* a "major belief or doctrine of Christianity"? Evangelicals can't have it both ways: inerrancy isn't an article of faith, and yet it is unfalsifiable (and therefore an article of *faith*).

simply isn't "in the Bible," and that no "biblical author" ever cites it "on the same level." But, this, too, was just a defensive caricature. The biblical authors didn't really have a sense of canon like we do—who *did*, in fact, cite and/or reference from the Apocryphal works precisely on the same level as our "scripture."[35] 2 Timothy 3:16 was supposed to amount to verbal plenary inspiration, but in actuality was an extremely mild statement, defining "God-breathed" as "useful," etc. And in constructing all of our constructions about the Bible, why wouldn't we "let the text speak for itself," instead of forcing a 19th-20th century bibliology into two verses in the NT regarding the whole topic of inspiration?[36] *Can we really determine what a book is before even reading it as a whole?* Presuppositional apologetics has its contributions against Modernism (e.g., exposing prejudices against religion). But this whole idea of being right in various opinions, just by definition, is no better than the JW that comes to my door and simply says "because God said so," which we all know is functionally synonymous with "because *I* say so."[37] In any case, the credibility of conservative biblicism continued to crumble in front of the most basic questions.[38]

And then came the origin of the Old Testament and Pentateuch. This one really bothered me, too. We're taught in Sunday School that Moses wrote the Pentateuch, without being told how or why other than "tradition" and a few arguments from inference (e.g., that of Hess, Dillard, and Longman).[39] Protestant evangelicals, aligned with "sola

---

[35] In particular, see Lee Martin McDonald, *The Formation of the Biblical Canon,* 2 vols (New York: T&T Clark, 2017), who has taken Roger Beckwith et al. to task on this for about a quarter century now. Similarly, see the extensive table on Paul's quotations and use of apocrypha in Timothy Lim, *The Formation of the Jewish Canon* (The Anchor Yale Bible Reference Library) (New Haven: Yale University Press, 2013).

[36] And it did no good to "adopt Jesus' own perspective on the Bible," as that line too was wrought with countless problems, anachronisms, and readings of verses that were novel and/or incredulous.

[37] Sometime during this period a JWitness came to my door not long after I had watched the film *The Island,* and it left a profound impact on me. I realized, to be fair and to truly "know," I had to genuinely believe and live like I could be *that person,* stuck in a self-referring world, a "cult," or whatever, and not know it. It was an uncomfortable, higher level of skepticism that, while I wouldn't obsess over (as many post-fundamentalists and post-Christians do), couldn't ignore, either.

[38] For more on this, see the attached "Introduction to the Introduction of the Bible."

scriptura" would normally shun this kind of reliance on tradition. But in this case, the question is the Bible itself, so relying on "tradition" apparently gets a free pass. It's a rather basic question: *where did most of the OT come from? How was it written?* While I was a student in RTS, everyone would praise students for asking about the New Testament and its reliability. Literary history, context, authorship, occasion—all the basics of exegesis were held in high esteem. These aspects were viewed as essential to understanding God's Word. But all of sudden, when the *same* questions were asked about the *Old* Testament, this was viewed as *threatening*. To simply acknowledge the fact that "we don't know by whom, when, why, where, or how Genesis 1 was written" was an affront to the faith itself. And since my simple questions were met with blank stares or dismissals, I obviously had to look elsewhere for something substantive (if I wanted answers at all).

In the meantime, I heard the prefab responses like "we have the text now; history doesn't matter," and "oh the documentary hypothesis; that doesn't have credibility anymore," to which I had to wonder: *do you even know what the documentary hypothesis is*, and its many variations? (I had read all the leading scholars on the subject—Schmid, Baden, Carr, Schneidewind, etc., but my colleagues had never even heard of them.) And regardless, lacking credibility *according to whom*? (Can it be denied the Enneateuch was assembled using sources when they're frequently explicit?)[40] I had already been attending ETS meetings and met many of the top scholars on these subjects and related ones and asked them these questions in person, to which there weren't any more satisfying answers.[41]

By this time, three things were becoming abundantly clear about the community of evangelical professors and publishers in which I once

---

[39] Strangely, it is even argued amongst some that questioning Mosaic authorship undermines "inspiration" (?). Of course, this argument isn't that strange when one realizes the "liberal" alternative: that multiple authors wrote it much later, and revised it in a process that can't be nailed down according to what tradition demands.

[40] E.g., Book of Jashar, Book of the Annals of Kings of Israel, The Book of the Kings of Judah, etc. See "Thinking Critically About the OT" (on my academia.edu page) for the most relevant discussion of this.

[41] I was a full member of ETS for two years (also a committee chair, and publisher in their journal *JETS*), which was quite enough.

placed my trust.

1. They were masters at outright bullsh*tting.[42] Some knew their stuff—but those were the ones who would either bail or keep their heads low until retirement.

2. They tended not to read from anyone but their own tribe (i.e., intellectual inbreeding); why read and genuinely learn at the feet of others when we already know they're wrong? (I.e., given their wrongness, "those people" should always be viewed with suspicion, and thus cannot be trusted. Hence the desire to find and elevate one or two figures we *can* trust and stick with them to the end.)

3. The Bible in this kind of religious community is *so insanely fragile*, that it cannot possibly function for anyone without a team of Navy Seals protecting it at all times. Whereas in traditional Christianity (e.g., the major streams prior to 20th century American evangelicalism) the Bible is incredibly *robust*, surviving translations, migrations, missing chunks, countless variations, and everything else thrown at it, the Bible was continually presented to me as this delicate flower in a petrified forest with the police walking around in pleated pants, ties, and wielding ESV and KJV Study Bibles always ready to taze your ass. It's no wonder that some of us could spend our entire lives defending the Bible.[43]

The problem seemed to be this: as an evangelical, you don't *get* to ask certain questions.[44] (And as some argue, they are not the kinds of

---

[42] Or just downright delusional—like Crossway publishing an unchanging, eternal version of their English Standard Version Bible. (Jeremy Weber, "Crossway Reverses Decision to Make ESV Bible Text Permanent," *Christianity Today* [September 28, 2016]).

[43] It reminds me of the twentieth century evangelical James Orr, who said during the rise of inerrantism in the 1970s-80s: "It is urged…that unless we can demonstrate what is called the inerrancy of the biblical record down even to its minutest details, the whole edifice of belief in revealed religion falls to the ground. This, on the face of it, is the most suicidal position for any defender of revelation to take up."

[44] Hence Mark Noll, *The Scandal of the Evangelical Mind* (Grand Rapids: Eerdmans, 1995)— the scandal is that 'there *is no* evangelical mind.'

questions *Christians would* ask; so there is self-justifying, coercive pressure at this point. Christians don't question inerrancy, don't ask questions that might possibly question the "authority" of the Bible, etc.)[45] In evangelicalism, "How the OT was written and who wrote it?" is like asking "How should two transgender parents raise a child?" It's an oxymoronic question that can't be answered.

How bizarre this was, to be rubbing shoulders and having drinks (non-alcoholic of course)[46] with all the commentators and main figures of evangelical scholarship and realize that "there was nothing at the top" — at least when it came to basic issues about the center of their own faith: the scriptures.[47]

HOW MY TEAM LET ME DOWN (PART II)

While all this was happening in 2011-2014, something even more significant occurred than in indulging in mere curiosity.

I met Jessica, who was more intelligent than me, extremely skeptical, and very sensitive to patriarchalism, sexism, and cultures of power. She never wanted to marry, because to her that meant the end of her distinct personhood, being subordinate to a man for the rest of her life. (After thinking about wedding and marital traditions, it seemed that this is actually what the tradition points towards.[48]) After a year of dating, this

---

[45] It is common rhetorical strategy to call people who simply disagree "professing" Christians (since we need to place a question mark over their identity, and monopolize Christian identity). There are times when this might be legitimate (since Christian identity can be questionable). But usually it's just to be a jerk and claim purity. This was the kind of self-righteousness that drove Jesus crazy—thus he intentionally ate with "sinners" and touched Samaritans and talked to women alone, basically crossed every line imaginable— seemingly just to piss people off *back* and trivialize their own absurd tribalisms.

[46] After attending the dry ETS receptions, SBL/AAR would setup the open bars in the same hotel rooms just a day later. (Is it really a surprise that such *dry theologies* habitually emerge from the former? Just sayn.)

[47] The term "bibliolatry" is actually used by religious studies authors in works on world religions, and it isn't restricted to Christian texts. (I just mention this so you know that the focus on the Bible over everything else—Christ, salvation, God, creation, etc.—is not an original observation with me or post-evangelicals, or just a rash criticism without a larger context.)

[48] E.g., "does this man *give this woman* to this man" (the language has always been of title/property transfer); "I now present to you Mr. and Mrs. [Groom's First Name] [His

struck me because it was something I had never considered. I had to ask: is this what *I* thought of marriage? As raw submission, as a unilateral relationship of hierarchy and authority? As an institution that was about *my* life and purpose and career, thereby eliminating the priorities of this other person?

I became as disgusted with the idea of marriage (in this way) as Jessica was, and knew that this wasn't what either of us wanted.[49] We simply wanted to be friends, partners and companions in life. Maybe we'd have kids and a family, maybe not. We just didn't want to be separate, and wanted the stability that a committed relationship provided. (This was something I also wasn't taught growing up: there are many different reasons why people get married, and thus many different types of marriage.) Even thinking selfishly, *I don't need a subordinate*. I need an equal who can hold me accountable and call me out. Wielding "authority" simply because I have testes swinging between my legs is both lame and cowardly (ironically, "unmanly"). So we did get married—changed some of the traditions (e.g., both our parents walked Jessica down the isle; Jessica's name was not erased from the pronouncement, etc.), and wrote our own vows, which were identical for each other.[50] (Not sure why I'm saying this since you were there. Thanks again for coming by the way, though I'm sure you regret it given the last few pages you've had to read.)

Meanwhile, we were attending what we both thought was an ideal church: a Confessional 1689 Reformed Baptist Church in the sticks of Caputa, SD, led by a rural American homeschooling dad with a stache. It had grand total of 15 members. As an elder-candidate and co-preacher, I taught through the Second London Confession and re-embodied that

---

Father's Last Name]" (the bride's first *and* last names are absent); and, of course, the regular sermon stuff on female subordination, etc.

[49] Many parents (that we know) go into marriage with essentially these assumptions, and the jury is out: this arrangement really doesn't help either the husbands or the wives. As a 50-year study by the Council on Contemporary Families also concluded, the divorce rates of evangelicals are worse than the general population ("Evangelical Protestants are more likely to be divorced than Americans who claim no religion."). This obviously doesn't include those who stayed married but regretted their marriage. See https://contemporaryfamilies.org/50-years-of-religious-change/

[50] If you recall, we also wrote "resolutions" that were custom for each other as individuals.

model of theology I outlined earlier. This model also included another major mechanism of relating theology to life that bears iterating:

1. Theology (true, timeless propositions extracted from biblical text) will result in a change of character and action. That is, if your theology is "right," your behavior will follow suit. Doctrine (theology in this case) is like software, and catechism/teaching is like programming: program yourself and others with the right stuff, and then people will behave in the right godly way.

2. Deduction: If people aren't behaving right, this simply means their software (theology) needs to be reprogrammed. Whether a person comes into your office for rape or stealing donuts from the cops, the problem is clearly "theological" or "doctrinal." (Time for "biblical counseling" to reprogram.)

It wouldn't be long before this doctrine-as-software model broke down quickly in the face of, well, sin and disillusionment with results.[51] (What happens if decades pass and the "right" theology isn't actually producing the results that it "should"? What then? It's not enough to just read a different book in Sunday school; the whole paradigm needs to be re-evaluated.[52])

Well anyway, the church we were attending was doing some weird stuff that neither Jessica nor I had ever encountered even within our own sheltered lives. For instance, *women didn't pray with men*. Like, at Bible/church camp, or at church or youth group, or whatever, women

---

[51] Cf. Jacques Ellul, *The Subversion of Christianity*, translated Geoffrey Bromiley (Eugene: Wipf and Stock, 2011, orig. 1986), 20: "We are so accustomed to thinking that conduct results from will or knowledge, that morality is made up of precepts that we have to apply, that quite spontaneously, when we confront such aberrations, such perversion, we attribute them to those who have formulated doctrine or elaborated theology. Yet we can no longer be content with this explanation, which has it that some theological mistake, however small, is the origin of every deviation and perversion."

[52] You can surely relate to this disillusionment in the corporate world between principle/theory and results. Something similar happens in economics: the goal is always "market equilibrium," even though it's mostly an unattainable abstraction that markets tend towards but don't actually achieve in the real world (because everything is constantly changing).

prayed with men. It wasn't a big deal. But here, it wasn't even allowed. Even as a "complementarian" at the time, I thought this was weird, and also unhelpful (since I wanted to hear from the other half of our congregation). I inquired from the church's sole elder (who was somehow "accountable" to elders of a different church over in Montana…). I was told that "oh the women pray, just to themselves, and God can hear that." But I pushed this shameless absurdity, and eventually we got women praying.

…But they were only allowed to pray with other women downstairs in the kitchen, while the men prayed upstairs in the sanctuary. (This segregation obviously made matters worse!) And then something else weird happened. I read the church's bylaws and documents, and it was saturated with proof-texts of every kind for every possible policy and procedure of the church, from the obscure to the general. Bible verses were cited even in support of "church response sheets" (which we never used). But then, in its prohibition of women deacons, not a single passage was cited. (How could it, since women deacons existed even in the first century church?). This was plainly hypocritical. We were supposedly a "biblical" church, and "always reforming," and here the sole pastor wasn't even willing to have a conversation about this plain, biased and extremely unfair rule that not even John MacArthur (Peace Be Upon Him) or Lord Grudem supported (!). It became clear that the culture of this tiny congregation had nothing to do with "scripture," or even "Christianity." Instead, it was just like any other organization of that type: an embodied projection of the opinions of the old white guy in charge.[53]

So I ended up doing my master's thesis on the topic (instead of "neurotheology" and theological anthropology). It was a complementarian Reformed Baptist case for women deacons, gladly endorsed by a Reformed Baptist Pastor, advised by a PCA minister and Greek professor, and with a foreword written by an OPC emeritus

---

[53] The pastor informed me in some discussions that he was not that radical because he used to not be able "to even look at a set of playing cards without panicking about the evil/demons involved." I genuinely feel sorry for the way he was raised.

church history professor of Westminster Seminary. (Anyone who continued to insist that being "reformed" and supporting women deacons was incompatible had to reckon with this!) We left the church and joined a PCA church with a plurality of elders and more stability etc., which we attended for several years. It would take Jessica and I a couple more years to learn the things I already mentioned (that happened in parallel above).

Before I transferred to RTS from Bethel Seminary around 2010, I took a critical thinking class that required students to debate with another classmate. I chose women pastors just to push my curiosity and see where it went. Being a somewhat analytical thinker and having already gotten my feet wet on this topic, I put my efforts to work making an argument *against* women pastors—because who debated what was determined by the flip of a coin, not us. And so that's what happened. My partner and I exchanged writings, and I just used 1 Tim 2:12 to pin him to the ground. Dunzo.

While I was somewhat victorious, even I could see that there were problems. First of all, I knew that the lack of someone's explanation is not actually evidence of either (a) a good argument or (b) a true state of affairs. Anyone can say anything to anyone, but just because a person's response to what's been said is silence, or unsound, or illogical, does not necessarily say anything about the premise in question. (In that case, I could win arguments all day long by arguing in an empty room, or with my dog, because no one is there to refute me.)[54] Second of all, it was weird that one verse could result in the prohibition of all women preaching the gospel at their own churches for all eternity. (Was this really the author's intention? This was [according to evangelicals] *Paul*, the evangelist dude who risked his life and said cutting penises—in his own ongoing apologetic against those "mutilators of the flesh"—is worth

---

[54] Sadly, this is functionally the game many "apologists" play. They tilt the lights, rig the room, showcase front row seating, and train the audience to see the game as if it's the only one in town. They never lose because they never play a game they can't win. (And then scoff at others for being cowardly when declining to engage in "public dialog.") It's no wonder most self-proclaimed apologists mock academia: you could never possibly play this game!

it to "win some"?[55] And was this really how Christian ethics worked, in general?)[56] Third of all, I had no idea what 1 Tim 2:12 was actually prohibiting. While I could *use* it to argue against women ministers in the 21st century, it made no sense from a biblical-studies, discourse-analysis, contextual perspective that this was in fact the intention and purpose. It made no sense to me—nor to virtually any NT scholar—that the author's intention was simply to ban women from the distinct function of elder and/or office of it. The context of the chapter strongly suggested that women weren't learning in the way good students should, not that entire ministries in general were being addressed and fenced-off. The *manner of learning* was the issue.

Since the whole debate seemed to revolve around this question, I studied *everything* on it.[57] And it became clear that Grudem and company were downright lying about the authors they were critiquing. I knew my dissertation was going to be peer-reviewed by people at multiple universities from multiple religious perspectives, so there was no "faking it."[58] To whatever extent my work at aomin.org and realapologetics.org was the art of rhetoric (i.e., blowing smoke), I knew this wasn't going to work anymore.[59] So I had to read both sides as honestly as possible (that

---

[55] For the record, I think Paul may have authorized someone to write the Pastorals (or chunks of them) on his behalf. He may not have even read the letters himself before sending off. (This makes me terribly "conservative" in the world of NT studies, by the way, where the Pastorals are said to be written by his colleagues a generation or two later, post 70).

[56] For most of my life, I didn't even realize that I was *doing* ethics. To me, I was simply "reading and applying the Bible." That's all "ethics" was.

[57] The bibliography for my dissertation ("A New Case for Female Elders: An Analytical Reformed-Evangelical Approach") was 45 pages alone. And I managed to recycle one chapter into three journal articles just on 1 Timothy 2:12 (*JETS, PP, JSPL*), two of which are attached.

[58] My own advisor (from Zimbabwe) was a "post-feminist" Catholic nun, the meaning of which I'm still not quite sure about.

[59] And this is largely why figures like James White, Ravi Zacharias, John MacArthur, Frank Turek, and a dozen others do not have genuine research doctoral degrees (and have been caught lying about their credentials), and why (here's more intellectual inbreeding) people of a kind get degrees of "their kind" (e.g., SB getting PhDs from SBTS; NeoCalvinists getting PhDs from Calvin Seminary; confessional reformed getting PhDs from Westminster Seminary; dispensationalists getting PhDs from Talbot, Masters, and Dallas; fundamentalist Arminian Baptists getting PhDs from Liberty, etc.). It's a giant circle of internal validation. Heck, on that matter, JWC was accredited by an offshoot of ICR

Proverbs 18:17 thing again). And to my dismay, it turned out that the work of Rebecca Groothuis, Stan Grenz, and other evangelical "egalitarians" was not that of the horned, pitch-fork carrying "liberals" marching over the hills looking to torch Western civilization with the galaxy-threatening innovation of (gasp) women publicly speaking and doing stuff in trousers, that I had been told about. Nor could the debate be relegated to such imaginary corners of apostasy. It was *reformed* denominations (RCA, CRC, PCUSA, etc.) that had changed their denominations to allow women ministers many years ago—not to mention there being a history of women preachers in Baptist traditions (in 1800s and early 20th century) that was only recently suppressed. So here again, I was coming to realize that the pet issues of American evangelicalism were peculiar, a product of their time (like other competing frameworks), and that the "complementarian" story of its own history was (as many self-telling histories are) incredulous and inevitably biased.

The contradictions of the whole complementarian paradigm—a theory of gender that didn't exist prior to 1977[60] and yet claimed to be eternal—were caving in. The fact that Grudem was willing to change the doctrine of the Trinity (establishing himself as a *bona fide* heretic—like the *real* kind of heretic),[61] was so absurd that almost even his fellow fundamentalists distanced themselves from this whole scandal.[62] And

---

(TRACS)—an accreditor recognized by the DOE whose sole purpose is to validate (and perpetuate) young-earth creationism! It's almost as bad as those mattress companies that buy mattress review websites to give themselves a good name.

[60] I.e., the year George Knight III published *Role Relationships of Men and Women* (Grand Rapids: Baker, 1977, republished in 1989). As you know, the standard view of the church and theology was that women are inferior to men, not that women are equal to men and only "functionally" (e.g., "role") subordinate to men.

[61] Kevin Giles, *The Rise and Fall of the Complementarian Doctrine of the Trinity* (Eugene: Cascade, 2017). Cf. Michael Bird and Scott Harrower, *Trinity Without Hierarchy: Reclaiming Nicene Orthodoxy in Evangelical Theology* (Louisville: Kregel, 2019).

[62] In San Antonio, in a hotel room filled with a thousand ETS Members during the annual 2016 ETS meeting on "The Trinity," I asked Grudem himself (who was standing in front of another mic after giving his lecture) about both his changing and unorthodox doctrine of God, and the answers were…well, let's just say this signaled the official end of his popularity amongst many evangelical profs. (Everyone is still waiting for his promised emended version of *Systematic Theology*.) See the attached transcript of this short interaction (which received over 200 views just 24 hrs after I posted it a month or so ago).

then there were all the other standard problems in the literature.[63] There appeared to be no length too extreme, no argument too uncanny, to keep women in positions of subordination. What was up with this? Why the heck were all the manly men being such pansies about everything? Eventually, I realized that this is what the problem was—with...*me*—and other men, who feel threatened by women in positions of power. It had very little to do with "what the Bible says." Our prejudices and, especially, our irrational fears, were what was doing all the talking.[64]

By that time I began communications with a potential doctoral advisor at UNISA, and I was willing to put down "A New Case for Female Elders" as one of the four potential topics for my dissertation. One other was a "biblical theology of gender," since no one had actually written this yet, and two other topics not related. I hoped and prayed that basically my advisor wouldn't choose the elders one. It would mean...well we all know what it would mean.

She chose the elders one, and the rest is history.

---

[63] E.g., no acknowledgement that it is once again our own choice and opinion to prohibit women from teaching men after the 8th grade, or from teaching Greek at seminaries (but not counseling) or vice versa, etc. Sigh. It would be nice if the people who said "we shouldn't give human opinion the weight of scripture" would actually do it on this score.

[64] Like, if women are as weak as they supposedly are, what problems could possibly occur? And, if women can be mothers and influence boys over their most influential phases of life, why not when they are actually mature enough to make decisions on their own? (I'm really not sure what the theoretical worse-case scenario of gender problems was, or how it was so much more alarming than, say, heterosexual male pastors molesting thousands of people, or whatever...)

~

I developed as a speaker and was travelling the world delivering profundities from various platforms about everything certain and absolute. People cheered. I had found truth.

In our structure-building phase of life, we often find safety and solace in organizations that exude confidence and assurance. For religious institutions that hold to literalism of the Bible as a form of orthodoxy the framework of certitude and conviction are irresistible for anyone seeking guarantees or formulas that will work in this wild ride called life. Unless we foster a strong culture of critique and self-reflection in these settings, we will mistakenly confuse our flourishing ego as faith and our elitism as community. With such a narrative, held in place by praise and success, it becomes increasingly difficult to change and grow...My ego had hired my love for certainty and structure as labourers—it was a perfect match. Success and accolades dull the senses. They have us cling to fantasies and keep us blind. Maybe that is why I didn't question hierarchical structures or patriarchal dominance for such a long time. My love affair with certainty ensured that I obediently nodded to ideas and doctrines that were presented as absolute truth, yet jarred deeply with my values. At least I submitted in the early years, when influential leaders would propagate the myth of male headship. However, both my husband and I began to fall down the rabbit hole as we opened ourselves to voices outside our tight-knit community, and the wheels of change began to slowly move and creak. Questions started to arise, often uttered in hushed tones...This was not easy. Holy Cows are very precious. However, paradox was calling.[65]

~

---

[65] Nicole Conner, "Falling Down the Rabbit Hole," in *Neither Here Nor There: The Many Voices of Liminality*, ed. Timothy Carson (Cambridge, UK: The Lutterworth Press, 2019), 133.

HOW I SALVAGED AND BEGAN REBUILDING MY FAITH

By the time I finished in 2014, not much was left to untangle in my own spiritual and intellectual deconstruction, as I had reached a point of raw skepticism and doubt. Evangelicals are trained to do just that: stay or leave. It's all or nothing. You're in or out. You cross lines, you're out. Or, here's a better analogy: When a chicken flies the coop, the big and unfamiliar world seems to suggest that there are no directions or points of reference at all, even though that's obviously not the case. It's just a bigger world we have to learn to navigate. But that's not how we're trained; it's evangelicalism or atheism (of one form or another).

But I also realized I had absolutely no idea what systematic theology really was. All I knew how to do was repeat Bible verses and regurgitate stuff that other people had said (a true intellectual, indeed!). And the high of having public fans and being right all the time was short lived, and the hangover set in. I once enjoyed being in a bubble, but now it was stifling. So with this formal education behind me, the once-impenetrable "biblical worldview" mangled in front of me (from my own surgeries trying to save it), and some time on my hands, I began a massive project of re-educating myself and intentional humbling. I became a member of the American Academy of Religion, Society of Biblical Literature, Canadian-American Theological Association, Academy of Religious Leadership, and American Scientific Affiliation, among others.[66] I started

---

[66] I began to notice who was there (lots of Christian scholars whose books I began reading—and noticeably nonwhite nonmale dudes) and who wasn't (Grudem, MacArthur, Piper, White, Zacharias—well actually any Christian apologist.) Let me repeat for emphasis: There are no Christian apologists, and generally few conservative evangelicals, to my knowledge, that attend and present at the American Academy of Religion and its publications. (The Society of Biblical Literature is similar, though one can find someone like Larry Hurtado or Richard Bauckham, for example, doing important "apologetic" work.) And no, it's not because evangelicals are too smart for everyone else, or too holy, or because they'd be "persecuted." The main reason is (among other things already mentioned) mainstream high-school level apologetics is only for those who are already convinced of its positions, and it does not seek correction of any kind. In other words, *mainstream/most apologetics is actually anti-intellectual.* (I know how weird this sounds, but I've found it to be true over and over again.)

looking at other universities and other courses and catching up on everything I possibly could, reading big names that I wasn't familiar with, and reading lesser-known authors that spent their entire lives dedicated to a few issues.

More importantly, I tried to get involved instead of observing from a distance. I was tired of being intimidated. I was tired of being scared about everybody else and their confidence in ideas that I found incredible. And I was annoyed with my inability to have a prolonged intellectual conversation with other people with whom I disagreed—agnostics and former Christians, unitarians, Buddhists, and even those horrible Catholics and mainline Protestants that I really knew virtually nothing about—without erecting these massive high walls and trapping myself in apologetic mode.[67] And the only way forward was live ammunition. That meant presenting papers for the traditional academic guilds (in a room of experts that would tear you apart 20 minutes later) and publishing journal articles in a variety of venues (with editors that were almost always smarter than you and would likewise shred your beautiful ideas). In other words, engage in the bread and butter of diverse scholarship that supposedly I was already doing as a professor, but wasn't because, again, that type of thing isn't encouraged in the bubble.

After a couple years of mostly rejections (many embarrassing, but I knew this was necessary), I finally got a sense for what decent research actually is, and also read enough to know the flow of an academic conversation. Scholarship is like that: you're in a hallway with a bunch of conversations going on in rooms all around you, and these conversations have been going on for centuries. But I haven't been part of them, so I had to listen to even know what's going on. Eventually I might have

---

[67] Robert Wilken, *The Spirit of Early Christian Thought* (New Haven: Yale University Press, 2005), 172, 183: "The first task of a serious interpreter is to give oneself to the author. It was a point T. S. Eliot learned when studying Indian philosophy: 'You don't really criticize any author to whom you have never surrendered yourself…You have to give yourself up, and then recover yourself, and the third moment is having something to say, before you have wholly forgotten both surrender and recovery.' The student begins by putting himself or herself in the hands of a teacher who knows and loves the work…Love must precede argument."

something interesting to say. So it started clicking around 2015-2017, where I was traveling all over presenting papers and publishing some decent stuff in pretty good journals of a large variety. The way in which these organizations and experiences shaped me was immeasurable for my intellectual and spiritual growth. First, of all, I actually had to listen. And I learned how to disagree in conversation and discourse without simply arguing. Second, there was no more "them." The gatekeepers and innovators of theological thought and biblical studies were in the rooms and available for questions, not just names on a book cover. New relationships also naturally began to form, and locally, I became a favorite professor of the college.[68]

I also began to realize that the post-evangelical experience was extremely common, happening to thousands upon thousands of millennials and other people around our age every single month. 6,500+ people leave Christianity every day. 3,000+ churches shut down every year. And "the nones" are the largest religious category (*and* fastest growing) in America. Countless books and autobiographies going back to the 1980s were written about this transition, but I was either too ignorant or too scared to read them.

---

[68] I'm skipping lots of other interesting things—launching our Airbnb business, getting the college accredited, home remodels, and other projects going on at this time I might catch you up on.

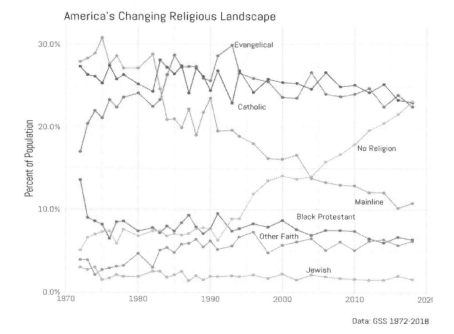

And I knew in another moment of maturation that there's no going back. History only goes forward, and the models of church and theology that we've made in the last century will soon be the equivalent to the Amish. So to attach ourselves to a specific version of Christianity was to endanger the vitality of the Christian faith itself. Now I understood what people like Brian McLaren, Sarah Bessey, Rob Bell, Rachel Held Evans, Peter Enns, David Gushee, and others were actually saying and trying to do.[69] All of my former enemies threatening to destroy the faith once delivered to the saints were actually doing their best to *preserve* it and give it the space people needed in order to grow. They were able to discern the aforementioned difference between an *expression* of Christianity and how that looks different through time. Even so, they were trying to be attentive to the historic movements and traditions of the church, Bible, and Christianity.

In hearing culture, they actually realized the "sovereignty of God"

---

[69] Were they really just *too dumb* to "get it right?" This never satisfied me as an explanation even a decade ago. Though, I suppose I fooled myself into believing that.

better than I did: God changes us and the world through culture. To plug our ears to what's happening in the world is to erect the sacred/secular dualism of modernity that's allowed Christians to hide their faith except on Sundays, and reinforce its overall irrelevance. But I was too fixated on the few things I thought were wrong or the results that were just weird to me, and too ignorant of Christianity's own spirit of innovation to be open to different possibilities. (Christianity wasn't exactly orthodox in the first century! As it's been said, everything that is now traditional was once innovative. To borrow from Paul's language, the "wild shoot of the Gentiles" appears to be all over.)

While I could piece things together in the larger picture of modernity and post-modernity, I still had to figure things out myself (and still today, I'm finding the far edges of Christian thought, and ground level for the credibility of Christian claims). But three notable shifts of thought were that:

1. Change is the rule, not the exception; ethics, theology, our physical world, never stops changing (studies in cosmology/evolution helped catalyzed this one, but so did studies in Old Testament—how polytheism, which evolved out of animism, evolved into henotheism, then ethical monotheism, then ontological monotheism, then binitarianism, Trinitarianism of many variants, and on and on. The story of religion is one of change. This is especially true for Christianity.)

2. The dominant expressions of "Christianity" today, American evangelicalism and Roman Catholicism, are mostly *deviations*— not representations or re-embodiments—of the early spirit of Christianity.

3. What is "biblical" is *not* the same as what is "Christian" (e.g., slavery, stoning gays, polygamy, wars, female subordination, etc. are all "biblical," but are anything but Christian.) The Bible is simply a window—neither spotless nor shattered—into the redemptive work of God. It is a *pointer*, not the point itself.

So my story is the same as Rachel Held Evans', and I couldn't put it better than she does in her now classic work *Faith Unraveled*:

> I used to be a fundamentalist. Not the Teletubby-hating, apocalypse-ready, Jerry Falwell type of fundamentalist, but the kind who thinks that God is pretty much figured out already, that he's done telling us anything new. I was a fundamentalist in the sense that I thought salvation means having the right opinions about God and that fighting the good fight of faith requires defending those opinions at all costs. I was a fundamentalist because my security and self-worth and sense of purpose in life were all wrapped up in getting God right—in believing the right things about him, saying the right things about him and convincing others to embrace the right things about him too. Good Christians, I believed, don't succumb to the shifting sands of culture. Good Christians, I used to think, don't change their minds...
>
> The problem with fundamentalism is that it can't adapt to change. When you count each one of your beliefs as absolutely essential, change is never an option. When change is never an option, you have to hope that the world stays exactly as it is so as not to mess with your view of it....For fundamentalists, Christianity sits perpetually on the precipice of doom, one scientific discovery or cultural shift or difficult theological question away from extinction. So fearful of losing their grip on faith, they squeeze the life out of it.
>
> Fortunately, the ability to adapt to change is one of Christianity's best features, though we often overlook it....I was under the impression that the most important elements of the faith had not changed over the years but had simply gotten lost and rediscovered. They were right there in the Bible, as simple and clear s could be, and it was our job as Christians to defend them and protect them from change.
> But the real story of Christianity is a lot less streamlined...

While I'm also still upset at what's happened (e.g., finally getting fired from the College for my publications, etc.) and what is happening to my friends (similar stories; some leave Christianity entirely, others I am helping counsel and walk through dark places together), I can appreciate aspects of my upbringing and tradition, and recognize that different denominations and religious expressions represent difference phases of our own lives, and are there for that purpose.

But there is a rather strong presence of problematic attitudes that betray the spirit of the movement—or at least what it has become. In other words, there appeared to be not only inherent *intellectual* weaknesses in current American evangelicalism, but inherent *moral* weaknesses as well. Let's put it this way: if I followed you around with a camera for a few weeks recording absolutely everything you did, and showed it to a group of people, and asked them to write down "his theology," what if this *actually constituted* your theology? It's quite a thought. And I'm haunted by this idea, because I think it's really what Jesus and Paul (and esp. James) are getting at—whether in dealing with Pharisees or Judaizers or whatever. As Vanhoozer puts it, "doctrine" is best conceived as spirit-led performance. The scripture is our "script," giving us cues and framing the whole drama.[70] It's absurd to think that when we die God (or anyone else) will say "so glad you fully subscribed this Confession of Faith. Well done! Everyone here is a middle-class heterosexual 1689 confessional reformed Baptist amil partial preterist..." In a strange way, this is almost anti-Christianity, because it is devoid of the Spirit and gives trust not so much in God as in our own power of calculation. It also requires virtually no sacrifice, love, or faith. (How, then, could it be *"true"*?) Despite my love for creeds and confessions, rank *confessionalism* is the closest thing to first-century Pharisaism I can think of.[71]

This led to another discovery that deserves mention in our case: a big contradiction within Reformed epistemology. While I still have some sympathies with Reformed thought,[72] I definitely don't have a horse in the race of classical Arminian/Calvinist debates. More importantly, I learned that the Reformed thought of the English Puritans simply is not the thought of Luther and Calvin, and represents a scholastic version

---

[70] Kevin Vanhoozer, *The Drama of Doctrine* (Louisville: WJK, 2005).

[71] Be sure to read Hübner, "The Diversity of Contemporary Reformed Theology."

[72] Like Luther's original objection of taking advantage of people's consciences to profit, of religious superstition in Rome, and the spirit of *Semper Reformanda*, etc.

that is highly influenced by the dominant themes of Modernism — namely, heavy optimism regarding what the human mind can achieve.[73] The big contradiction is this: *sin has deeply affected the human mind, but these minds can still somehow write notoriously large and detailed creeds and confessions that can demand people's assent, and even threaten them one way or another.* These are mutually exclusive ideas. People who write confessions are not immune to the "noetic effects of sin." (In fact, given their willingness to enforce them, we might question their own minds more than others.) *If we take total depravity seriously, we can never be in a position to demand assent to any human document, no matter how much we think it rightly represents the truth.* This isn't the relativist boogey-woman; it's not even anti-creedalism.[74] It's just being prudent. Human beings are human beings. The authorship, dogged adherence to, and enforcement of articulations (of any kind) presumes the same set of assumptions that underlie socialist command-economies: a remarkable confidence in the ability of a single group to comprehend, centralize, and execute an idea.[75]

Even if we stay within a propositionalist model of epistemology and doctrine, this incoherence is really a subset of a larger statistical problem: *what are the chances that my unique combination of doctrinal beliefs are right?* I had never thought of this before. All of us are born into and adopt, mostly by influence from others, a specific collection of ideas on all kinds of topics. Like, say we go with Grudem's organizational schema of doctrine, and outline the possibilities:

---

[73] I wish I could elaborate more on how "reformed theology" today means something very different than the thought of Luther and Calvin. Many have pointed this out—and I experienced it during our debate prep when reading Arminius's own works—but it's often more significant than it sounds. Like, Luther would not enjoy reading Turretin's *Institutes of Elenctic Theology*—and for good reasons, and the WCF is not simply a projection of Calvin's theology.

[74] "Creeds and Confessions" was my favorite course in college, and one of my favorites that I taught as a prof of Christian Studies (later renamed to "the history of theology").

[75] And why do we stop at 1648 or 1689? Good heavens, *Semper Reformanda*, where is the church in writing new creeds and confessions? (Well, it's there in reformed churches, but again I was isolated from it because these were the 'liberal' ones; the 1982 Brief Statement of Faith by PCUSA is one of my favorite confessions of all time; it's like a modern, poetic Nicene.)

1. On what theology is, it's goals, sources, methods, etc. (say only 30 variants; includes all views about the Bible's use, "inspiration," attributes, and theological methods of past 2,000 years, etc.)

2. God and creation (say only 30 variants; includes views on God's attributes and being; everything about evolution, age of earth; all the views on sin and the fall, etc.)

3. Humanity (say only 30 variants; includes anthropology, origins, all variants of psychology and gender, biology, relationship and differences with animals, numerous views on "imago dei" and "dominion," etc.)

4. Christ and Holy Spirit (say only 30 variants; includes all the debates on Christology and Trinity, views of incarnation and its forms; historical Jesus theories; Gospel differences in Christology and evolution of Christology in NT theology; etc.)

5. On Redemption/Soteriology (say only 30 variants; includes all versions of Calvinism/Arminianism and in between; all variants of justification, sanctification, atonement theories; Trinitarian implications; molinism and foreknowledges; scope and extent of "salvation"; etc.)

6. Doctrine of Church (say only 30 variants; includes all variations of church governance, of spiritual gifts, discipline, worship models, theories of missions and evangelism, etc.)

7. Doctrine of the Future (say only 30 variants; includes all hermeneutical models of interpreting OT prophecy, of Revelation, of Olivet discourse; all variants of millennialism; variants of resurrection of the body, of prophetic connections between Testaments, etc.)

The odds of "getting it right" (assuming there is only one right answer in each category) as a whole is less than 0.000000003%. The odds of getting just two categories "right" is less than 0.3%. Even if we decreased the odds by ten-fold, there's still not more than a 1% chance of "nailing" the right combination. But here's what's even more interesting,

Hans: *the chances of getting one's propositional doctrine right decrease exponentially as one gets more detailed/specific.* This was perhaps the biggest thing I've learned from classical modern liberal theology. It's actually more "conservative" to be more general (epistemologically), and far more risky and uncertain to be specific—especially in multiple areas.[76] It's like setting up more targets on the shooting range at twice the distance. (No one is impressed by this needless display of self-competence!) The upshot of this fact is twofold (and this was and is big for my journey):

A. Because the chances of having (especially being born into) the "right doctrine" are astronomically tiny, *changing one's theology should be constant (since it can be assumed it needs regular modification), and such change is a sign of maturity.*

   a. Deduction: *Not* regularly changing one's beliefs is a sign of *immaturity.* Permanency and fixation on a certain, inevitably time-bound formulation, is childish.[77]

B. It's fine to write down all that we think is true, and it is sometimes necessary. But *it is never reasonable (or moral) to enforce such statements of opinion on other Christians that would violate their own conscience.*[78]

As the Christian philosopher and mathematician Blaise Pascal argued, "While we can discern a great deal from reason, we are

---

[76] So for example, I would rather bet "It will rain tomorrow" than "it will rain 2 inches tomorrow between noon and 2pm."

[77] This is especially true for younger thinkers. In other words, if one's beliefs have not evolved past what I thought when I was in college, I'm probably not on the right track.
What's bizarre about all this is that *Semper Reformanda* is most ineffectively performed by the "conservative" or "confessional" reformed"—for which it was originally associated!

[78] E.g., if a church required assent to a creed or confession for membership, the qualifier "I assent, *realizing these are human documents and are limited, inadequate, etc.*" must always be attached. When President Wells was conducting his heresy hunts on me at JWC, he didn't get this and simply disagreed: all persons at the college had to pretend that the college's Statement of Faith was in a position of coercive authority and not qualified by its inherent humanness. (Again, we can *say* it isn't "at the level of the Bible," but such documents *are treated as if they are.*)

---

ultimately forced to gamble."[79] So if we want to "win," it is better to adhere ourselves to a handful of broader, important convictions, not to a subset of a subset of a subset of a particular faith that depends upon hundreds of details.[80] (So we should do our doctrine like we live the rest of our lives: mitigate risk and keep probabilities on our side.)

Of course, this whole model assumes that on any given topic only one perspective is right. But that's probably not even right, either. Human experience challenges this one-dimensional, monolithic orientation every day. If I were to describe one side of a mountain and you the other, our descriptions would be similar, but different. Neither of us is simply right nor wrong. If we understood where we stood and that this is what we were doing, our descriptions would complement each other in a way that only one perspective wouldn't. (I think theology is sort of like that, and why God gives us a pluriform of scriptures—and perhaps even different faith traditions—with a huge range of images to compare and contrast.[81]) In other words, *multiple* perspectives and explanations does not necessarily mean *competing* perspectives and

---

[79] Summarized by Mandy Ford, *God, Gender, Sex, and Marriage* (London: Jessica Kingsley, 2019), 117.

[80] Apparently I came to the same conclusion as William James a century ago in his *The Varieties of Religious Experience* (New York: Oxford University Press, 2012), 256, which I only recently read: "He who acknowledges the imperfectness of his instrument, and makes allowance for it in discussing his observations, is in a much better position for gaining truth than if he claimed his instrument to be infallible. Or is dogmatic or scholastic theology less doubted in point of fact for claiming, as it does, to be in point of right undoubtable? And if not, what command over truth would this kind of theology really lose if, instead of absolute certainty, she only claimed reasonable probability for her conclusions? If *we* claim only reasonable probability, it will be as much as men who love the truth can ever at any given moment hope to have within their grasp...dogmatism will doubtless continue to condemn us for this confession."

[81] All religious language is inherently metaphorical anyway—a topic I wish we had time to explore more thoroughly. But suffice to say, theologians tend to forget that their language about God is metaphorical (God is not literally a "Father," Jesus is not literally a "Son," or the Spirit a literal blast of "wind," nor is the Bible the literal "word of God.") I used to feel threatened by this kind of observation until I realized that this was my modern bias towards favoring literal, quantifiable, and measurable language and my prejudice against metaphorical/analogical/figurative language. There's nothing inherently "better" about one language form or another. Although, it should be said, theology would not exist without figurative and metaphorical language, and the biblical authors (not to mention Jesus) definitely preferred figurative/metaphorical over any other.

explanations. (I spent years of my life arguing on this false premise; so anything different than my own view or knowledge was automatically viewed as threatening. This can really make a person overly-defensive!).

Well anyway. Returning to the previous point: From the "outside," I could see that my actions as an evangelical were often hypocritical, and even when they weren't, were often inconsistent with the Golden Rule, Fruits of the Spirit, and Greatest Commandment. If I want to know the "theology" of Jerry Falwell Jr., I'll look at how his friend Michael Cohen (now in prison) covered up some of his scandals, and how Falwell ousted board members merely for not voting for Trump. If I want to know the "doctrine" of a small church, I'll look at how they treat a random Native American who wonders into church one Sunday morning. If I want to know the doctrine of a 1689 Reformed Baptist church, I'll see how they respond to another pastor coming out as gay, trans, or nonbinary. It's kind of like what Jon Stewart recently argued in front of Congress June 11, 2019: Everyone says "Never Forget 9/11," but the congressional chairs in front of him to help assist the physical condition of first-responders are empty.

I know you already generally "get" this—because you've already lived it. The goodness of your heart (to the extent it is) is visible and known to everyone around you (including me). And this is, after all, the real meaning of "creed" (from *Credo,* "I believe.") When the spears are held to your chest and you are asked to denounce Christ while standing in the Roman arena, what you do and say in that moment is your confession, your creed—not what documents you've assented to, nor to what denomination one is affiliated, or whatever.

So the question is, are the time-bound models and modes of worship and thought—all of which are necessary to construct to have any framework of interpretation (just like the need of having a language)— really worthy of anyone's uttermost loyalty?

"There's no perfect church." "*Everyone* is a hypocrite." Yes I know, but these are often just standard clauses used to legitimize illegitimate behaviors—and galvanizing one's position along the way. And people are more clearly seeing the mechanisms through which institutions of power perpetuate their dominance—the narratives and rhetorical strategies used to circle the wagons. Everyone knows, for example, that the laundry list of events regarding sexual abuse in the past decade of the Southern Baptist Convention—the public apologies issued from Mohler, Chandler, Patterson and the committees—are almost entirely politically driven. The way and manner and content of apology and actions of recourse are structured to *benefit the institution itself* and persons controlling it. They couldn't care less about the victims (as is so evident in the way the victims have been systematically silenced and ignored). There's a game to win, and that's what matters. (…and that's why people are leaving both evangelicalism and Christianity in droves. People are leaving evangelicals to play their own destructive religious game with themselves.)

I saw and lived this out myself, so there's no reason to appeal to popular examples. I was expected to lie about enrollment numbers as Chief Academic Officer on behalf of the President (who's goal was to colonize the North with both an Southern Baptist-oriented church and college plant), and support a (failed) capital campaign that was financially insane—all of which would come at the expense of everyone's conscience, well-being, and conception of "faith" and "God's promises." And I watched James 2:2-5 get utterly trampled on by those whose job was to do precisely that. And I've had to sit through absurd propaganda at fundraisers spewing out of the face of Michelle Bachmann about Muslims that actually induced professing Christians to *give cash*—cash that went towards my paycheck. Something was terribly wrong if this is the "Christianity" I was supposed to support. The Spirit of Christ was nowhere to be found.

So in my view and experience, questioning people, the millions and millions of "nones," and former evangelicals like myself aren't looking for the perfect church. They're looking for churches that don't physically assault others and cover it up, question your faith for believing the earth is over 10,000 years old, and don't require subordination of various groups to others in irrational and uncritical ways. (Is that so unreasonable?) They're rightly looking for fewer double standards—

especially searching people like me who used to be entrenched on the front lines as the bulldog apologist (and wrote his first monograph refuting bad theologies and endorsed by an apologist hero at age 18, blah blah blah).

All of this is to say is that, with others, I've found evangelicalism as spiritually and morally bankrupt as intellectually bankrupt. If this—and even half of what has been observed thus far—is true, the faster this dead wood burns, the better it is for the survival of the forest (i.e., a vibrant and meaningful Christian faith). Again, no religious expression or model is permanent—especially after what we've seen can change since the Christ event. As Evans already pointed out above, what makes Christianity so remarkable is its ability to adapt through entire epochs and worldviews and linguistic systems, living through different cultures, political arrangements, geographies, and philosophies.

I must quote again at length just to recap:

> You might say that the apologetics movement had created a monster. I'd gotten so good at critiquing all the fallacies of opposing worldviews, at searching for truth through objective analysis, that it was only a matter of time before I turned the same skeptical eye on my own faith. It occurred to me that in worldview class, we laughed at how transcendentalists so serenely embraced paradox and contradiction, but then went on to theology class and accepted without question that Jesus existed as both fully God and fully man. We criticized radical Islam as a natural outworking of the violent tone of the Qur'an without acknowledging the fact that the God of Israel ordered his people to kill every living thing in Canaan, from the elderly to the newborn. We sneered at the notion of climate change yet believed that God once made the earth stand still. We accused scientists of having an agenda, of ignoring science that contradicted the evolution paradigm, but engaged in some mental gymnastics of our own, trying to explain how it's possible to see the light from distant stars. We mocked New Age ambiguity but could not explain the nature of the Trinity. We claimed that ours was a rational, logical faith, when it centered on the God of the universe wrapping himself in flesh to be born in a manger in Bethlehem.

Most worrisome, however, was how we criticized relativists for picking and choosing truth, while our own biblical approach required some selectivity of its own....I was taught that the Bible served as a guidebook for Christian dating and marriage, but no one ever suggested that my father had the right to sell me to the highest bidder or to take multiple wives, like Abraham. Homosexuality was preached against incessantly, but little was said of gluttony or greed. We cried the death of each aborted baby as a violation of the sanctity of human life but shrugged off the deaths of Iraqi children as expected collateral damage in a war against evil. We celebrated archaeological finds that supported the historical claims of the Bible yet discounted massive amounts of scientific evidence in support of an old earth.

Despite my emerging doubts, I went on looking for ways to glue the pieces of my faith back together... (Evans, *Faith Unraveled*, 79-80)

Or as McLaren recounts:

...this reservoir of questions and unsatisfying answers overflowed and I experienced a kind of spiritual crisis that started me on a quest: a quest for honesty, for authenticity, and for a faith that made more sense to me and to others...My disillusionment was intensified by what was happening in the Christian community in America....A large number of both Protestants and Catholic leaders had aligned with a neoconservative political ideology, trumpeting what they called 'conservative family values,' but minimizing biblical community values. They supported wars of choice, defended torture, opposed environmental protection, and seemed to care more about protecting the rich from taxes than liberating the poor from poverty or minorities from racism. They spoke against big government as if big was bad, yet they seemed to see big military and big business as inherently good. They wanted to protect unborn human life inside the womb, but didn't seem to care about born human life in slums or prisons or nations they considered enemies. They loved to paint gay people as a threat to marriage, seeming to miss the irony that heterosexual people were damaging marriage at a furious pace without any help from gay couples. They consistently relegated females to second-class status, often while covering up for their fellow males when they fell into scandal or committed criminal abuse. They interpreted the Bible to favor the government of Israel and to marginalize Palestinians, and even before September 11, 2001, I feared that through their influence Muslims were being cast as the new scapegoats....

Their stridency and selectivity in choosing issues and priorities at first annoyed, then depressed, and then angered me. They had created a powerful, wealthy, and stealthy network to mobilizing fighters in their 'culture war.'...They had turned the way of Jesus, I felt, into the club of the Pharisees....The terms 'evangelical' and even 'Christian' had become like discredited brands through their energetic but misguided work. I increasingly understood why more and more of my friends winced when the name 'Jesus' was mentioned in public. It wasn't due to a loss of respect for Jesus, but for those who most used his name....

Morning after morning I woke up in the brutal tension between *something real* and *something wrong* in Christian faith. The sense of *something real* kept me in ministry and in Christian faith; the sense of *something wrong* kept me looking for a way out. Somehow, by the grace of God, I held on to the *something real* long enough to begin to figure out what the *something wrong* might be. And eventually, I began to get some sense of what to do to disentangle the one from the other, to hold on to this *something real* and let the other go. (McLaren, *A New Kind of Christianity*, 7-8)

It's no irony, then, that the greatest apologists *against* Christianity are all former conservative evangelical Christians. Robert Price, Bart Ehrman, James Robinson, Robert Funk, William Provine, and on and on. Is this just a coincidence? Could I just ignore this fact as irrelevant, especially as a person still interested in apologetics?

Speaking of, while I was teaching my apologetics classes, I had students read Craig Evans' *Fabricating Jesus*. And in the first chapter he explains how an unrealistic view of the Bible paved the way for the apostasy of some of the leading critics of the historical Jesus.

Ehrman's struggle with faith—and I feel for him—grows out of mistaken expectations of the nature and function of Scripture, mistaken expectations that he was taught as a young, impressionable fundamentalist Christian...I have heard fundamentalists say, 'Show me one mistake in the Bible and I will throw out the whole thing.' I suspect Ehrman heard that more than once in his Moody Bible Institute days. His reasoning today, even as a professing agnostic, still has a fundamentalist ring to it. (Evans, *Fabricating Jesus*, 31)

I had also came across the recent story of Jahaziel (UK's most popular Christian rapper), who left the faith for reasons which included, "When I first joined Christianity, I was told 'you must believe this book is God's infallible word'...Before I'd even read the book!! How can one decide for themselves whether a book is accurate and true BEFORE they have even read & investigated the book thoroughly?!" He was right.

Years later, I heard from students who took my intro to Bible course (see attached materials) who said "I would have left Christianity and probably everything if you hadn't shown me that it's OK to have a different view of the Bible than I was raised with—because that's what everyone is saying should happen." Others in my apologetics class said, "all my siblings left Christianity because they were told that they had to be a conservative evangelical to be a Christian at all, and if they asked questions about the Bible and had different views of ethics, they couldn't be Christian. I'm glad I took this course and learned to have a more realistic view."[82]

This was a microcosm of a cosmic phenomenon. Tens of thousands of evangelicals, for example, would have become hopeless wanderers were it not for the works of the "progressive Christians." And I used to think Christian-evolution organizations like BioLogos were evil organizations perverting the church. Now I realize their entire purpose is to keep biology majors and scientists from needlessly becoming atheist— and they have pages and pages of testimonials from persons all over the world demonstrating some success in this regard.

And it's no different for other issues. One in twenty persons are gay/lesbian/bisexual, and the evangelical church has made it more than

---

[82] These remarks were made to me in private since it wasn't safe otherwise.

clear that this group is simply not welcome ("Come as you are…but stay at arms-length because of your disease").[83] But, since 15-40% of the homeless are NH/C[84] (families kick out children and family members when they learn of the person's orientation)—and the suicide rate is extremely high in these populations—and Christians are called to serve the vulnerable, does one keep treating them as lepers?[85] The Hebrew prophets and ministry of Christ make it very clear: *we don't get to choose who are the vulnerable and oppressed in society.* And those groups will rarely be socially convenient or publicly respectable to help. (That seems to be why Jesus said following him would result in societal rejection; and those who serve the least of these, honors Christ himself. If this sounds like foolishness, you're permitted to re-listen to John MacArthur's exposition of 1 Corinthians 1…)

So, "Fight the good fight"; "Get your doctrinal shit together." Cool, been there done that. But, what are we doing to keep our friends and family from putting guns to their heads every single day? "Protect the unborn." Great. What about the thousands of toddlers being drone-bombed with full approval by both political parties, regardless of theological inclinations? I think you smell what I'm steppin in.

INTERLUDE

So while I haven't "arrived," I've come to some provisional (and absurdly unoriginal) conclusions about what Christianity is about. It's about (a) protecting the vulnerable, (b) giving a microphone to the voiceless, (c) calling truth to power and exposing the empire (whether

---

[83] Or worse, "there is no such thing as a gay Christian" (a sentiment upheld by White, MacArthur, etc).

[84] Non-heterosexual, non-cisgender.

[85] About 40% of transgender persons have attempted suicide, and teens who are NH/C are 100-500% more likely to commit suicide. Also, note Megan Lytle, John Blosnich, Susan M. De Luca, Chris Brownson, "Association of Religiosity With Sexual Minority Suicide Ideation and Attempt," *The American Journal of Preventative Medicine* 54:5 (2018): 644-651, "Overall, increased importance of religion was associated with higher odds of recent suicide ideation for both gay/lesbian and questioning students." Regardless of our views on gender, we can all agree the church needs to attend to this vulnerable population in a more helpful and less shaming manner.

that empire is public or private, political, religious, economic, or otherwise), (d) loving one's neighbor as themselves, (e) living a life of repentance and humility before God and others, living as though one's life matters—living in hope. If that's really the case, and if religious neutrality is impossible (there's no view from nowhere), and there is something proprietary within the pages of Matthew, Mark, Luke and John, then there's little incentive to exit. In fact, this "way" even seems worthy of committed adherence. That's the intellectual side, anyway. On the more spiritual and personal side, I can't run from God because of what I've seen happen and have experienced in my own life (events that cannot be here recounted), and believe this universe is intensely personal anyway. So I trust worshipping God through Christ in the Spirit—who (among all the persons, objects, and phenomena of this universe) seems worthy of that mediatorial role—is adequate and proper, good for my soul and others, and respectable in its own right.

Deep sigh.

I could write more, but that's just a little sliver. Though, it's a lot to take in, and you never asked for any of this. I also can't imagine how many buttons I've pushed. ("Faithful are the wounds of a friend"?) But two things to briefly mention before this introduction ends and I get to the actual letter I was intending to write. (Sorry for how terribly brief this exchange has been. I'll be sure to make it longer next time.)

First, as it has already been indicated, most stories are not as "fortunate" as mine. I still identify as Christian and am inspired by the Christ event and the positive power it unleashed to change the world, whereas many others have fully joined the nones and agnostics with no motivation for anything—and stay that way. (Though, sad to say, many probably have good reasons for going that route, in some sense. I sympathize with them, and wouldn't ever think of shaming them for leaving.) It really seems that, at least in one's upbringing up to this part of life, the harder to the right, the tighter and smaller the box, then the further left and bigger the explosion when the lid opens. I've seen it with dozens of my friends in the last ten years, and I suspect you may have seen similar things. (And, of course, it's true vice versa in moving in other directions.[86]) It's a "blowback" effect, I guess. I only mention this to again underscore that dogmatic and fundamentalist variants of religious faiths (whether Christian, Hindu, Muslim, or otherwise) are intellectually, spiritually, and societally dangerous. It's the soil and seeds from which acts of violence generations later come into fruition—whether the next 9/11 or public shooting.[87] I'm not only running as far away from that as possible, but encouraging others to do the same in many of my publications (attached). (Jesus and Paul were incensed at the fundamentalists more than the 'liberals' it seems—and presumably for good reasons.)

Second, it's super important to underscore that the ensuing discussion above is *not* specifically meant to persuade you or anyone else of *any* particular doctrine. I wouldn't want it and would be scared if anyone finds what I say convincing at face value, anyway. I'm not writing to "convert." So although I probably sound a bit polemic and impassioned, and much of my experience and criticism inevitably addresses your own views (that's part of the reason I found them worth sharing), I'm just trying to let you get inside my head for a few minutes to understand how faith "deconstruction" can happen—because it's a taboo subject that's clouded by stereotypes, even if that's sure to make others pretty disturbed. But to be clear: I don't expect nor necessarily want you to change specific views on anything, and that's not why I'm writing, and that's not why I'm sending you these gifts.

And that brings us to…phew, finally. The purpose of this letter—explaining the gifts!

---

[86] Although, it is extremely rare for a person to become more "conservative" as they get older. See all the autobiographies of the Christian scholars in John Byron and Joel Lohr, eds., *I Still Believe: Leading Bible Scholars Share Their Stories of Faith and Scholarship* (Grand Rapids: Zondervan, 2015)—all but one move from "right" to "left." This book, by the way, was encouraging to me in some dark times.

[87] The April 2019 shooting at the Chabad Synagogue by the young OPC perpetrator, who enjoyed talking reformed theology and Calvinism, comes to mind in mentioning this—though there obviously is no bounds to who can commit such atrocities.

ON THE BOOKS

Even given the qualifiers above, I have already given you all the ammunition you need to completely discard all the contents in the box you have before you, and to discredit myself from being a trustworthy conversation partner in things related to theology. For I am now "one with the enemy," "on the dark side," "defected from the faith." In many ways (though not all), I stand at the opposite end of the spectrum of my former life, and everything I say can and say will be held against me, and I am a true danger to your soul (let's laugh at this together, because if I'm really that threatening, good heavens…).

So let me give you *more* reasons why you shouldn't accept these gifts or trust me in any way: (1) I'm overconfident, and it obviously got the best of me early in life; (2) I'm still young (though the gray hair is appearing, and my frontal hairline is retreating like Custer's last stand); (3) you don't really want to experiment with your perfect theology (fingerprints on that crystal glass, golly!); and (4) you would be embarrassed to have to explain why there are odd and unfamiliar books in your (once) holy and unblemished household.

But, there is a sliver of hope in this dark sky that I haven't wasted all my time and money. Very briefly. First, *none of the books in this box are strictly chosen to persuade you to change your views on anything.* That's a fact. Second, *none of the books are purely a representation of "what I think" on a given topic.* That's a fact.[88]

So then why the heck did I give you the books that I did? What's the point?

For three reasons, and for three reasons only, my Lord Hans: (1) to put an end to the embarrassing public spectacle of when bystanders gaze upon the "theological library" in your office and henceforth initiate vomiting in their own mouths[89]; (2) to at least somewhat catch you up on

---

[88] My own writings included in this box are, well, they are what they are. Read at your own risk.

[89] For your own sake—from the bottom of my heart—and for the sake of your descendants and their name, I forbid you from ever referring to that pile of (almost) entirely waste-paper filth behind your desk as a "theological library"—or even a "library," ever again.

the most important issues related to Christianity by the highest quality monographs on given subjects (i.e., "education"),[90] and to do so in a way that is (mostly) more enjoyable than threatening; (3) above all (as Owen Barfield once put it), to do what poetry does best: expand your consciousness. That's it. That's all I'm hoping for. To "challenge" you? Yes, of course, that will inevitably happen in some sense. Very few of the books are from a perspective you're familiar with—and the books wrapped in red lean in that challenging direction. But, even as you need some challenging (as we all do), spurring both empathy (a form of intelligence) and intellectual understanding is the point.[91] In the end, I'm not simply trying to push your buttons. If I wanted to convince you of something, I would have kept 15% of these selections and changed the other 85%. Especially for the books wrapped in gold paper, this is more of a platform for discussion, common ground, and shared inspiration.

How, then, does this orientation come to bear in the categories?

THE BOOKS WRAPPED IN GOLD

The books wrapped in gold paper are there precisely because they are that: *gold*.

These are six[92] of the highest quality books on Christianity that I have ever read, that are meant to build up your faith one way or another.

Your parents have both failed you in this respect, and they will receive their own discipline in due time. Until then, just know that you'll thank me later.

[90] It's impossible to do what a seminary education could do—but, you'll be pleased to know that most seminaries have you read poopie books anyway (as evidenced in the fact that *none* of the works I'm bestowing to your possession were part of *any* of my three degrees in religion/Christian studies).

[91] I clarify "empathy" as a form of intelligence because too often in conservative evangelical circles, appeals to "emotion" are somehow viewed as "anti-rational" and automatically discounted, as if emotional reactions can be assured to be untruthful. This again reveals fundamentalism's sell-out to modernist thought (and it's fictional dualism between reason and emotion), and also skews our perception of things. (For example, even if emotions could be entirely detached from rationality and reason, they still indicate truth in ways that words and contemplation could not—as when a number of German SS officers wept when witnessing their first execution of Jews under Hitler.)

[92] We leave the seventh book for the scriptures themselves, of course. (This is just my way of saying: I intended seven but it didn't work out that nicely.)

I chose them not because they're my favorite (though some are), or because they represent my views (though some do), or because you will simply find them challenging. I chose them because of their overall *quality* and *importance* of issues to which they speak. So if there are any volumes in Christian thought that I think you ought to read sooner than later, these would be it. These are the ones you "don't want to miss,"[93] and will hopefully inspire you to be a better person and a more confident witness to the world.

Books to the scholar, as you know, are like friends. They deserve affection and at least some words of introduction. So let me introduce you to some of my friends…

Fleming Rutledge. *The Crucifixion of Jesus.* Grand Rapids: Eerdmans, 2015.

One of the most important books ever written on the crucifixion in the English language. Yes, that's quite a claim for a book that is less than a decade old. But when you read it, its endorsements, and experience its contents, you'll understand.

Rutledge is a preacher of renown in the mainstream Protestant world. As such, her analysis, stories, and prose make the themes and paradoxes of the cross come to life in a way that stands unmatched to perhaps its most similar work—*The Crucified God* by Jürgen Moltmann (also highly recommended). I enjoyed reviewing the book for a journal I edit. She covers a lot of standard stuff (e.g., atonement theories, problem of evil, etc.), but in enlightening and original ways.

Suggestions for reading: Set aside petty quibbles, drink a few ounces of Talisker (Distiller's Edition, not that Storm crap), and let the wisdom of this sage minister course through your veins.

James Cone. *The Cross and the Lynching Tree.* Maryknoll: Orbis Books, 2013.

One of the most notable books in theology of recent times, also

---

[93] And if you do miss them—bury them under some disgraceful stuff that doesn't even deserve the dignity of being named—well, it's your funeral.

centered on the paradoxes and meaning of the cross with an eye-opening parallel to the lynching period in American history. His chapter on his predecessor at Union, the great Reinhold Neibuhr, and the ignorance with which the most socially-liberal theologians of the time had while brothers and sisters in Christ were hung up, fingers cut off, and lit on fire with gasoline, was stunning to read about. Even more so was the remarkable parallels between Roman crucifixion and lynching in the early 1900s and late 1800s.

I was talking with an Airbnb guest the other night on issues of theology (he is a Methodist with similar interests), and he said "I've come to learn more and more that white Christians don't have much of a story to tell. But in black preaching, you just hear how theology comes to life in the real story of forgiveness and suffering that they've lived through." My experience has been the same. I've never felt that "the gospel" is more relevant to the world than listening to African American Christians preach and unfold the meaning of the cross, whether in music or prose.

Sound crazy? Sound too "liberal" for your impeccable sensibilities, pious brother? I hereby dare you to read this book and see for yourself just whose theology needs an injection of RedBull.

Daniel Migliore. *Faith Seeking Understanding*. Grand Rapids: Eerdmans, 2014.

This selection would not be complete without a systematic theology or topical introduction of some kind. I chose Migliore for its thematic completeness, pastoral wisdom, and something I think you would also enjoy.

I've taught through this volume several times in the classroom, and was thoroughly gratified and edified by it each time. Although the first chapter(s) is a little wordy and abstract, the book as a whole is an excellent demonstration of a sagacious scholar (Charles Hodge Professor of Systematics at Princeton, no less) distilling a lifetime of scholarship into theology that matters in practical ways for the church. Broadly reformed, somewhat Barthian and with sensitivies to 20th century theologies (with a hilarious conversation between some recent theological giants in the back matter), *Faith Seeking Understanding* is, yes, another book "you won't want to miss." (My mom read it this past year and, though she found it challenging at times, deeply appreciated the journey.)[94]

Alan Kreider. *The Patient Ferment of the Early Church: The Improbable Rise of Christianity in the Roman Empire*. Grand Rapids: Baker Academic, 2015.

There is no short supply of competing narratives when it comes to Christianity's earliest identity, growth and eventual dominance in the West. The contemporary accounts vary widely: the popular conspiracy theories of mainstream lore (e.g. *The Da Vinci Code*, the original *Zeitgest* film); the contrarian, debonair reflections of Elaine Pagels (*The Gnostic Gospels* [New York: Vintage, 1989]; *The Origin of Satan: How Christians Demonized Jews, Pagans, and Heretics* [New York: Vintage, 1996]) and Bart Erhman (*How Jesus Became God* [New York: HarperOne, 2015]); the refined, in-house projects of Christian academia (e.g. N.T. Wright's *Christian Origins and the Question of God* series, the works of Larry Hurtado); the proposals of historians like Rodney Stark (*The Rise of Christianity: How the Obscure, Marginal Jesus Movement Became the Dominant Religious Force in the Western World in a Few Centuries* [San Francisco: HarperOne, 1997]), Ramsay MacMullen and Erhman (*The Triumph of Christianity: How a Forbidden Religion Swept the World* (New York: Simon and Schuster, 2018); and everything else in between and beyond (such as the work of Candida Moss). The modern fight for Christianity's origins continues.

This was the first paragraph of my review of *The Patient Ferment* in *The Journal of Greco-Roman Christianity and Judaism*. As I indicate, there is a big debate going on in academia in the last few decades on the origins

---

[94] I used this volume side-by-side with Thomas Oden's one-volume *Classic Christianity*, also highly recommended as it is a great distillation of more traditional theological themes in the "great tradition," but with his widely-known command of the primary sources (Oden edited the whole Early Christian Commentary series and is a patristic scholar.)

of Christianity (yes, you read it right: no one agrees on how or why Christianity came into existence or why it didn't go extinct). But this book is more than an explanation to this question: it's a window into the early ethos and culture of the first Christians.

I'd explain more but let me put it this way: after reading this book, I remembered why I'm still a "Christian." And as I write in the conclusion of the review:

> It merits the highest priority for any English speaker wanting to know what on earth Christianity is all about and also for those who are interested in second- and third-century church history. It is the first (and perhaps last) book that I have reviewed without a single complaint or quibble. The only exception would be directed at the publisher for not signature-binding. For a monograph that might as well have been smyth-sewn in calfskin leather, it is a shame that the first printing boasts such a quotidian format. If the work sells, is translated and is distributed worldwide as it ought, perhaps the next printing will give the book the dignity it deserves.

Suggestions for reading: Take everything you thought about what "early Christianity" is and throw it out the window. Then read this with humble curiosity.

David Bentley Hart. *Atheist Delusions*. New Haven: Yale University Press, 2009.

A classical theist, Eastern Orthodox scholar, and the most eloquent (if not flamboyant) writer I've ever encountered, Hart is not just quotable in nearly every paragraph, but a force to be reckoned with when it comes to Christianity and atheism.

This is one of the few single volumes that have literally changed the way I've thought about my place in the world in the 21st century, as it encourages everyone not only to revisit the original challenge of Christianity, but to accept the new era of post-Christendom with a sense of honor and hope—especially since "we live now in the wake of the most monstrously violent century in human history, during which the secular order (on both the political right and the political left), freed from the authority of religion, showed itself willing to kill on an unprecedented scale and with an ease of conscience worse than merely depraved. If ever an age deserved to be thought an age of darkness, it is surely ours." We never chose it, but we live in a certain period of history that entails certain responsibilities. At least that's how I'm thinking now.

Friends have called it demeaning and arrogant. I guess I just found the tone entertaining more than irritating. Regardless, it was thoughtful and inspiring. So let me make it easy for you: You probably have not experienced "Christian apologetics" in book form until you've read *Atheist Delusions*.

N. T. Wright. *Jesus and the Victory of God.* Minneapolis: Fortress Press, 1996.

Perhaps the same could be said for this one—though in the realm of biblical studies instead of theology and philosophy.

Jesus and the Victory of God is probably the most significant explanation of Jesus from a "traditional" perspective. But since "N. T. Wright" already has negative connotations in the world of both fundamentalists *and* mainstream biblical studies, I'll have to unfold a bit more why this is, what it means, and the place of this book.[95]

First, on the "New Perspective," which has nothing to do with this book, but since you're unfortunately one of the souls that have gotten wrapped up (to some degree) in this bizarre Christian-anti-Wright spirit in America, it merits some explaining.

In 1977, a NT scholar by the name of EP Sanders published a book that changed the face of NT studies forever. It's called *Paul and Palestinian Judaism*. Among Sanders' discoveries (as an expert in Second-Temple Judaism, the period from post-exile to 70 CE) was that first-century Pharisees were not 16th century Roman Catholics. Crazy huh? You see, Luther's doctrine of justification developed by conflating his

---

[95] A PCA church I once attended forbade the reading of N. T. Wright, if that says anything! (And it was funny how none of them ever read any of Wright. It seemed to be another case of "we're too smart to read other books.")

Roman Catholic opponents with the "Judaizers" in Paul's letters (and of conflating his own experience with Paul's). The trouble, of course, is that they aren't the same—and Sanders proved it. There *was* no group of Jews in the time of Jesus that taught the Protestant idea of "works righteous salvation." This type of "legalism" (Medieval Catholic) couldn't be found in the primary sources of the period.[96] So then what exactly were Paul's Jewish *opponents* really saying, and what did *Paul* mean by "justification by faith"?

Well, just look at the name: "the circumcision party." The "works of the law" were specifically the Jewish ethical codes like circumcision and food laws. Paul isn't contrasting his teaching with "generic good deeds" (at least most of the time, and at least in his earlier letters). "Faith" contrasted with this how? That's explained in Galatians 1-3 (and Romans 1, etc.), again contrasted with these specific ethical codes. "Faith" is life in the "fruits of the Spirit"—a life lived in Christlikeness, which is in freedom. This is "the law of Christ" (as opposed to, the famous "law of Moses" at large).

What then is "justification," since people are "justified by faith"? Again, it's right there in Galatians (which comes *before* Romans, mind you), especially 2:11-16: Peter was rebuked by Paul because he acted in a way contrary to Christ. He stopped eating with Gentiles. That is, he reneged on his "faith" and went back to "the law" (i.e., of ceremonial

---

[96] Or in the words of N. T. Wright and Michael Bird, *The New Testament in Its World* (Grand Rapids: Zondervan Academic, 2019), 126-128: "Passage after passage in Jewish writers of the period...emphasizes that the Jewish laws were not designed as a legalist's ladder up which one might climb to heaven; they were the boundary-markers for a beleaguered people...The clash between Jesus and the Pharisees...must be seen in terms of two alternative political agendas, generated by the alternative eschatological beliefs of two competing renewal movements...Jesus was announcing the kingdom in a way that did not reinforce, but rather called into question, the agenda of revolutionary zeal that dominated the horizon of the leading group within Pharisaism. The coming of the kingdom, as Jesus announced it, put before his Pharisaic contemporaries a challenge, an agenda: give up your interpretation of your tradition, which is driving you towards ruin....Jesus' clash with the Pharisees came about not because he was antinomian, or because he believed in 'grace' and 'faith' while they believed in 'justification by works', but because his kingdom-agenda for Israel demanded that Israel leave off its frantic search for national purity and regional hegemony, reinforced as it now was by the ancestral codes, and embrace instead the proper vocation to be the light of the world, the salt of the earth."

separation, because the gospel is actually *inclusive*). *This* is the context of justification, according to Paul. And it means (according to Dunn, who followed up on Sanders) an indicator of "*staying in* the covenant people," or (according to Wright, who followed up on Dunn) "*knowing who is* in the covenant people."[97] In either case, justification is a *visible badge*. It's like you're at a party and the bouncer looks around for the badge of membership, and he sees you and the badge and says "Ok, you're good; you're justified" (and doesn't throw you out.) If this doesn't make sense, just turn to James and his discussion of justification, and it's pretty clear. (So yes: Paul and James *are* generally talking about the same thing. The reason Protestants have to say James is talking about something different than Paul is not because James is deviant, but because *their* understanding of *Paul* is deviant.)

All this gets jumbled up into language of "salvation," of course, because "getting in" or "staying in" has to do with God's work of being saved as covenant people. But "justification" is not simply "salvation," but has to do with (for Paul) who you're eating with and other visible displays of identity. (See diagram of all this below, as best as I could summarize.)

---

[97] "… 'justification by works' has nothing to do with individual Jews attempting a kind of proto-Pelagian pulling themselves up by their moral bootstraps, and everything to do with the definition of the true Israel in advance of the final eschatological showdown. Justification in this setting, then, is not a matter of *how someone enters the community of the true people of God,* but of *how you tell who belongs to that community,* not least in the period of time before the eschatological event itself, when the matter will become public knowledge…it was not so much about 'getting in', or indeed about 'staying in', as about 'how you could tell who was in'…wasn't so much about soteriology as about ecclesiology; not so much about salvation as about the church." N. T. Wright, *What Saint Paul Really Said* (Minneapolis: Fortress Press, 1997), 139. Yes, I read Piper's book in response—and also read Wright's response to Piper in *Justification.* FYI: Even many evangelicals today no longer accept "imputation." See Michael Bird, *Evangelical Theology* (Grand Rapids: Zondervan, 2011), 562-63: "The problem humanity has is not a lack of moral merits. The problem is a broken relationship. What is needed is not merit, but reconciliation…The standard proof texts lined up to prove imputation fail to say exactly what some Reformed theologians think they say…no text explicitly says that the obedience of Jesus is imputed to believers as their righteousness. [It's better to talk of 'incorporation']."

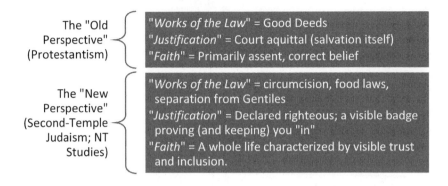

For anyone in biblical studies, this is another fascinating case of taking a standard theological dogma for granted. And there's little reason to reject the thesis (or at least its broad contours). But for conservative evangelicals and their Protestant tradition, *the sky is falling*. We don't mess around with these "sacred words" of Lord Luther—even if it only shows our own ignorance of Paul and the New Testament. Sigh.

Well anyway, none of this has much to do with Wright—unless, again, that's all you've heard "N. T. Wright" to be associated with. It's barely even a side-hustle to his work. His main goals have been re-orienting the whole project of Christian New Testament Studies since the advent of higher criticism, and clarifying Jesus, Paul, and Christian origins. In other words, making sure that the Christian faith as a whole doesn't get swept entirely aside. What then, is he responding to? Well, big trends and ideas like:

1. Jesus was just a cool teacher, or just an apocalyptic prophet, or another contemporary revolutionary who got squashed by the Romans, or a cynic, lunatic, etc. (Wright's thesis is based on a theological interpretation of the Old and New Testaments: the God in Christ is becoming King [hence his book titles, *How God Became King* and *Jesus and the Victory of God*]—inaugurating the "take-over" period of God's kingdom coming to earth.)
2. Paul was a Jew who never intended to invent Christianity, but believed Jesus was the Messiah. Christianity was invented later by the Gospel writers (80s-120 CE), who were anti-Semitic and

desperate to "win."

3. Paul was a Christian who invented Christianity—against Jesus' own wishes and context (because he wasn't Messiah, or he was, but only for the Jews).

4. Paul perverted Christ's message and the gospel writers, which was Christianity against Judaism (or against religion in general) and a more universal religion for all.

And on it goes. You can see then, *this is a pretty big deal in the big picture.* Is Christianity a legitimate faith tradition or not? If you care about apologetics, this question dwarfs about anything else…

The resurgence of the study of Second-Temple Judaism in the last half century—due to its previous neglect in Jesus studies[98]—spawned the new field of "Christian Origins," which is frequently taught by Jewish professors at universities in chairs by that title. The basic line, using some of Ehrman's material and stuff on gnostic gospels (like Pagels), is #2 above. Christianity was an accident (see works of P. Eisenbaum, P. Fredricksen, etc.). *It never should have gotten off the ground in the first place, and isn't actually a legitimate religion today any more than it was then.*[99] The books on this are now fast and some very popular. It's gaining a larger (and premature, I might add) consensus in various universities, and more "traditional" histories of Christianity are fading into the background (hence the importance of Kreider and others mentioned below).

Again, if you're an "apologist" or care about the credibility of Christianity, this is about as relevant as it gets. But virtually no popular apologist is even aware of these movements (they seem too preoccupied

---

[98] The "Greco" in "Greco-Roman" world was sort of the default orientation of scholarship since the late 1800s and into the early 20th century, instead of the Jewish aspects.

[99] Of course, one could argue that neither then is Judaism a "legitimate' faith, since it evolved out of polytheism and henotheism. This again gets back to the dynamic, evolutionary work of God in history mentioned earlier. What if this whole process is part of God's plan, and not simply depositing a one-time injection of "authoritative revelation" in a particular religious identity? (If this sounds heretical, consider the outsider Melchizedek blessing Abraham, or Paul's use of pagan poetry and the "unknown God" in his encounters with the Greeks, etc.)

arguing amongst themselves about middle-knowledge and whether Noah's flood was global…).

Anyway, hence Larry Hurtado's *The Lord Jesus Christ* and *Destroyer of the Gods,* hence Richard Bauckham's *The Jewish World Around the New Testament* and *The Christian World Around the New Testament,* hence James Dunn's three-volume *Christianity in the Making* series, and hence N. T. Wright's multivolume "Christian Origins and the Question of God" — which brings us to the book you hold. As a former historian who worked at Cambridge and Oxford, Wright is in a unique position to assess this whole debate. This six-volume project is set out as one of the most significant works in Christian thought and New Testament, and even "apologetics" (this term is not respected and used in academia for its notorious anti-intellectualism already discussed above). Among many unique contributions, he comes to essentially "traditional" conclusions about Christianity and Judaism[100] —including (in contrast to some others) the bodily resurrection.[101] In general, Wright is too conservative for many or most NT scholars in academia (including me, though NT isn't technically my space).[102] But (like Richard Bauckham and gospel research), because he comes to rather ordinary ("traditional") conclusions for good reasons, and because of his command of the Greco-Roman world and lucid writing style, many appreciate his work (as I do) and some non-fundamentalist evangelicals in America love him. And thus, being on the front lines, he gained the notoriety that he has around the world.

---

[100] His own metaphor regarding this relationship is "Christianity is a mutation of Judaism."

[101] Less "conservative" Christian scholars in this space like, Sanders and Meier, typically leave the resurrection as a historical "mystery" or just outside the bounds of historical work. More "liberal" ones, like Borg, take the classic modernist route (i.e., something weird happened and the disciples made up the resurrection, or they intentionally made it up in response to the trauma of losing their leader, or it gradually evolved into a metaphor for something.)

[102] As an elder British Anglican, Wright naturally defaults to many traditional positions on social issues, and does not know the space of systematics very well (I asked him in person at an IBR conference what his favorite work in more recent theology was and he said, "well Paul…" I should have seen that coming), and also is uncritical/overly critical about what post-modern criticism brings to the table. Though, I have to say I am sometimes surprised at his progressive outlook on various matters (e.g., being interviewed on the Christian Transhumanism podcast).

So I laugh every time I hear about mainstream apologists getting their knickers in a twist about N. T. Wright and the "New Perspective" (1977 isn't new)—when he may have done more to establish the credibility of traditional accounts of early Christianity in the last two decades than perhaps any other single individual.

Well anyway, Wright completed the first volume in 1992 (setting the context of the exile and Jewish people), second volume (the one you have) in 1996, third one on the resurrection in 2003, fourth in 2013 on Paul, and the fifth (and final?) is due to come out next year or so. (Yes, it's about a thirty-year project.)[103] Each one is significant in its own right (no pun intended). But this second one is probably the most popular and notable because it deals directly with Jesus. By the mid-1990s, the Jesus seminar and most schools of thought on the subject had pumped out their representative works. *Jesus and the Victory of God*, then, is simply one of the most brilliant works of New Testament scholarship ever written about Jesus from a Christian perspective. Although some have (legitimately I'm sure) accused him of painting too clean of a picture,[104] the dots that he does connect in *so much* of what we've been taught— from Sunday school parables to the "end times"—is impressive to almost anyone. (I own all of his "NT for Everyone" commentaries—which includes his own translation of the entire NT—and it has been the best investment of that sort I've made, at least when it comes to really understanding the NT in its own context.)

So if you couldn't care less about whether Christianity is actually a faith worth being part of, no need to read the book. It would be boring. But if you do, and if you grasp the potential weight of what's happening in terms of perceptions of early Christianity—and the immeasurable implications they might have, and if you want a quality work, this is a "must-read."

---

[103] All of them will be helpfully condensed into one volume by Bird entitled *The New Testament in Its World*.

[104] See Dunn's critiques in *Jesus Remembered*.

THE BOOKS WRAPPED IN SILVER

Inevitably, there were books that just *didn't quite* make the cut. Instead of just forgetting them like most people (I'm not like most people, you see), I decided to include them in a second tier. The top two are Daniel Migliore's *The Power of God and the Gods of Power,* an excellent resource for small groups or studies that show the relevance of Christian theology to everyday life. And Dorothee Soelle's *Thinking About God: An Introduction to Theology.* It's a birds-eye view of theological method that's really easy to read, and very clever in its orientation. The book clobbered me pretty hard in helping me step outside my box; I'm guessing it will challenge you in similar ways. But, like Schneider and Ray's *Awake the Moment,* it's a highly underrated work by a brilliant thinker that I wish I would have read in seminary.

Robert Wilken's *The Spirit of Early Christian Thought* is probably the best work I've ever read that explains how Christian theology evolved from the first century to the dogmas of the West. It's a gem that is unmatched in that task, at least in terms of readability and familiarity with primary sources and history. (His earlier work, *The Christians as the Romans Saw Them,* is just as great and original.) There are other items included here as a "bonus." (We all agree that you've earned it).

THE BOOKS WRAPPED IN RED

This entire wedding gift began as a response to your gift to me— which included the book on dispensationalism. I wanted to send back a couple zinger books in response for fun, but as you can tell, things got a little bit out of hand.

But I ended up with three/four books to at least stretch your thinking a bit in some of the classic dogmas of evangelicalism. This small selection of heresy (in your eyes, of course) is simply to lay out what might help you at least *understand* other points of view (since I know you are willing to do that).[105]

---

[105] Though, as someone recently told me in a handwritten letter, "But if the Lord wills to

I included James Barr's *The Bible in the Modern World* (co-shared with your brother) and Christian Smith's *The Bible Made Impossible* to help you get a sense for "bibliolatry" and "biblicism" and why it's a problem (cf. the book for your brother by Carlos Bovell).[106] *How I Changed My Mind About Women in Ministry* is self-explanatory, as is David Gushee's *Changing Our Mind* and McLaren's *A New Kind of Christianity*. I was going to include some on evolution, like Peter Enns *The Evolution of Adam* or McKnight and Venema's *Adam and the Genome*. But since I already wrote a 55-page article on that topic, I figured I'd let you read it from the "horse's mouth" and save a few dollars. That brings us to the final categories.

SELECTIONS FROM MY LIBRARY

There are two collections from my library of material that you might be interested in reading that are included in this box.

The first are a selection of articles and book reviews, which I have aptly labeled "heresy." The second selection are drafts of teaching materials and syllabi, which I think are helpful points of reference for much of what has been covered in this letter, and also for future discussions on related topics. I think you'll find perusing these teaching documents quite fun and interesting; most of the syllabi represent my current inclinations as to how I would teach a course at a Christian university or church or what have you.

Tables of contents are provided on the first page of each bound collection so you can find your way around. In the back of the teaching materials one, I've also provided my CV so you can identify those works that I have and have not included.

We've reached the end.

---

unblind your eyes…who am I to object?"

[106] I really like Barr, probably because he's like me (intentionally presses the forbidden questions). And if I have the money someday, I'll buy his recently published collected works by Oxford (3 vols). He's actually a British Hebrew scholar and linguist who wrote three volumes on American fundamentalism (strange indeed), which—along with this book on the Bible—was probably the single most "unplugged from Matrix" experience I've had in my journey.

In conclusion, I love you, and hope the years get better for you as time goes on, and that God would bless you and keep you, that your marriage would be for happiness and not just for holiness,[107] and that we will see each other sooner instead of later. I'm so happy to have gotten to meet you and learn from you, and I have often been jealous of not being a brother in your family. Stay in touch!

So enjoy these petty gifts and petty words as you continue to lose hair, beauty, and Lord knows what else. The Grim Reaper draws near.

In Christ,
Grace and Peace,
Jamin
Summer, 2019

---

[107] Yes, you read that right.

Appendix A:

Table of Contents of
Publications Originally Included With Letter

(Reader's Note: **Bold** ones are included in this book as appendices)

*"Selections from Hübner's Library of
Horrifyingly Horrendous Heresies"*

"The Evolution of Complementarian Exegesis." *Priscilla Papers* 29:1
(Winter, 2015):11-13.

Review of John Piper, *A Peculiar Kind of Glory: How the Christian
Scriptures Reveal Their Complete Truthfulness* **(Wheaton:
Crossway, 2016) for** *The Canadian American Theological Review* **5:1
(2016):91-95.**

"Revisiting αὐθεντέω in 1 Timothy 2:12: What Do the Extant Data
Really Show?" *The Journal for the Study of Paul and His Letters* 5:1
(Spring, 2015):41-70.

"Revisiting the Clarity of Scripture and 1 Timothy 2:12." *The Journal for
the Evangelical Theological Society* 59:1 (2016):99-117. Revised and
republished by CBE in *Priscilla Papers* 30:3 (2016):18-25.

"The Anatomy of Nationalism: A Fresh Appraisal Based on Recent Case
Studies." *Libertarian Papers* 10:2 (2018):137-177.

"The Progress (or Extinction?) of Modern Creationism: A Critical Review
of Crossway's *Theistic Evolution.*" *The Canadian-American Theological
Review* 7:1 (2018): 1-55.

"A Critical Review of The Nashville Statement." *Priscilla Papers* 33:1
(Winter 2019):19-30. First published in *Eyes to See and Ears to Hear
Women: Sexual Assault as a Crisis of Evangelical Theology.* Ed. Tim
Krueger. Minneapolis: CBE International, 2018. Pp. 83-113.

"Selections from Hübner's Library of
Scholarly Pedagogy"

"What Does 'Modern' and 'Postmodern' Really Mean?"

"Intro to Intro to the Bible."

Syllabus for CHR101: "Introduction to the Bible" (or "The Origin of the Bible")

Syllabus for CHR331: "Theologia Principia I: God and Creation"

Transcript of Q & A During 2016 ETS Annual Meeting Trinity Panel Between Wayne Grudem and Jamin Hübner

Syllabus for CHR207: "Christian Apologetics"

Syllabus for CHR422: "Pauline Epistles"

Appendix B:

DECONSTRUCTING BEFORE RECONSTRUCTING
A Concise Annotated Bibliography

These books are primarily meant for readers who remain convinced American evangelical views on key issues are intellectually credible, but are willing to challenge them. (These are in addition to my own publications in Appendix A.)

Baden, Joel. *The Book of Exodus: A Biography.* Princeton: Princeton University Press, 2019. A short little book on the meaning of Exodus and how its significance has changed through time. Baden (Professor of Hebrew Bible at Yale Divinity School) also presents a concise explanation of its historicity and literary origins. Easy to read and very fascinating. The challenge for evangelical readers here is twofold: (a) the latest scholarship by the best experts on the subject do not hold to the evangelical view on the historical Exodus for good reasons, and (b) the Bible's meaning is plural and evolutionary (or "living"), and (fortunately) not fixed and bound to time ("dead").

Barr, James. *The Scope and Authority of the Bible.* London: SMC Classics, 2002. Barr (Professor of Hebrew Bible at Oxford) was my gateway drug to historical-critical readings of the Bible. While some read him as a bit cold and rational, he's really just a rigorous modern thinker and, underneath, really cares about his readers. This volume remains one of the most concise and penetrating discussions about how any Christian thinks about the Bible. (Best read alongside his *Beyond Fundamentalism: Biblical Foundations for Evangelical Christianity.*)

Breed, Brennan. *Nomadic Text: A Theory of Biblical Reception History.* Indianapolis: India University Press, 2014. Perhaps the most important work on the concept of "interpreting the original text," especially with regard to the Old Testament. He reveals that a fixed singular autographic text ("the original") is an abstract fiction, and much about "the meaning of the text." (Cf. Van Der Toorn, *Scribal Culture,* listed below.)

Boswell, John. *Same-Sex Unions in Premodern Europe.* New York: Vintage, 1995. For one reason or another, many evangelicals today are under the impression that same-sex relationships are "new," and that Christianity has never interacted with them (and certainly not blessed them) before. This book offers a historically-grounded narrative that demonstrates otherwise and is helpful in re-situating our assumptions about same-sex relationships, regardless of what our conclusions or starting points are.

Bovell, Carlos. *Rehabilitating Inerrancy in a Culture of Fear.* Eugene: Wipf and Stock, 2012. A Westminster Seminary graduate explains why such things as the Chicago Statement of Inerrancy are intellectually and spiritually bankrupt. (Cf. his *Inerrancy and the Spiritual Formation of Younger Evangelicals*)

Brownson, James. *Bible, Gender, Sexuality: Reframing the Church's Debate on Same-Sex Relationships.* Grand Rapids: Eerdmans, 2013. The seminal work on the gay/lesbian and Bible debates by a reformed biblical scholar. Particularly good for those who are caught up in the hermeneutical issues of "what's biblical" and haven't bothered to ask the "why" question.

Burge, Gary. *Whose Land? Whose Promise?: What Christians Are Not Being Told about Israel and the Palestinians.* Cincinnati: Pilgrim Press, 2013. Ever since the rise of dispensationalist theology in the late 1800s, the traumatic events of two world wars, and the establishment of the state of Israel in 1948, conservative evangelicals in America have come to conflate the people of "Israel" in the Bible with the secular, political state of "Israel" of today. This Zionist theology has facilitated war, racism, and one of the greatest refugee crises in modern history (with over 700,000 Palestinians displaced). This book, written by an evangelical New Testament professor at Wheaton College, re-examines the biblical and theological claims of evangelical Zionism and finds them severely wanting. (See also his *Jesus and the Land*, to learn about Jesus' own anti-nationalist perspective on this matter.)

Date, Chris, et. al. *Rethinking Hell: Readings in Evangelical Conditionalism.* Eugene: Cascade, 2014. Many people become evangelical Christians for one reason only: to avoid the eternal fires of hell. It's strange, however, how this unchristian (and even "unbiblical") dogma became a centerpiece of evangelical theology. This book is written by over a dozen evangelicals who don't buy eternal conscious torment.

DeFranza, Megan. *Sex Difference in Christian Theology: Male, Female, and Intersex in the Image of God.* Grand Rapids: Eerdmans, 2015. A fine research project of theological anthropology and historical theology surrounding concepts of sexuality and intersexuality. Challenging for those who simply want to ignore the importance and implications of such subjects, and a must-read for those who believe sexual and gender binarism is "traditional."

Ellul, Jacque. *The Political Illusion,* trans. Konrad Kellen. New York: Knopf/Random House, 1967; republished by Wipf and Stock, 2015. An eccentric work by an eccentric thinker, a French sociologist and lay theologian. A brilliant classic in Christian anarchism that puts mainstream politics, media, and the state in a realistic—and eye-opening—perspective.

----------. *The Subversion of Christianity,* trans. Geoffrey Bromiley. Eugene: Wipf and Stock, 2011, orig. 1986. Ever wonder how and why Christianity got so far off track since the first century? This book is one of the most thoughtful, socio-theological answers to that question ever penned. Readers will have their whole understanding of Christianity turned upside down and inside out.

Enns, Peter. *Inspiration and Incarnation: Evangelicals and the Problem of the Old Testament.* Grand Rapids: Baker Academic, 2015 (orig. 2005). A more popular work that brings to bear some of the problems of the OT on traditional bibliology by a former Westminster Seminary Professor.

----------. *The Evolution of Adam.* Grand Rapids: Brazos, 2012. A clear and concise explanation why Genesis 1-3 should be interpreted in its context (i.e. post-exilic). Contrary to what most evangelicals have taught, these stories were written later and not earlier in Israel's history; Gen 1-3 are likely a parable of Israel's birth, call to obedience, and fall into exile. An injection of sound reasoning regarding the most abused chapters in the Bible.

Giles, Kevin. *The Rise and Fall of the Complementarian Doctrine of the Trinity.* Eugene: Cascade Books, 2017. A short and eye-opening narrative of how evangelicals hi-jacked the doctrine of the Trinity to maintain female subordinationism, and why it was hopeless from the start. Written by an Anglican pastor-scholar.

Greenwood, Kyle, ed. *Scripture and Cosmology: Reading the Bible Between the Ancient World and Modern Science.* Downers Grove: InterVarsity Academic, 2015. A scholarly collection of studies on reception history of Hebrew cosmology. That is, the various authors look at how the Genesis creation account (and other things) has been interpreted through time, and reveal all kinds of interesting points. (Why is the story of Eve not found anywhere else in the Hebrew Bible? Did you know "Adam" in Hosea 6:7 is referring to a city, not a person? Etc.) Despite being a superb Hebrew Bible scholar, Greenwood (and other members of Colorado Christian University's theology/biblical studies dept) was laid off for his research. (Like other conservative institutions, the admin again made it clear that anti-intellectualism and indoctrination are more important than scholarship).

Groothuis, Rebecca. *Women Caught in the Conflict.* Eugene: Wipf and Stock, 1997. An influential work of mild, introductory feminist thought by a conservative evangelical. A great introduction to those who aren't at all familiar with feminist thought and its relation to Christian thought. (Cf. her sequel, *Good News for Women.*)

Joyce, Kathryn. *Quiverful: Inside the Christian Patriarchy Movement.* Boston: Beacon Press, 2009. If you grew up thinking your greatest purpose in life was bearing children and obeying your husband, think again. A very eye-opening work of social history that reveals how the conservative homeschool subculture is not exactly a place of safety and nourishment.

Klein, Kay Linda. *Pure: Inside the Evangelical Movement That Shamed a Generation of Young Women and How I Broke Free.* New York: Simon and Schuster, 2019. Whether you're a fan of sexual abstinence or not, there is certainly a right and wrong way to handle and talk about sex—especially for teenagers, since these are often traumatic experiences. This book shows how tactics of shame in evangelicalism needlessly destroys one's sense of worth, a healthy view of the body, and more healthy sexual relations with other persons. (Best read in conjunction with Jami Finch, *You Are Your Own* and Sellers, *Sex, God, and the Conservative Church.*)

Law, Timothy. *When God Spoke Greek.* New York: Oxford University Press, 2013. An excellent work showing how the early church used the Greek translation of the Old Testament instead of "the original" Hebrew text for their Bible. Essential for autograph-onlyists, and anyone who prioritizes the Hebrew Masoretic text over the Septuagint.

Lim, Timothy. *The Formation of the Jewish Canon.* New Haven: Yale University Press, 2013. Chronicles the tale of how certain books came to be in our Old Testaments, and why the "apocrypha" cannot be binarily rejected (as generally is by today's evangelicals). With Lee McDonald, Lim pulls up the rug from the views of Roger Beckwith, Michael Kruger, and others who manufacture arguments in order to "settle" the canon as evangelicals have it today.

McSkimming, Josie. *Leaving Christian Fundamentalism and the Reconstruction of Identity.* New York: Routledge, 2017. A sociological field-study of people who left conservative evangelical churches in Sydney, Australia. Very fascinating with lots of insight through real subjects and interviews, but more importantly, shows how perceptions radically change when one sees things from the outside instead of the inside. (Everything makes sense from "the inside"!)

Schmid, Konrad. *The Old Testament: A Literary History.* Minneapolis: Fortress Press, 2012. A standard literary history of the OT from a leader of the "European school" on this subject. An incredible journey with many twists and turns; dense but extremely incisive in its research. A must for anyone wanting to know about how the OT was written.

Smith, Mark. *The Origins of Biblical Monotheism: Israel's Polytheistic Background and the Ugaritic Texts.* New York: Oxford University Press, 2003. Many Christians have a simplistic view of the Old Testament and theology. In theory, Yahweh (God) simply revealed unique theological truths to Israel and these were passed down faithfully ever since. This seminal work by a Christian scholar shows how monotheism was something that evolved gradually in Israel's own history, and explains Yahweh's place in that story. A must-read for those who contend that there is only one theology in the Old Testament. (Best read in conjunction with Thomas Römer, *The Invention of God* and Konrad Schmid, *A Historical Theology of the Hebrew Bible.*)

Sprinkle, Preston. *Fight: A Christian Case for Nonviolence.* Colorado Springs: David C. Cook, 2013. It's an absolutely bizarre turn of events how Christians came to embrace the military, war, and the U.S. empire. Sprinkle, a conservative evangelical New Testament scholar, walks through the biblical and theological problems with this relationship. (Best read in conjunction with Keith Giles, *Jesus Untangled,* and Brian Zhand, *Farewell to Mars.*)

Van der Toorn, Karel. *Scribal Culture and the Making of the Hebrew Bible.* Cambridge: Harvard University Press, 2009. Clearly explains how the Old Testament was written and another "must" on the subject. While idiosyncratic, his basic theses regarding what scribes did and how they wrote is a great introductory guide for this controversial subject. A great example of a Christian researcher following the evidence as best as possible, and letting history inform our understanding. (Best read in conjunction with Sarah Milstein, *Tracking the Master Scribe.*)

Venema, Dennis, and Scot McKnight. *Adam and the Genome: Reading Scripture after Genetic Science.* Grand Rapids: Brazos, 2017. Shows how common ancestry from two progenitors is impossible, and why standard evolutionary accounts have achieved the consensus they have—and what implications this has on Christian readings of human origins. (Best read in conjunction with Cavanaugh and Smith, *Evolution and the Fall.*)

Appendix C:

RECONSTRUCTING AFTER DECONSTRUCTING
A Concise Annotated Bibliography

These selections span progressive evangelicalism to neo-orthodox to revisionist/constructionist to mainstream liberal to postliberal and otherwise. Like any book, I have reservations with all of these volumes and only generally recommend them. Some readers will find some more relevant to their situation and interests than others. In any case, in addition to the books I recommended in the letter above, they are useful points of triangulation I've found for re-constructing.

Books

Adams, Marylin-McCord. *Opening to God: Childlike Prayers for Adults.* Louisville: Westminster John Knox, 2008. A collection of simple prayers by a marvelous professor of philosophy. Particularly helpful if you don't know what genuine prayer can or should look like, or if this vital aspect of spiritual living has gotten lost in deconstruction.

Barfield, Owen. *The Rediscovery of Meaning.* Middletown: Wesleyan, 2013, orig. 1977. Barfield was an eccentric and original thinker ahead of his time. He challenged and made a profound impact on his close friends, J. R. Tolkien and C. S. Lewis. As a non-university intellectual, a theosophist, and a linguist focused on the problems of reductionistic modernism and the evolution of human consciousness, this collection of essays has vital insight into the meaningless world in which we find ourselves (best read alongside William James, *The Varieties of Religious Experience*).

Bass, Diana Butler. *Christianity After Religion: The End of Church and the Birth of a New Spiritual Awakening.* New York: HarperOne, 2012. A perceptive archeology of American Christian faith in recent times, and a provocative thesis about what the future of Christianity already looks like, and why. Saturated in statistical studies and complemented by helpful anecdotes in explaining deconstruction from many different angles.

Beck, Richard. *Reviving Old Scratch: Demons and the Devil for Doubters and the Disenchanted*. Minneapolis: Fortress Press, 2016. Focuses on one popular topic of classic western theology, re-thought by a prison minister and professor of psychology. Part of Fortress Press's wonderful "Theology for the People" series.

Bessey, Sarah. *Miracles and Other Reasonable Things.* New York: Howard Books, 2019. An intense, lucid work of spiritual and personal autobiography that never stops moving. Recounts her traumatic car accident and a number of other adventures in experiencing God, life, meaning, and the search for direction. Particularly helpful for those wanting to enter into authentic human experience that's both challenging and encouraging. (For a different and yet similar, experience, consider reading in conjunction with Nolz-Weber's *Pastrix*.)

Borg, Marcus. *Convictions: How I Learned What Matters Most.* New York: HarperOne, 2016. Sagacious reflections from a seventy-year old religion scholar on what matters most in religion—especially Christian faith. Borg, an Episcopalian and former conservative evangelical, has written many theologically and ecclesiologically-constructive works re-orienting those for the new path ahead; tends to lean more "left" than others on some pivotal issues (see his debates with N.T. Wright), but is well-rehearsed in and dependent on the biblical tradition.

---------, and Wright, N. T. *The Meaning of Jesus: Two Visions.* San Francisco, CA: HarperSanFrancisco, 1999. A dialog between two leading Jesus scholars, one progressive, one traditional. (I found both perspectives gratifying and complementary as much as competitive.)

---------. *Days of Awe and Wonder: How to be a Christian in the Twenty-First Century.* New York: Harper One, 2017. The last book by Borg, a topical selection of his previous essays and sermons. A great digest of his re-framing of Christian life and thought.

Brandt, Cindy Wang. *Parenting Forward: How to Raise Children With Justice, Mercy, and Kindness.* Grand Rapids: Eerdmans, 2019. All of the problems we're dealing with as adults can virtually be traced to the way in which we've been raised. What happens in the world today is a continuation of what has been happening in the world of childhood. With insightful, clear, and extremely important observations and suggestions, Wang addresses not only parents, but provides alternative strategies for anyone wondering about the nuts and bolts of our constructed world, and making an impact. Fresh and intentionally non-traditional, non-authoritarian, and pro-freedom.

Byron, John and Joel Lohr, eds. *I Still Believe: Leading Bible Scholars Share Their Stories of Faith and Scholarship*. Grand Rapids: Zondervan, 2015. A marvelous collection of short autobiographies of Christianity's most accomplished biblical scholars of the twentieth-century. One of the most personally enriching volumes I've read, containing many heart-breaking—and yet encouraging—stories of spiritual, social, and intellectual deconstruction and reconstruction.

Carson, Timothy, ed. *Neither Here Nor There: The Many Voices of Liminality*. Cambridge, UK: The Lutterworth Press, 2019. An eccentric compilation of essays, primarily autobiographical, regarding that "inbetween" space. Includes essays addressing the experience of bi-racial persons, religious pilgrimage, stories of transformation in the Torah, poverty, cancer, and chaplaincy, war, natural disaster, transracial adoption, climate change and desert spirituality, leaving evangelical fundamentalism, cyborgs and science, life in and out of prison, post-apartheid Africa, transgender lives, and living as a Bedouin in the Negev desert. (Oh, and nearly drowning during a 180 feet scuba-dive!). Many genres and something for everyone, written mostly by a variety of Christian authors.

Claiborne, Shane. *The Irresistible Revolution, Updated and Expanded: Living as an Ordinary Radical*. Grand Rapids: Zondervan, 2016. A now classic popular work of post-conservative evangelicalism. Like Bolz-weber's *Pastrix,* prepare to get down and dirty and witness the intense radicality of living by the Spirit of Christ in a social and political world gone crazy.

Cobb Jr., John. *Resistance: The New Role of Progressive Christians.* Louisville: Westminster John Knox, 2008. A more topically complete, systematic single volume in this category by multiple thinkers. Begins with a very helpful discussion delineating "liberal" from "progressive," and includes topical chapters on everything from politics, to ecology, economics, scientism, feminism, forgiveness, and otherwise. Particularly good for those who have heard about "progressive" evangelicalism/Christianity, but don't know what it means or what it's logic consists of.

Corey, Benjamin. *Unafraid: Moving Beyond Fear-Based Faith*. New York: HarperOne, 2019. In the preface to this book I highlighted the coercive, fear-based nature of American evangelicalism. Corey (popular in the blogging space) confronts this topic full-throttle.

Charry, Ellen T. *God and the Art of Happiness.* Grand Rapids: Eerdmans, 2010. An insightful, original, and encouraging study of both historical and practical theology by a Princeton theologian—and on a controversial subject for Americans concerned about getting things right. She argues that happiness has a more central place in western theology than originally perceived, and that "Christian doctrine has not adequately linked piety to pleasure, thus leaving a theological gap between goodness and happiness." Academic in tone and a bit dense read.

Clayton, Philip. *Transforming Christian Theology: For Church and Society.* Minneapolis: Fortress Press, 2009. Introductory reflections on how theology must now change, by a leading science-theology expert and philosopher. (If you are interested in this intersection or just love science as a Christian and haven't read much of Clayton before, be sure to check out *God and Gravity: A Philip Clayton Reader.*)

De La Torre, Miguel. *Doing Christian Ethics from the Margins.* 2nd ed. Maryknoll: Orbis Books, 2014. An introduction to Christian ethics that is intentionally non-Eurocentric and liberationist. Highlights the problem of developing "Christian ethics" that is uncritical of its social and temporal location, bringing critical social analysis to bear on this key subject area of faith and gives a microphone to marginalized perspectives. Less broad and systematic than Gushee's *Kingdom Ethics*—and in fact argues for a very different understanding of "kingdom"—but equally biting in its challenge.

Drietcer, Andrew. *Living Compassion: Loving Like Jesus.* Nashville: Upper Room Books, 2017. What if our purpose in life is to heal the world through compassion? What if that's what Jesus was teaching us to do? Then it's about time we *learn how to do this!* An entry-level book on how, practically, we love people and what it looks like; appropriate for small groups and laypeople. (Read with the sister book by Rogers, *Practicing Compassion.*)

Dunn, James. *Christianity in the Making* (series). 3 vols. Grand Rapids: Eerdmans, 2003-2015. Confused about how Christianity came into existence and what it meant in the Greco-Roman world? This is (to my knowledge) the most comprehensive, scholarly, and credible account of Christian origins by a Christian author. Highly academic, well-written, and represents the accumulated finds of a truly great New Testament researcher. (Best read in conjunction with John

Dominic Crossan, Marcus Borg, EP Sanders, Bart Ehrman, Richard Bauckham, NT Wright, Richard Horsley, Larry Hurtado, and Michael Bird's work.)

Evans, Rachel Held. *Inspired: Slaying Giants, Walking on Water, and Loving the Bible Again.* Nashville: Nelson Books, 2018. It's common for post-conservatives to chuck their Bibles after deconstruction. This is one of the more direct and thorough books oriented around appreciating the Bible for what it is in a much less triggering and dogmatic way. (Cf. Marcus Borg's *Reading the Bible Again For the First Time: Taking the Bible Seriously But Not Literally.*)

Goldingay, John. *Biblical Theology: The God of the Christian Scriptures.* Intervarsity Press, 2018. While evangelically rooted, Goldingay pulls together the rich insights of his career into a single, marvelous volume in an impossible project of theology directly based on "the Bible." He moves beyond many of the stale categories of traditional Protestant systematics in a unique synthesis, crafted by someone who loves the scriptures and the profound stories within them. Get lost in this biblical-theological wonderland.

----------. *Models for Scripture.* Toronto: Clements, 2004. The best book on bibliology (doctrine of scripture) that I'm aware of. If you aren't sure how a religious anthology of literature could or should function in the Christian/believing community more than any other kind of anthology, this is a must-read. (Best read in conjunction with his sequel, *Models for Interpretation of Scripture* and Gorman's *Scripture and Its Interpretation,* a great Bible intro.)

Gonzalez, Guillermo. *The Privileged Planet.* Washington D.C.: Regnery, 2001. Unfortunately framed as an apologetic for the "Intelligent Design" and creationist movement, because it is a marvelous look at what astronomy and geophysics can imply about humanity's place in the universe. Mainly hard science with reflections, and good for anyone interested in this intersection and skeptical that human beings aren't important "in the big picture." This one really expanded the frontiers of my understanding of creation. (Best read along with Deb and Loren Haarsma's *Origins,* Haught's *The New Cosmic Story,* and especially Goodenough's *Sacred Depths of Nature*).

Gushee, David, and Glen Stassen. *Kingdom Ethics: Following Jesus in Contemporary Context.* 2nd ed. Grand Rapids: Eerdmans, 2016. The most principled, systematic, and robust framework of Christian ethics I am aware of. Super useful for disoriented persons who don't know where to start after biblicism in constructing ethical principles and rules for their lives and those around them. The models implemented are also competent enough to deal with virtually any ethical situation—and with real, substantive import from the Christ event.

Gushee, David. *After Evangelicalism.* Louisville, Westminster John Knox, 2020. Haven't read it yet because it hasn't been released. But based on early quotes and a table of contents David posted, I'm certain it's a good fit for this short bibliography. (He owes me one for recommending it pre-pub!)

Hartgrove, Jonathan-Wilson. *Reconstructing the Gospel: Finding Freedom from Slaveholder Religion.* Downers Grove: InterVarsity Press, 2018. A reconstructive project oriented around racial/ethnic justice. Passionately re-prioritizes the intersection between faith and politics. Hartgrove is part of the "new monasticism," which is something this book unfortunately did not address.

Haught, John. *The New Cosmic Story: Inside Our Awakening Universe.* New Haven: Yale University Press, 2017. Similar in general orientation to Kaufman, Primavesi, and McFague, but almost entirely dedicated to the question of religion's place and role in light of modern science and the universe's "waking up." Religion is not an outdated framework that needs to go extinct to further evolution. Just the opposite: it is the *latest achievement* of evolution (God's creative activity) that should be furthered; the phenomena of religion introduces a whole new era of cosmic history that also *tells us* something about cosmic history. Deep and profound for anyone who sees religious life as playing an important role in the future and is interested in science-religion relationship. (Consider reading alongside the much different angle of sociologist Christian Smith, *Religion.*)

Hartke, Austen. *Transforming: The Bible and the Lives of Transgender Christians.* Louisville: Westminster John Knox, 2018. A remarkable book exploring the struggle and journey of transgender Christians (primarily evangelical), including their experience of biblical texts and themes, transition, and new identity. Uniquely informed by both biblical studies and personal testimonies. Essential for any Christian who isn't sure where to begin on this intersection of topics.

Hodgson, Peter C. *Winds of the Spirit: A Constructive Christian Theology.* Louisville: Westminster John Knox, 1994. Perhaps the best one-volume systematic theologies for theologians I'm aware of—and an excellent fit for this bibliography. (Sort of an expanded version of

Schneider and Ray's *Awake the Moment*). Learned, culturally and historically sensitive, committed, honest, intellectually prudent, contemporary, challenging, original, methodical, hopeful, and self-aware. Similar to the work of Kaufman and David Tracy being revisionist and sophisticated, but less intimidating. Not quite as grounded/accessible as Migliore and Schneider/Ray. His uncritically critical view of the gospels and resurrection also need some work (Markham does better on this score). Nevertheless, his working metaphor for theology (sailing, "catching the wind") is appropriate and helpful. A thoughtful and underrated work that serves as a great point of departure for post-evangelical thinkers who believe in the work and discipline of constructive (previously "systematic") theology. (See his condensed version, *Christian Faith*, for something less thorough.)

Hurtado, Larry. *Destroyer of the Gods: Early Christian Distinctiveness in the Roman World*. Waco: Baylor University Press, 2017. How was Christianity different in the Greco-Roman world? A substantial work of history, religion, and humanities by a renowned professor of Christian origins. (Best read in conjunction with Kreider, *The Patient Ferment of the Early Church*. If you're still into claims of credibility or "apologetics" as a post-fundamentalist—particularly those surrounding Christian origins—see also Hurtado's seminal work, *The Lord Jesus Christ*, Wright/Bird's *The New Testament in Its World*, and Keener's *Christobiography*.)

James, William. *The Varieties of Religious Experience*. (Oxford World Classics.) New York: Oxford University Press, 2012, orig. 1902. The ultimate classic in de- and re-construction. Has a psychological and modern bent, but was (still is!) far ahead of its time and covers an incredible amount of territory. While one may not follow James all the way on each point, his re-framing of religious experience and honest assessment about its role in modern society is extremely insightful. Aside from psychological aspect, very similar to Kaufman's *In Face of Mystery* in its overall approach and conclusions.

Kaufman, Gordon. *In Face of Mystery: A Constructive Theology*. Cambridge: Harvard University Press, 1993. Very heady, adventurous, and radically liberal, full-scale reconception of Christian thought. Basically a modern version of William James' *Varieties of Religious Experience*, only without the psychological bent. Like Rohr, Primavesi, McFague, Hodgson, Clayton, Haught, et. al., he stresses the necessary integration of evolution into our theological paradigms. Like Hodgson, revisionist (re-constructionist) but does not adopt traditional loci and organization in systematics, more targeted themes, and less fleshed out. Heavy emphasis on language and human responsibility in our imaginative reconstructions; very skeletal and definitely begs for help from others (like NT theologians), but a ground-level starting point in its own right. Essential for any sophisticated, critical (and risky) thinker.

Markham, Ian. *Understanding Christian Doctrine.* 2nd ed. London: Wiley-Blackwell, 2017. Similar to Migliore's *Faith Seeking Understanding,* Markham (Episcopalian) presents an even more concise—and yet penetrating—introduction to Christian doctrines and thought. Excellent for graduate students, advanced church/Bible-study students, and curious seekers who want something very thoughtful, up-to-date, small, and clearly written. Constructive like Hodgson but implements more contemporary scholarship in biblical studies, and focuses deeply on theodicy as a primary focus of Christian thought.

McFague, Sallie. *Models of God.* Minneapolis: Fortress Press, 1987. Still a classic work on metaphor and theology, encouraging everyone to think critically about how we speak and think of God on a planet that faces the threat of extinction. (Cf. her other works on eco-theology.) Refigures, for example, the Trinity in terms of "Lover, Savior, Friend" (all of which are "biblical" themes, interestingly). Similar to Primavesi's *Sacred Gaia* but far less sophisticated and more targeted towards theology proper. (See also McFague's excellent *The Body of God: An Ecological Theology.*)

Middleton, J. Richard. *A New Heaven and a New Earth: Reclaiming Biblical Eschatology.* Grand Rapids: Baker Academic, 2014. A fine work of "biblical theology" by a friend and colleague. A great place to start if you're lost when it comes to "end times" and the Bible. (Best read in conjunction with N. T. Wright, *Surprised by Hope.*)

McLaren, Brian. *A New Kind of Christianity: Ten Questions That are Transforming the Faith.* New York: HarperOne, 2011. A very thoughtful and clearly written re-conception of basic Christian ideas by a pastor with a background and interest in literature. A great exploration about how Western theology is peculiar and what its deconstruction means for future possibilities.

------------. *The Great Spiritual Migration: How the World's Largest Religion is Seeking a Better Way to Be Christian.* New York: HarperOne, 2016. Perhaps the best book in this category; a one-stop work of realistic and committed deconstruction and reconstruction for faith in the 21st century. Enjoyable, learned, generous tone, easy reading, highly recommended for all audiences.

------------. *Why Did Jesus, Moses, the Buddha, and Mohammed Cross the Road?: Christian Identity in a Multi-Faith World.* New York: Jericho Books, 2012. A very penetrating, easy to read book on what it means to be Christian in a pluralistic world. (Best complemented by Placher, *Unapologetic Theology* and relevant chapters in Hodgson's *Winds of the Spirit* and Migliore's *Faith Seeking Understanding.*)

Moltmann, Jürgen. *The Living God and the Fullness of Life.* Louisville: Westminster John Knox, 2016. Written in his 90s, the distillation of one of the twentieth-century's premier German Protestant liberation theologians. In a disenchanted age where everything is objectified and materialized, this work challenges us to think of God as something *living;* he critiques such stale (and Greek) ideas in theology proper as "immutability" and "impassibility," while also revealing the problems of modernism. Short, profound, and a pure joy to read; Moltmann, a WWII POW survivor, is one of the few theologians who makes me feel hopeful and inspired after every time I read his work. (Do read his five-volume systematic theology by Fortress Press for the full experience!)

Padgett, Alan and Patrick Keifert, eds. *But Is It All True?: The Bible and the Question of Truth.* Grand Rapids: Eerdmans, 2006. An excellent little selection of essays by various authors exploring many angles to the question of this book's title. A great starting point if you have trouble imagining how the Bible might be "true" if it isn't verbally inspired and inerrant. Most chapters are easy to read, a couple more focused and technical. (Best read in conjunction with Goldingay's *Models for Scripture.*)

Primavesi, Anna. *Sacred Gaia.* New York: Routledge, 2000. A remarkable, scholarly, lucid re-construction of theology in ecological terms. It's radical proposal? That creation is an organism, and that theology can be conceived as an earth science. Extremely valuable for post-western theologies sensitive to reductionism, scientism, and destruction of our planet. Special attention is given to how Western theology gave rise to violence. Short, incisive, and advances in somewhat different directions than McFague and other eco-feminist works.

Roberts, Matthias. *Beyond Shame: Creating a Healthy Sex Life on Your Own Terms.* Minneapolis: Fortress Press, 2020. A radically different perspective on sexuality than most Christians are used to, from the ground up; filled with practical signposts for victims of purity culture. Written by a Christian therapist. (Best read in conjunction with Sellers, *Sex, God and the Conservative Church.*)

Rogers Jr., Frank. *Practicing Compassion.* Nashville: Fresh Air Books, 2015. "Everybody believes in compassion," writes McLaren's endorsement, "but nobody tells you how to practice it." This book is the first for the Center for Engaged Compassion, and it is an extremely practical and accessible guide to what it means to actually love people. Couldn't be more important for the church in any age. Ecumenical, interfaith, and saturated with the wisdom of a scholar-teacher, great for small groups, and necessarily meditative/mystical in orientation instead of rationalist. (Read with sister book already cited above, *Living Compassion*).

Rohr, Richard. *The Universal Christ: How a Forgotten Reality Can Change Everything We See, Hope For, and Believe.* New York: Convergent Books, 2019. Rohr brings his spiritually and theologically acute perspectives to bear on the concept of "Christ." Primary focus on psychology, meditation, and spirituality, though I find his theological insights particularly interesting and thoughtful (though sometimes sloppy and confusing); they propose a deft and sweeping reconstruction as to what Christianity and Christ was and is all about. Similar to Barfield, he speaks from the Theosophy/Perennial Tradition, and similar to Moltmann and McFague, speaks from panentheism. Yet, rooted in biblical traditions and church history. Also extremely easy to read.

Schneider, Laurel, and Stephen Ray. *Awake the Moment: An Introduction to Theology.* Louisville: Westminster John Knox, 2016. A superb introduction to theology—which is, in this perspective, not a mere summary of beliefs or doctrines, but a way of life and framework of interpretation that changes us and the world for the better. In the authors' own words, "If Christian theology does not help us to figure out how to stand up for those being hurt who are right around us and those far away, then it is not worth doing or studying." One of the best fits and highest recommendations for theology junkies reading this bibliography.

Sellers, Tina Schermer. *Sex, God, and the Conservative Church: Erasing Shame from Sexual Intimacy.* New York: Routledge, 2017. Written by therapists and for therapists, this scholarly work reveals the depths of sexual trauma created by purity culture, and provides towards practical ways towards healing.

Stenberg, Mark. *51% Christian: Finding Faith After Certainty*. Minneapolis: Fortress Press, 2015. A quick, down-and-dirty, re-constructive overhaul of theological ideas and doctrines in everyday language. While Hodgson and Kaufman are more for "professionals," this work is for amateur theologians who want to cut to the chase and have some fun while being dead serious.

Taylor, Barbara Brown. *Learning to Walk in the Dark*. New York: HarperOne, 2015. A metaphorically rich account of appreciating periods in life where you're lost and not sure why what it's about. Those who love the outdoors and/or farm life will particularly appreciate its earthy stories. Easy, enjoyable read.

Tickle, Phyllis. *The Great Emergence: How Christianity is Changing and Why*. Grand Rapids: Baker Books, 2008. A sort of archeology of the church through the lens of social and ideological change, and a contemporary description of what it is North American Christians are experiencing right now in the big picture. She analyzes several models of Christianity that have responded to all its evolutionary development and suggests ways forward.

Podcasts[1]

Homebrew Christianity. Hosted by Tripp Fuller. Not really deconstructive or reconstructive in its orientation. However, many have found this project refreshing because it spans so widely across Christian ideas and frameworks; stays on the cutting edge of theology and its intersections with philosophy and science.

The Bible for Normal People. Hosted by Pete Enns and Jared Byas. Not really either a deconstructive or constructive project as much as just reading and interpreting the Bible in a non-biblicist paradigm. Has an excellent span of guests.

Exvangelical Podcast. Hosted by Blake Chastain. An worth-while resource of continual, quality interviews and conversations about the post-evangelical space. Focuses more on people and their biographies.

The Liturgists. Hosted by Michael Gungor and others. Mostly focused on

---

[1] There are many more that should be included and I apologize. To emphasize: this list is incomplete; much good content is missing (not least of which are my friends' podcasts: *The Sinnergists, Split Frame of Reference, The Lone Microphone, GodArchy, Libertarian Christian Podcast*, etc.). There are dozens of podcasts just under the "progressive christian" sections of various hosting sites.

what to do and how to live after leaving conservative evangelicalism. Very exploratory, wide-ranging, and has longer, more thoughtful, irregularly-released episodes.

Queerology. Hosted by Matthias Roberts. "How might we live better as queer people of faith and allies? Matthias brings together theologians, psychologists, poets, thinkers, and change makers for conversations around belief and being." Particularly good at providing an inside look at the faith of the marginalized and the lives of allies in religious conflict surrounding gender/sexual minorities. I've benefited tremendously listening to such testimonies of faith.

Appendix D:

Review of John Piper's *A Peculiar Glory*

(in original formatting)

> *A Peculiar Glory: How the Christian Scriptures Reveal Their Complete Truthfulness*. John Piper. Wheaton: Crossway, 2016. ISBN: 9781433552632. Pp. 302. $24.99 (USD).

The earthquake of higher criticism continues to reverberate throughout the church, and John Piper's *A Peculiar Glory* is another addition to the library of books confronting the persistent question about the Bible's truthfulness. In contrast to others, the book takes a multifaceted approach, the main thesis of which is "that the glory of God in and through the Scriptures is a real, objective, self-authenticating reality" (15). Put differently, the *Westminster Larger Catechism* reads "The scriptures manifest themselves to be the word of God, by . . . the scope of the whole, which is to give all glory to God." "This book," writes Piper, "is an effort to press. into that answer as deeply as I can" (13). He does this in the following five sections.

The first ("A Place to Stand") provides an autobiographical sketch of Piper's "journey" with the Bible, from early years to doctoral study and full-time ministry. He recounts his co-writing of Bethlehem Baptist Church's doctrinal statement, which declares the Bible to be "the Word of God Written" and "verbally inspired by God," meaning the inerrant autographic text of the Protestant sixty-six-book canon (34).

The second part is entitled "What Books and Words Make Up the Christian

91

CANADIAN-AMERICAN THEOLOGICAL REVIEW | 2016 ❦ Volume 5 • Issue 1

Scriptures"? In short sentences, steady pacing, and readable prose, Piper answers this question by giving brief arguments for why Protestants have the table of contents that they do. This section also explains why restricting "inerrancy" and inspiration to the autographs is a good idea, not a bad one. In fact, his whole bibliology, it is argued, can be located in the Bible itself.

The third section is a review of how the New Testament authors used the Old Testament, and what Christians today can learn by Jesus's use of Scripture. It also addresses the nature of divine discourse and how God speaks through people—whether prophets or apostles.

The fourth section asks "How Can We Know the Christian Scriptures are True?" As one might expect from Piper, the answer to this question is interlaced with quotations and insights from Jonathan Edwards. He also presses into the image of seeing God's glory and being blind to it. In a word, the Scriptures are 'true" because they can be *seen* to be true, and (deferring to Calvin's argument) this internal testimony is of the Spirit. He says that doubts may come, but "the miracle of seeing 'the glory of God in the face of Jesus Christ' through the Scriptures can happen to a person who never will be able to explain sufficiently why he trusts the Bible" (173). Over and again, Piper stresses that trust in the Bible is not a leap in the dark—not because there is affirming evidence, but simply because 'we have seen his glory."

The last section outlines several major ways in which the glory of God is revealed in the scriptures, such as the Incarnation, fulfillment of prophecy, miracles of Jesus, and "in the people the word creates" (253). This somewhat apologetic section concludes with reflections on the place of historical criticism and how there always remains work to do in order for the glory of the scriptures to shine through:

> My conclusion is that "the Bible, consisting of the sixty-six books of the Old and New Testaments, is the infallible Word of God, verbally inspired by God, and without error in the original manuscripts," and that this can be known with a well-grounded confidence because the peculiar glory of God shines in and through these Scriptures. (281)

For some—including those who regularly study and teach the Bible—*A Peculiar Glory* may come as a welcome reminder that the Scriptures are a remarkable collection of writings. And although great attention is given to the form of the Bible, Piper's overall thesis brings out the profundity of its content and story. Among other commendable features, the book also functions as a primer on how American evangelicals currently think of the Christian Scriptures.

On the whole, however, the volume represents perhaps the most overt act of

CANADIAN-AMERICAN THEOLOGICAL REVIEW | 2016 ❦ Volume 5 • Issue 1

published bibliolatry/biblicism in recent times. Countless Christian scholars have been trying to correct this unfortunate development now typical of American evangelicalism.[1] *A Peculiar Glory* just adds fuel for the flame, functioning like similar books of its kind[2] by circling the wagons and turning a blind eye to the debates themselves. Among other things, this results in poor scholarship, which is most immediately revealed in noticeable ignorance of key contributions from the most important works on pertinent subject areas, and in strange conclusions: for example, that the Hebrew Bible, not the Septuagint, was the primary Bible of Jesus, Paul, and the early church.

There are also the more typical errors and misleading arguments characteristic of this shamelessly fundamentalist perspective, such as the idea that:

1. Christianity in general should see (and has always seen) the canon in terms of binary categories (inspired/non-inspired), when in fact the canon has always had a common core with blurred edges—including today throughout global Christianity.[3]

2. There is a single autographic text, as if biblical authors sat down and wrote one version of a book that was then transmitted through the ages, when in fact this concept can apply neither to most biblical writings be-cause of their developmental origination (e.g., Psalms, Proverbs, and others are compilations of scribes that underwent adaptation, revision, in-

---

1   See, for example, Craig Allert, *A High View of Scripture?: The Authority of the Bible and the Formation of the New Testament Canon* (Grand Rapids: Baker Academic, 2007); Carlos Bovell, *Inerrancy and the Spiritual Formation of Younger Evangelicals* (Eugene: Wipf and Stock, 2007); idem, *Interdisciplinary Perspectives on the Authority of Scripture: Historical, Biblical, and Theoretical Perspectives* (Eugene: Wipf and Stock, 2011); idem, *Rehabilitating Inerrancy in a Culture of Fear* (Eugene: Wipf and Stock, 2012); James Dunn, *The Living Word* (Minneapolis: Fortress Press, 2003); Peter Enns, *Inspiration and Incarnation: Evangelicals and the Problem of the Old Testament* (Grand Rapids: Baker Academic, 2005); idem, *The Bible Tells Me So: Why Defending Scripture Has Made Us Unable to Read It* (New York: HarperOne, 2014); Christopher Hays and Christopher Ansberry, ed., *Evangelical Faith and the Challenge of Historical Criticism* (Grand Rapids: Baker Academic, 2013); Christian Smith, *The Bible Made Impossible: Why Biblicism is Not a Truly Evangelical Reading of Scripture* (Grand Rapids: Brazos Press, 2012); Kenton Sparks, *Sacred Word, Broken Word* (Grand Rapids: Eerdmans, 2012); idem, *God's Word in Human Words: An Evangelical Appropriation of Critical Biblical Scholarship* (Grand Rapids: Baker Academic, 2008); Thom Stark, *The Human Faces of God: What Scripture Reveals When It Gets God Wrong (And Why Inerrancy Tries to Hide It)* (Eugene: Wipf and Stock, 2011); Ben Witherington, *The Living Word: Rethinking the Theology of the Bible* (Waco: Baylor University Press, 2009). Earlier efforts can be traced to Jack Rogers and Donald McKim, *The Authority and Interpretation of the Bible: An Historical Approach* (New York: Harper and Row, 1979) and to James Barr's three volumes on scripture and additional three volumes on fundamentalism.

2   E.g., Steven Cowan and Terry Wilder, ed., *In Defense of the Bible: A Comprehensive Apologetic for the Authority of Scripture* (Nashville: Broadman and Holman Academic, 2013); Craig Blomberg, *Can We Still Believe the Bible?: An Evangelical Engagement with Contemporary Questions* (Grand Rapids: Brazos Press, 2014); Wayne Grudem, Thomas Schreiner, and John Collins, ed., *Understanding Scripture* (Wheaton: Crossway, 2012). Blomberg's book, it should be mentioned, is more nuanced and critically-minded than the others.

3   See Lee Martin McDonald, *The Biblical Canon* (Peabody: Hendrickson, 2008) and *The Formation of the Biblical Canon*, 2 vols (New York: T & T Clark, 2017).

93

tegration, expansion, etc. over time[4]), nor to many NT writings (where authors often kept a copy for themselves, revised another for a particular congregation, sized a copy down to fit a scroll, etc.),[5] so that speaking of "the original Bible" makes as much sense as saying "the original internet" or "the original Wikipedia."

3. 2 Timothy 3:16 teaches verbal plenary inspiration of the original autographs, when in fact (a) the text is extremely mild in its claims, defining "God-breathed" in terms of making one "wise for salvation" and equipping the person of God for "every good work", and (b) "scripture" likely refers to the Septuagint (a translation) and not to the Hebrew text at all.[6]

4. "Verbal plenary inspiration" is simply the default Protestant (even *Christian*) bibliology, when in fact there are entire Christian and evangelical denominations that do not hold this view, and Reformed theologians such as Herman Bavinck who intentionally *distanced* themselves from this rigid perspective (touted by his American friend B. B. Warfield) in favor of "organic inspiration" or "genetic-synthetic" bibliology.[7]

5. The idea that Jude wasn't quoting 1 Enoch (Jude 14–15) as "scripture" or "authoritatively," when there's no reason to believe (except preconceived bias) that he is doing anything different.

In addition to these and other elementary problems, there are the typical unanswered questions that readers are bound to have, such as:

1. If verbal plenary inspiration and words—as opposed to the message and meaning of the Bible—are so important, why do Jesus and the early

---

4 See Karel Van Der Toorn, *Scribal Culture and the Making of the Hebrew Bible* (Cambridge: Harvard University Press, 2007).

5 See E. Richards, "Reading, Writing, and Manuscripts" in *The World of the New Testament*, ed. Lee Martin McDonald and Joel Green (Grand Rapids: Baker Academic, 2015), 362. After elaborating this point, he reflects, "While I personally hold a high view of Scripture, I must admit that there are challenges to the concept of original autographs." Cf. Michael Holmes, "From 'Original Text' to 'Initial Text,'" in Michael Holmes and Bart Ehrman, ed., *The Text of the New Testament in Contemporary Research* (Boston: Brill, 2014); John Brogan, "Can I Have Your Autograph?" in Vincent Bacote, Laura Quay, Dennis Ockholm, ed., *Evangelicals and Scripture* (Downers Grove: IVP Academic, 2004).

6 See Timothy Law, *When God Spoke Greek* (New York: Oxford University Press, 2013), along with many exegetical commentaries.

7 "[The Bible is] a living whole, not abstract but organic. It is not given to use simply to parrot its exact words and phrases but so that we, drawing from the entire organism of Scripture, as free and thoughtful children, think God's thoughts after him. . . . Taking the text of Scripture seriously as the Word of God does mean that we do not read it atomistically, as though each word or letter by itself has its own divine meaning. Words are included in thoughts and vowels in words . . . not every text or passage or book is equally close to the circle of faith's center. Not all of the books of the Bible are of equal value." Herman Bavinck, *Reformed Dogmatics*, trans. John Vriend, abridged (Grand Rapids: Baker, 2011), 17, 106.

CANADIAN-AMERICAN THEOLOGICAL REVIEW | 2016 ❦ Volume 5 • Issue 1

church feel free to create their own unique readings that comprise a mixture of the LXX and Hebrew text?[8]

2. If verbal plenary inspiration and words—as opposed to the message and meaning of the Bible—are so important, why is it continually repeated as being significant that textual variation doesn't affect essential Christian doctrines? This is significant for Christians who *don't* adhere to verbal plenary inspiration, not for those who *do*. (Piper seems unaware of the possibility that words/wording only matter to the extent that they affect meaning, as opposed to having independent divine value regardless of their functioning in sentences and semantics).

3. Why is it significant that the New Testament writers don't quote from and allude to Apocryphal writings when (a) they actually do[9] and (b) they don't quote from many other canonical books as well (e.g., Judges, Ruth, Esther, Ezra, Obadiah, Zephaniah, Song of Solomon, Lamentations)?

As far as I can tell, *A Peculiar Glory* is written to Christians of American fundamentalist persuasion who need re-affirmation that their own bibliology isn't irrational. It is worth pondering why this has to be continually argued in the first place, especially within a Christian context. In the end, whether the bigger picture or the specific issues are concerned, Piper's work largely points in the wrong direction. One is better off reading *Models for Scripture*[10] and *Scripture and the Authority of God*,[11] supplemented by *Engaging the Christian Scriptures*,[12] *The Word of God for the People of God*,[13] and *The Abingdon Introduction to the Bible*[14]—at least if one desires an equally impassioned but more informed, realistic, and tempered presentation.

Jamin Hübner
John Witherspoon College

---

8   E.g., Mark 7:6–7; Luke 4:17–18; John 1:23; Acts 15:16–18; Rom 2:24; 9:33; 10:20–21; 14:11; Heb 10:5–7; etc.

9   E.g., Sir 4:1 in Mark 20:19 alongside Deut 5 and Ex 20; Sir 17:26 in 2 Tim 2:19-20 alongside Num 16; Wis 14:22–31 in Rom 1:24–32; Wis 2:23–24 in Rom 5:12–21; Ascension of Isaiah 11:34 or Elijah Apocalypse in 1 Cor 2:9; 1 Enoch 1:9 in Jude 14; 1 Enoch in 2 Pet 2:4 and 3:6; Wis 7:25–26 in Heb 1:3.

10 John Goldingay, *Models for Scripture* (Toronto: Clements, 2004).

11 N. T. Wright, *Scripture and the Authority of God* (New York: HarperOne, 2013).

12 Andrew Arterbury, W. H. Bellinger, Derek Dodson, *Engaging the Christian Scriptures* (Grand Rapids: Baker Academic, 2014).

13 Todd Billings, *The Word of God for the People of God* (Grand Rapids: Eerdmans, 2010).

14 Joel Kaminsky, Mark Reasoner, Joel Nohr, *The Abingdon Introduction to the Bible* (Nashville: Abingdon, 2014).

Appendix E:
An Introduction to the
Introduction of the Bible

(*Reader's note*: This is an unpublished teaching document used for the first couple days of an "Intro to the Bible"—a course and a document that has proven transformative for many students. I obviously had to oversimplify and generalize.)

"Introduction to the Bible" is one of those "core" courses that aims at building new foundations of learning. As such, it functions a lot like basic training functions in the military:

1. *Break down*
    a. Unlearn
    b. Find extreme limits and boundaries; go to unknown places
    c. Ask forbidden questions
2. *Rebuild*
    a. Acquire new knowledge and skills
    b. Gain new confidence
    c. Obtain a better, more realistic understanding

As you can imagine then, introductory courses are more traumatic than they are comforting. "But I was taught" and "but my parents always told me" and "but we learned in Sunday school" are some of the most common responses of students in classes like these. Like liberal arts institutions as a whole, these courses are meant to *educate*, not indoctrinate. That means opening doors and minds and exploring new worlds and frontiers of knowledge, not conforming to immediate consensus and popular views. No professor exists to re-affirm what students think they already know. Certainly, teachers want to encourage and not dishearten students. Good teachers also don't take pleasure destroying the entire worldviews and opinions of students (though I know some profs that unfortunately do).

But no matter what the case is or what a student's particular beliefs are when they come into the classroom, they *will be challenged*. That's a necessary part of the posture of learning, and a necessary part of shaping our lives and worldviews in a way that leaves us less intellectually and spiritually vulnerable.

In the case of an Intro to the Bible course, there are varying reactions depending on the student's perspective. To help illustrate what I mean, let's look at two extremes: challenges faced by the modern "secularist" and faced by the religious fundamentalist.

Navigating Between Extreme Perspectives on the Bible

For those who don't find themselves in the Christian faith, it is natural to absorb the views of the Bible that immediately constitute their contemporary environment. This might include the mainstream media (e.g., history channel), popular (non-academic) books, the university, and other veins of culture. Such secular views tend to be rather critical—often, *unreasonably* critical—of the Bible. **Here are a handful of examples of what popular, secular, academic views of the Bible sometimes look like:**

1. Many, if not most, events in the Hebrew Bible ("Old Testament") are fictional and nonfactual. The Exodus and other events never happened; Israel itself, along with King David, Solomon, and other figures, are considered pious, pseudo-historical constructions at most, otherwise imaginary characters whose lives were blown way out of proportion by both Jews and Christians for some contemporary theological purpose.
2. Most of contents of the Hebrew Bible was written late (3rd-4th century BC), but if it was written earlier, it is hopelessly lost in oral tradition and due to primitive writing technology.
3. The ethical law codes, and even some of the poetic literature, are little more than rip-offs of contemporary works and civilizations and therefore have no special significance (e.g., "do not murder" is anything but revelatory/proprietary).
4. The prophetic books (and future-telling sections) are late productions written *after the fact*, intending to convince (well, *deceive*) readers that something was foretold and fulfilled.

5. Deuteronomy, like other books in the OT, are fraudulent writings (e.g., planted and was then "discovered" by people like King Josiah), written to deceive an illiterate people—whether with good or ill intent.

6. Jesus himself is either a fictional person or, if real, was merely a pious teacher, prophet, and revolutionary no better than contemporary Messiah/revolutionary figures (of which there were many). He was ultimately mistaken about the coming of God and/or end of the world (just as he says on the cross in the earliest gospel: "Why did you forsake me?") and never intended or wanted to be viewed as "divine" (as Paul implies in Rom 1: the resurrection belief is what instigated the "son of god" stuff).

7. Paul isn't the author of the books Christians attribute to him (though there are some exceptions), nor did any of the Gospel writers write any of the Gospels; they are intentional forgeries written in the 80s-120s CE.

8. Paul may have completely misunderstood Christianity and invented his own version entirely apart from (or against) Peter and the early church before him. Given his writings, we may not need to consider him a "Christian" at all; he was simply a Jew who saw Jesus as the Jewish Messiah.

9. The New Testament documents are generally unreliable; there are too many copyist errors to be trustworthy in any meaningful sense; or, some were forgeries; or, they were written for political or theological purposes that have no bearing on historical reality.

10. Second and third-century "gnostic gospels" or "non-canonical gospels" were really first-century Christian gospels; Matthew, Mark, Luke, and John were conspiratorial documents designed to vindicate pro-Messianic traditions and cover up the earlier, authentic tradition.

11. The canon of scripture (table of contents) as we have it today in our Bibles was the product of a vote at council whose agenda was to cover up the real early Christian written tradition.

12. The Bible is logically used to justify violence—against Jews, women, gays, and that is inevitably part of universal Christian ethics today.

13. Yahweh is a racist, sexist, homophobic, misogynist, masochistic, genocidal, torturous god—a tribal deity that never existed with any dominance prior to 587 BCE and got blown way out of proportion by the Temple Scribes.

One could go on. But you can see the general attitude towards the "modern critical" perspective. In its worst form, it seems bent on tearing down traditional assumptions, being contrarian, and often, assuming the worst-case whenever possible. In its best form, it is a slanted reading of certain facts, and for that reason cannot be dismissed, but not simply believed, either.

Students who come from this uncritically critical orientation are surprised when they learn things like:

1. the acute ability of those in Jewish culture to memorize and preserve oral tradition.
2. that there is credible archaeological evidence for the basic contours of Israel's story and other Hebrew narratives.
3. that the NT documents are probably the most reliable and well-attested literature of the ancient world, with over 5,700 copies (far more than Plato, Aristotle, etc.) and many early copies within 200 years of the events.
4. that most NT copyist errors don't even change the meaning of a sentence.
5. that Luke-Acts, the largest piece of literature in the New Testament, proves to be particularly reliable when it comes to historical details (e.g., names, places, geography, customs, etc.).
6. that the NT Gospels were written in the first century and not later (and that Gnostic gospels are almost certainly the late, creative constructions with little historical bearing).
7. that archaeological evidence of the early Christian story (names, geography, customs, events, buildings, etc.) is robust.
8. that the traditional Christ-story as a whole bears all the distinguishing marks of historical and contextual authenticity (e.g., "criteria of embarrassment," multiple witnesses, double attestation, etc.)—at least as much as we could expect from that time and culture.
9. that multiple, reliable contemporary external references to Jesus and Christians exist and generally fit what is found and told of in early Christian literature.
10. that many of the narratives of scripture have proven to be positively influential, leading to various reformations, inspiration for art, architecture, music and literature,

transformed entire societies and civilizations (not to mention individuals), gave reason for hospital and orphanage building, philanthropy, business and financial prudence, property rights and judicial procedures, virtuous living, etc.

11. that despite abuse and misuse, the Bible has remained a vital source for progressive social change, from women's suffrage to the civil rights movement.

12. that Yahweh's/Elohim's instruction in Mosaic law often actually protects individuals (including women, slaves, and aliens) from harm in their original context, that all but one of Israel's wars were defensive (and all of which had very strict ethical rules attached at that), and that ethical law-codes of that period are much more sophisticated than can be crudely interpreted by 21st century English-speakers. Mosaic law in some sense was an "advance" or "step forward," at least in its ancient context (which is what is immediately significant).

You can see, then, that it is difficult to simply throw out the whole Bible as a book of irrelevant fairy tales. But, for a student who isn't used to this unlearning process, swallowing these realities (at least as I understand them) is as intellectually painful as the first week of basic training in the military. The scriptures are not simply an outdated book of "make-believe." They need to be reckoned with.

For those who *do* find themselves in the Christian faith, it also is only natural to absorb the views of the Bible that immediately constitute their contemporary environment. This includes views perpetuated in popular Christian culture, like magazines, songs, books, church and Sunday schools, seminaries, Christian homes/homeschools, social media, and other channels of culture. Many of those Christian views tend to be rather unrealistic and uncritical—often, *unreasonably* uncritical of the Bible. (And by "critical" I do not mean full of *criticism*; I mean thoughtful, probing, asking tough questions). **This is particularly true in "biblicist" or evangelical fundamentalist circles that tend to be very rigid, unrealistic, hopelessly demanding, and affirming of such ideas as the following:**

1. That books of the Bible are generally written by *one* author (presumably in a single sitting), even though they bear immediate evidence of being written over decades by multiple authors.

2. That books of the Bible are independent of all external sources, standing "alone" as it were—even when biblical authors themselves explicitly cite and name external sources.

3. That books and chapters are forced to bear historical details and modern standards of journalism and historiography even though they were never meant to (and probably never could).

4. The explicit distinction that biblical authors draw between what *they* say and what *God* says (e.g., "thus saith the Lord," "it is the Lord and not me who says…" etc.) is collapsed and erased, so that all the writings are flattened into one "divine" category of "the Bible," "what God said," etc.

5. The distinction between a variety of genres (prophecy, poetry, song, narrative, etc.) are collapsed into one ambiguous genre (e.g., "Word of God," "Bible," etc.), again flattening an otherwise rich and dynamic collection.

6. That the prophecies in the First (or "New") Testament (Hebrew Bible) are generally or always precise, literal, and unconditional instead of (for example) more general, conditional, and/or spiritual.

7. That the ethical and moral content of the Bible is exclusive and purely revelatory (i.e. "brand new") in relation to contemporary culture, without any possible overlap, parallel influence, or cross-fertilization.

8. That discrepancies of chronology and detail in the four gospels can be ignored, or forcefully harmonized into a superficial synthesis (…so that (ironically) none of the gospel authors are actually speaking accurately).

9. That only the "original autographs," or just the *Textus Receptus*, or some other theoretically fixed text-form of the Bible is authoritative, true, infallible, inerrant, etc. (in contrast to the—often partial and derived—biblical texts that Jesus, the apostles, and that Christians *actually used*).

10. That the biblical books are "binary," being either "inspired" or "uninspired," and that there is a divinely fixed number to the "inspired" collection that is universally applicable to all Christians past and present.

11. That the Bible's *primary value* is its serving as a collection of true propositions and as an ultimate standard for all truth claims of any kind.

12. That the Bible (however defined) was copied inerrantly

throughout history.

13. That the Bible (however defined) was copied inerrantly throughout history in certain "textual families" or manuscripts or translations (which were divinely preserved).
14. That "Apocryphal" books are only used by Roman Catholics, and were historically rejected by most Christians.

One could, again, go on to list more examples. But you can see the attitude of fixation, rigidity, lack of nuance and qualification, naiveté, and even a bit of triumphalism. It is often assumed that *the more flexible and less certain a view of the Bible is, the less truthful and less Christian it is.* But, as we will learn in class, just the reverse is the case: it is precisely the Bible's *organic nature* and *ability to adapt and speak to the present* that makes it "true," robust through time, and meaningful to every kind of people around the world.

In extreme cases in this perspective, anyone who raises questions about the Bible—even basic ones like who wrote it, to whom, and why, is viewed with suspicion and potentially as an enemy of the faith. Even having conversations with people of other views is considered spiritually dangerous.

So when students come from this type of orientation take Intro to the Bible, they are shocked to learn such things as the following:

1. That the five-volume collection called the "Pentateuch" wasn't known as such after its composition, but much later (i.e., 400s-600s BCE).
2. That Genesis through Kings is generally a single literary work (of two major parts) assembled sometime around 600-400s, already based on previous literary sources (e.g. southern and northern traditions)—and not a collection of separate literary works first written by Moses during his time and then others being systematically added immediately thereafter.
3. That there is currently no well-established, direct archaeological evidence for either the Exodus or the Fall of Jericho, and possibly won't be in the future.
4. That biblical authors, like any authors, exaggerate.
5. That biblical authors, like others in the ancient world(s), can and do write under other people's names, sometimes intentionally and other times maybe not (e.g., pseudonyms and

pseudepigraphs).

6. That the personal opinions of the biblical authors cannot be simply separated from "the biblical text" that they wrote, and that the biblical text contains opinions that should be treated as such (even as Paul, for example, explicitly argues in 1 Cor 7).

7. That the ethical content of the Bible sometimes strongly parallels contemporary documents/cultures (e.g., ancient treaties, poems, etc.).

8. That the ethical content in the Bible exhibits change, within Testaments (e.g., Num 27) and across Testaments (e.g., Acts 10; Gal).

9. That historical fiction and parabolic history are some of the many genres of biblical writings (e.g., Jonah, Job, Esther, Gen. 1-11; cf. 3-4 Macc, Judith, Tobit, etc.).

10. That in talking about any literary semantic content, *truthfulness* and *factuality* are not necessarily the same thing (e.g., there can be "true" and "false" parables, etc.), and that neither exist as binary categories but exist on a spectrum and in different senses.

11. That biblical authors are generally more concerned about theology and ethics than historical or factual accuracy.

12. That most prophecies in the OT are relatively loose in fulfillment, some appearing to lack accurate or any fulfillment (Ez 26:1-21 and fall of Tyre by Babylon; Is 13:17-19 and Jer 51:11-12 and destruction of Babylon by Medes; Jer 34:1-5 vs 52:3-11; Jer 22:30 vs. 2 Kings 24:6 and 2 Chron 36:8; Mt 16//Mk 13, etc.), others being revised/reinterpreted (Ez 29:18-19; Mt 1:23; etc.), and, perhaps, some given after the event itself (Daniel).

13. Many prophecies and foreshadowing/typology have fulfillment in the New Covenant and in Christ in ways that no one predicted (e.g., the Messiah being the atoning sacrifice; the Messiah dying and rising back to life, the New Covenant having the sign of baptism, etc.).

14. That the period between the OT prophets and the NT was not "silent" but filled with a plethora of writings addressing the same matters as canonical works.

15. That the gospel accounts (among other works) contain discrepancies of various kinds (historical details, sayings of Jesus and discourse, chronology, etc.) that cannot be resolved—and that to force harmonization would sometimes render all accounts incredulous.

16. That discrepancies that do exist in historically-oriented literature actually often demonstrate their *authenticity*, not their unreliability, anyway.

17. That the gospel accounts primarily existed in oral form for up to two or three decades before being formally written down—and that the differences that we witness in the gospels today are partly due to different ways of remembering or performing in different localities.

18. That, given what we read in the New Testament, Jesus and the NT authors generally cared more about *what* a biblical text was saying than preserving the original textual *form.*

19. That there have always been *multiple* "original autographs" (e.g., Greek vs. Hebrew versions of OT writings; multiple editions of epistles, archived original copies and distributed versions, etc.), which Christians continue to dispute regarding authority and priority (e.g., "published version," "canonical version," original oral form, etc.). In some cases (like in OT documents), the idea of an "original" may not even function at all (any more than saying the "original internet" or "original Wikipedia.")

20. That (therefore) Christians disagree on what constitutes an "original" text-form to begin with, even though they may be unaware of it.

21. That most of the First Testament was regularly under development and revision, both orally and literarily; such revision involved adding and revising text of prophetic and historical works—and that this continues to the present day.

22. That there are textual variants—disagreements—between copies, some 400,000 in the NT manuscript tradition alone; as one result, modern Bibles are "missing" (i.e., "adding") entire verses (e.g., John 5:4; Acts 8:37; Mt 17:21, 18:11, 21:44, Mk 7:16, etc.).

23. Some portions or the whole of biblical texts, at least in their "original" forms, are "missing" (e.g., 1 Sam 10:27ff; 13:1; some of the court documents cited in Sam-Kgs; Paul's third letter to Corinthians; unmentioned letters written by apostles; possibly the literary source of Matthew and Luke, etc.).

24. That translation always involves the loss of information (so, if you believe all meaning in the Bible is of equal value, using translations is a serious problem.)

25. (Yet) That the Bible translations we have today might be just as (or *more*, given their completeness and availability) authoritative

and useful as the Bibles during the ancient church—despite having inevitable errors emerging from the translation team, the translation itself, publishing and printing process, manuscript selection, etc. (E.g., the ESV has "revised" versions, despite Crossway's attempt in 2016 to create a "permanent text" edition that would be "unchanged forever, in perpetuity.")

26. That Jesus and the NT authors quote the Greek Old Testament (a translation) more than the Hebrew ("original"), sometimes even mixing readings between them (Mk 7:6-7; Lk 4:17-18; Jn 1:23; Acts 15:16-18; Rom 2:24; 9:33; 10:20-21; 14:11; Heb 10:5-7; etc.).

27. That (thus) Jesus and the NT authors give just as much (or more) authority to *translations* of biblical texts than any theoretical originals.

28. That much of the Greek NT text is probably *itself* a translation of Aramaic discourse, and that some texts can't be fully understood without reference to reverse translation into Aramaic (e.g., the effect of "camel" and "needle" phrase in Mt 19:24//Mk 10:25//Lk 18:25).

29. That the New Testament contains over a dozen allusions or references to "Apocryphal" and "Pseudepigraphal" writings, sometimes in precisely the same way "canonical" works are cited (e.g., Sir 4:1 in Mark 20:19 alongside Deut 5 and Ex 20; Sir 17:26 in 2 Tim 2:19-20 alongside Numb 16; Wis 14:22-31 in Rom 1:24-32; Wis 2:23-24 in Rom 5:12-21; Ascension of Isaiah 11:34 or Elijah Apocalypse in 1 Cor 2:9; 1 Enoch 1:9 in Jude 14; 1 Enoch in 2 Pet 2:4 and 3:6; Wis 7:25-26 in Heb 1:3, etc.).

30. That a copy of Romans in the first century would have cost around $2,200, and that virtually no synagogue during Jesus' day had copies of every book in the OT, or even the whole Torah (this may explain why Jesus mainly cites from three books— Deut, Psalms, and Isaiah).

31. That "scriptural books" as binary is largely (though not entirely) a modern construction and unrecognizable to many or most Christians throughout history—who saw books on a spectrum in relation to the Jesus story and what the historic church used in worship.

32. That still today, at least five different *Christian* canons (table of contents) for the Bible still exist, only one of which adds up to 66 books; Christians have always had (as a general principle) and still have today, a choice as to what books of the Bible will be in

their Bible (e.g., when we go online or visit a bookstore to purchase scriptures, etc.).

33. That the earliest copies of the NT (Codex Sinaiticus and Codex Vaticanus), the original 1611 King James Bible, and Martin Luther's German Bible translation all contained the "Apocrypha."

34. That the Dead Sea Scrolls contained multiple copies of "apocryphal" works, but not a single copy of the book of Esther.

35. That Genesis 1-3 was probably written after the exile (580s-400s BCE) as a parable of Israel's creation, call to obedience, and exile from the promised land, also (esp ch 1) in refutation to Babylonian cosmologies, not written in the second millennium BCE about the physical creation of the world.

36. That the contents in the Bible are rarely written to simply deposit facts, but are more often used to make promises, invoke worship, establish historical identity, tell a story and provide social and ethical orientation, etc.

37. That the Bible as "word of God" has generally been (until the reformation and modern age) considered a metaphor, not a description, by the Christian church.

38. That Christians, organizations, and denominations disagree on what it means for the Bible to be "true" and to be "the Word of God" (and yet legitimately remain "Christian").

39. That 2 Timothy 3 defines "God-breathed" as being "useful," and does not amount to Hodge/Warfield's doctrine of "verbal plenary inspiration."

40. That *books* don't technically "say" anything; *persons* do.

41. That what biblical authors *do* in text can be just as (or more) important as what they *say* in text.

42. That there are multiple legitimate ways of interpreting biblical texts.

43. That there may be more than one legitimate "meaning" in a text.

44. That Christians have disagreed on what biblical texts mean, and yet (in principle) legitimately remain "Christian."

45. That the Bible contains multiple theologies; Israel's understanding of God evolved just like ours does today—and the scriptures testify to the movement from polytheism, to henotheism, to various versions of monotheism (ethical, ontological, binitarian variants, Trinitarian variants, etc.).

46. That the Apostle Paul's theology underwent development as he

wrote to churches—and that all theology emerges (whether as "revelation" or not) from our on-the-ground work of following Christ and loving each other.

Again, like the secularist who discovers the remarkable profundity of the Bible, many (especially religious fundamentalists) are a bit shocked when coming across these various observations. It requires serious unlearning and re-learning, again, like the traumatic first weeks at basic training. But, again, even though a bit of soreness will set in, there will be new humility and a wiser posture. This will enable us to re-appropriate the scriptures theologically and ethically for today in a way that is neither in fear or ignorance of scholarship, nor naïve to the reductionism of modernism that leaves us with a dead corpse of literature.

Appendix F:

Syllabus for CHR101[1]

Introduction to the Bible

I. **General Information**

Instructor:	Jamin Hübner	Email:	jhubner@jwc.edu
Office Hours:	Mon-Thurs, 1:30-4:30pm	Office	TBD
Mobile Phone:	[]		
Semester:	Fall 2018	Schedule: Mon 6:15-9:00pm	
Credits:	3	Location: TBD	

II. **Course Description**

A general introduction to the Bible giving specific emphasis on its origin and production. Students of the course will learn about the historical origins, nature, and production of the First and Second Testament and about various theories of bibliology. All of the basic "critical" fields of study—such as redaction, canonical, textual, and literary criticism—will be surveyed, along with the major literary groups within the Christian Bible.

III. **Course Objectives and Learning Outcomes**

The students who successfully complete this course will—whenever talking about, reading, or using the Bible—be able to competently:

1. Identify and understand the various theories of the Bible's authority and inspiration, the historical origins of the Old and New Testaments, and the process of textual transmission and criticism.
2. Recognize the various literary features of the Bible and its diverse canon of writings.
3. Recognize the various versions and translations of the Bible and explain how today's Bibles come from ancient Greek and Hebrew texts.
4. Identify and distinguish the basic challenges of translation.

These course objectives and outcomes require critical thinking and biblical studies, which are two of JWC's institutional objectives. They also fulfill the program goals of Christian Studies, such as to "explain and summarize the nature and contents of the New and Old Testament Scriptures, including an

---

[1] *Note*: Like all of the following syllabi, these were tailored for homeschool students with very little genuine exposure to alternative perspectives (and are therefore helpful to MacArthurites, like Hans).

understanding the origin of the Bible," and "be able to apply...biblical principles to contemporary situations," and the program goals of the Humanities Program, such as obtaining a "thorough grounding in biblical...studies, and the development of interpretive skills" and "Leadership development in the classical tradition based on wide-ranging knowledge of Western culture and literature."

IV.   **Course Professor**

Dr. Jamin Hübner is a entrepreneur, musician, and theologian from South Dakota. He is a graduate of Dordt College (BA Theology), Reformed Theological Seminary (MA Religion) and the University of South Africa (ThD Systematic Theology), and a student at Southern New Hampshire University (MS Economics) and currently serves as the Director of Institutional Effectiveness, founding Chair of Christian Studies, and part-time Professor of Economics at John Witherspoon College.

V.   **Prerequisites**

None.

VI.   **Required Texts/Resources**

Comfort, Philip, ed. *The Origin of the Bible*. Carol Stream: Tyndale House Publishers, 2012.
Arterbury, Andrew, W. Bellinger, and Derek Dodson. *Engaging the Christian Scriptures: An Introduction to the Bible*.
Van Der Toorn, Karel. *Scribal Culture and the Making of the Hebrew Bible*. Cambridge: Harvard University Press, 2007.

Other supplemental writings will be available for free download on populi, such as chapters and essays from books.

VII.   **Optional Texts/Resources**

General Introductions and Surveys
Arterbury, Andrew, and W. Bellinger and Derek Dodson. *Engaging the Christian Scriptures: An Introduction to the Bible*. Grand Rapids: Baker Academic, 2014.
Carr, David and Colleen Conway. *An Introduction to the Bible: Sacred Texts and Imperial Contexts*. Malden: Wiley-Blackwell, 2010.
Johnston, Philip, ed. *The IVP Introduction to the Bible*. Downers Grove: InterVarsity Press, 2011.
Kaminsky, Joel, Reasoner, Mark, and Joel Lohr. *The Abingdon Introduction to the Bible*. Nashville: Abingdon, 2014.
Pelikan, Jaroslav. *Whose Bible Is It?*. New York: Penguin Books, 2006.

First Testament Introductions and Surveys
Brueggeman, Walter, ed. *The New Interpreter's Bible: Old Testament Survey*. Nashville: Abingdon, 2006.
Carr, David. *An Introduction to the Old Testament: Sacred Texts and Imperial Contexts of the Hebrew Bible*. Malden: Wiley-Blackwell, 2010.

Coogan, Michael, and Cynthia Chapman. *The Old Testament: A Historical and Literary Introduction to the Hebrew Scriptures.* 4th ed. New York: Oxford University Press, 2017.

Goldingay, John. *An Introduction to the Old Testament.* Downers Grove: InterVarsity, 2016.

Hayes, Kristine. *An Introduction to the Bible.* New Haven: Yale University Press, 2012.

Hess, Richard. *The Old Testament: A Historical, Theological, and Critical Introduction.* Grand Rapids: Baker Academic, 2016.

Septuagint Introductions and Surveys

Dines, Jennifer and Michael Knibb, eds. *The Septuagint.* New York: Bloomsburg T&T Clark, 2004.

Silva, Moisés and Karen Jobes. *Invitation to the Septuagint.* 2nd ed. Grand Rapids: Baker Academic, 2015.

Second Testament Introductions and Surveys

DeSilva, David. *An Introduction to the New Testament: Contexts, Methods, and Ministry Formation.* InterVarsity Press, 2004.

Hagner, Donald. *The New Testament: A Historical and Theological Introduction.* Grand Rapids: Baker Academic, 2012.

Powell, Mark. *Introducing the New Testament: A Historical, Literary, and Theological Survey.* Grand Rapids: Baker Academic, 2009.

Craddock, Fred, and M. Eugene Boring. *The New Interpreter's Bible: New Testament Survey.* Nashville: Abingdon, 2006.

Apocrypha and Pseudepigrapha

Burke, Tony, and Brent Landau. *New Testament Apocrypha.* Grand Rapids: Eerdmans, 2016.

DeSilva, David. *Introducing the Apocrypha.* Grand Rapids: Baker Academic, 2018.

Charlesworth, James. *The Old Testament Pseudipigrapha.* 2 Vols. Peabody: Hendrickson, 2010.

Bibliology and Doctrine of Scripture

Barton, John. *People of the Book? The Authority of the Bible in Christianity.* Louisville: Westminster John Knox, 1989.

Bavinck, Herman. Trans. John Vriend. *Reformed Dogmatics, Vol 1: Prolegomena.* Grand Rapids: Baker, 2008.

Billings, Todd. *The Word of God for the People of God.* Grand Rapids: Eerdmans, 2010.

Bloesch, Donald. *Holy Scripture: Revelation, Inspiration, and Interpretation.* Downers Grove: InterVarsity, 2005.

Brettler, Marc. *How to Read the Bible.* Philadelphia: Jewish Publication Society, 2005.

Bryan, Christopher. *And God Spoke: The Authority of the Bible for the Church Today.* Cambridge: Cowley. 2002.

Dodd, C. H. *The Authority of the Bible.* London: Fontana, 1960.

Goldingay, John. *Models for Scripture.* Toronto: Clements Publishing, 2004.

Humphrey, Edith. *Scripture and Tradition: What the Bible Really Says.* Grand Rapids: Baker Academic, 2013.

Volf, Miroslav. *Captive to the Word of God: Engaging the Scriptures for Contemporary Theological Reflection*. Grand Rapids: Eerdmans, 2010.

Ward, Timothy. *Words of Life: Scripture as the Living and Active Word of God*. Downers Grove: InterVarsity, 2009.

Webster, John. *Holy Scripture: A Dogmatic Sketch*. Cambridge: Cambridge University Press, 2003.

Wolterstorff, Nicholas. *Divine Discourse: Philosophical Reflections on the Claim that God Speaks*. Cambridge: Cambridge University Press, 1995.

Wright, N. T. *Scripture and the Authority of God*. New York: HarperOne, 2013.

General Biblical Criticism

Abraham, William. *Canon and Criterion in Christian Theology*. New York: Oxford University Press, 2002.

Barton, John. *How the Bible Came to Be*. Louisville: Westminster John Knox, 1998.

----------. *The Nature of Biblical Criticism*. Louisville: Westminster John Knox, 2007.

Bruce, F. F. *The Canon of Scripture*. Downers Grove: InterVarsity, 1996.

Comfort, Philip, ed. *The Origin of the Bible*. Carol Stream: Tyndale House Publishers, 2012.

Evans, Craig and Immanuel Tov, eds. *Exploring the Origins of the Bible: Canon Formation in Historical, Literary, and Theological Perspective*. Grand Rapids: Baker Academic, 2008.

McDonald, Lee. *The Biblical Canon: Its Origins, Transmission, and Authority*. Peabody: Hendrickson, 2007.

----------. *The Origin of the Bible: A Guide for the Perplexed*. New York: Bloomsbury T & T Clark, 2011.

----------. *The Formation of the Biblical Canon*. 2 Vols. New York: Bloomsbury T & T Clark, 2017.

----------, and James Sanders, eds. *The Canon Debate*. Grand Rapids: Baker, 2001.

Wegner, Paul. *The Journey from Texts to Translations: The Origin and Development of the Bible*. Grand Rapids: Baker Academic, 2004.

First Testament Criticism

Baden, Joel. *The Composition of the Pentateuch*. New Haven: Yale University Press, 2012.

Berman, *Inconsistency in the Torah: Ancient Literary Convention and the Limits of Source Criticism*. New York: Oxford University Press, 2017.

Breed, Brennan. *Nomadic Text: A Theory of Biblical Reception History*. Indianapolis: Indiana University Press, 2014.

Carr, David. *The Formation of the Hebrew Bible*. New York: Oxford University Press, 2011.

Cassuto, Umberto. *The Documentary Hypothesis: And the Composition of the Pentateuch*. Jerusalem: Shalem Press, 2006.

Dever, William. *What Did the Biblical Writers Know and When Did They Know it?: What Archaeology Can Tell Us about the Reality of Ancient Israel*. Grand Rapids: Eerdmans, 2001.

----------. *Who Were the Early Israelites and Where Did They Come From?* Grand Rapids: Eerdmans, 2006.

----------. *Beyond Texts: An Archeological Portrait of Ancient Israel and Judah*. Atlanta: SBL Press, 2017.

Finkelstein, Israel. *The Quest for the Historical Israel.* Atlanta: Society of Biblical Literature, 2007.

----------. and Neil Silberman. *David and Solomon.* New York: Free Press, 2006.

Friedman, Richard. *Who Wrote the Bible?.* New York: HarperOne, 1987.

Grabbe, Lester. *Ancient Israel: What Do We Know and How Do We Know It?* New York: Bloomsbury T & T Clark, 2008.

Hess, Richard, and Bill Arnold. *Ancient Israel's History: An Introduction to Issues and Sources.* Grand Rapids: Baker Academic, 2014.

Schiedewind, William. *How the Bible Became a Book.* Cambridge: Cambridge University Press, 2005.

Schmid, Conrad. *The Old Testament: A Literary History.* Minneapolis: Fortress Press, 2012.

Lim, Timothy. *The Formation of the Jewish Canon.* New Haven: Yale University Press, 2013.

Levy, Thomas, Schneider, Thomas, and William Propp. *Israel's Exodus in Transdisciplinary Perspective.* New York: Springer, 2015.

Levinson, Bernard, and Gary Knoppers, eds. *The Pentateuch as Torah: New Models for Understanding Its Promulgation and Acceptance.* Winona Lake: Eisenbrauns, 2007.

Long, V. Philips, Baker, David, and Gordon Wenham. *Windows into Old Testament History: Evidence, Argument, and the Crisis of "Biblical Israel."* Grand Rapids: Eerdmans, 2002.

Van der Toorn, Karel. *Scribal Culture and the Making of the Hebrew Bible.* Cambridge: Harvard University Press, 2009.

Septuagint Criticism

Law, Timothy. *When God Spoke Greek.* New York: Oxford University Press, 2013.

McLay, R. Timothy. *The Use of the Septuagint in New Testament Research.* Grand Rapids: Eerdmans, 2003.

Second Testament Criticism

Barton, John. *Holy Writings, Sacred Text.* Louisville: Westminster John Knox, 1998.

Dunn, James. *Jesus Remembered.* Grand Rapids: Eerdmans, 2003.

----------. *The Oral Gospel Tradition.* Grand Rapids: Eerdmans, 2013.

Porter, Stanley. *How We Got the New Testament.* Grand Rapids: Baker, 2013.

----------, and Bryan Dyer. eds. *The Synoptic Problem: Four Views.* Grand Rapids: Backer Academic, 2016.

Thatcher, Thomas, ed. *Jesus, the Voice, and the Text: Beyond The Oral and the Written Gospel.* Waco: Baylor University Press, 2008.

Metzger, Bruce. *The Canon of the New Testament: Its Origin, Development, and Significance.* Oxford: Oxford University Press, 1997.

Patzia, Arthur. *The Making of the New Testament: Origin, Collection, Text, and Canon.* Downers Grove: InterVarsity, 2011.

Stein, Robert. *Studying the Synoptic Gospels.* Grand Rapids: Baker Academic, 2001.

Watson, Francis. *Gospel Writing: A Canonical Perspective.* Grand Rapids: Eerdmans, 2013.

Wright, N. T.. *The New Testament and the People of God.* Minneapolis: Fortress Press, 1992.

Textual Criticism

Aland, Kurt and Barbara. *The Text of the New Testament: An Introduction to the Critical Editions and to the Theory and Practice of Modern Textual Criticism.* Grand Rapids: Eerdmans, 1995.

Bratzman, Ellis. *Old Testament Textual Criticism: A Practical Introduction.* Grand Rapids: Baker, 1993.

Comfort, Philip. *New Testament Text and Translation Commentary.* Carol Stream: Tyndale House Publishers, 2008.

Ehrman, Bart. *The Orthodox Corruption of Scripture.* New York: Oxford University Press, 2011.

----------, and Bruce Metzger. *The Text of the New Testament: Its Transmission, Corruption, and Restoration.* Oxford: Oxford University Press, 2005.

----------, and Michael Holmes, eds. *The Text of the New Testament in Contemporary Research.* Boston: Brill, 2014.

Parker, D. C. *Textual Scholarship and the Making of the New Testament.* New York: Oxford University Press, 2014.

Tov, Emmanuel. *Textual Criticism of the Hebrew Bible.* Minneapolis: Fortress Press, 2011.

----------. *The Text-Critical Use of the Septuagint in Biblical Research.* Winona Lake: Eisenbrauns, 2015.

----------, and Armin Lange. *Textual History of the Bible.* 2nd ed. Multivolume. Boston: Brill, 2016-.

Ulrich, Eugene. *The Dead Sea Scrolls and the Origins of the Bible.* Grand Rapids: Eerdmans, 1999.

Wallace, Daniel. *Revisiting the Corruption of the New Testament.* Grand Rapids: Kregel, 2010.

Würtwein, Ernst. *The Text of the Old Testament.* Grand Rapids: Eerdmans, 2014.

Conservative and/or Fundamentalist Introductions and Apologetics

Archer, Gleason. *The New International Encyclopedia of Bible Difficulties.* Grand Rapids: Zondervan, 2001.

Beale, Gregory. *The Erosion of Inerrancy.* Wheaton: Crossway, 2008.

Block, Daniel, ed. *Israel: Ancient Kingdom or Late Invention?* Nashville: B & H, 2008.

Blomberg, Craig. *The Historical Reliability of the Gospels.* Downers Grove: InterVarsity, 2007.

----------. *Can We Still Believe the Bible?* Grand Rapids: Brazos, 2014.

----------. *The Historical Reliability of the New Testament: Countering the Challenges to Evangelical Christian Belief.* Nashville: B & H, 2016.

Carson, D. A. *Collected Writings on Scripture.* Wheaton: Crossway, 2010.

----------. ed. *The Enduring Authority of the Christian Scriptures.* Grand Rapids: Eerdmans, 2016.

Conn, Harvie, ed. *Inerrancy and Hermeneutic: A Tradition, a Challenge, a Debate.* Grand Rapids: Baker, 1988.

Cowan, Steven, and Terry Wilder. *In Defense of the Bible: A Comprehensive Apologetic for the Authority of Scripture.* Nashville: Broadman and Holman Academic, 2013.

Dockery, David. *Christian Scripture.* Eugene: Wipf and Stock, 2004.

Ewert, David. *A General Introduction to the Bible.* Grand Rapids: Zondervan, 1990.

Frame, John. *The Doctrine of the Word of God.* Phillipsburg: Presbyterian and Reformed, 2010.

Geisler, Norman, ed. *Inerrancy*. Grand Rapids: Zondervan, 1980.

----------. *A General Introduction to the Bible*. Chicago: Moody, 1986.

----------, and Thomas Howe. *The Big Book of Bible Difficulties*. Grand Rapids: Baker, 2008.

----------, and William Roach. *Defending Inerrancy*. Grand Rapids: Baker, 2012.

----------, and F. Farnell. *Vital Issues in the Inerrancy Debate*. Eugene: Wipf and Stock, 2016.

Grudem, Wayne, Collins, C. John, and Thomas Schreiner. *Understanding Scripture: An Overview of the Bible's Origin, Reliability, and Meaning*. Wheaton: Crossway, 2012.

Ham, Ken. *Demolishing Supposed Bible Contradictions*. 2 vols. Master Books, 2010, 2012.

----------, and Bodie Hodge, eds. *How Do We Know the Bible is True?* 2 vols. Master Books, 2011, 2012.

Hannah, John, ed. *Inerrancy and the Church*. Chicago: Moody Press, 1984.

Harris, R. *Inspiration and Canonicity of the Bible*. Grand Rapids: Zondervan, 1969.

Henry, Carl. *God, Revelation, and Authority*. Wheaton: Crossway, 1999.

Hoffmeier, James. *Ancient Israel in Sinai: The Evidence for the Authenticity of the Wilderness Tradition*. New York: Oxford University Press, 2011.

----------. *Israel in Egypt: The Evidence for the Authenticity of the Exodus Tradition*. New York: Oxford University Press, 1999.

----------, and Dennis Magary, ed. *Do Historical Matters Matter to Faith?: A Critical Appraisal of Modern and Postmodern Approaches to Scripture*. Wheaton: Crossway, 2012.

Kitchen, K. A. *On the Reliability of the Old Testament*. Grand Rapids: Eerdmans, 2006.

Kruger, Michael. *The Question of Canon: Challenging the Status Quo in the New Testament Debate*. Downers Grove: InterVarsity, 2013.

----------. *Canon Revisited*. Wheaton: Crossway, 2012.

Linnemann, Eta. Trans. Robert Yarbrough. *Historical Criticism of the Bible: Methodology or Ideology: Reflections of a Bultmannian Turned Evangelical*. Louisville: Kregel, 2001.

----------. *Is There a Synoptic Problem?* Grand Rapids: Baker, 1992.

----------. Trans Robert Yarbrough. *Biblical Criticism on Trial: How Scientific is Scientific Theology?* Louisville: Kregel, 2001.

Lightner, Robert. *The Case for Total Inerrancy*. Louisville: Kregel, 1997.

MacArthur, John, ed. *The Inerrant Word: Biblical Historical, and Pastoral Perspectives*. Wheaton: Crossway, 2016.

Merrick, J. and Stephen Garrett, eds. *Five Views on Biblical Inerrancy*. Grand Rapids: Zondervan, 2013.

Morrison, John. *Has God Said? Scripture, the Word of God, and the Crisis of Theological Authority*. Eugene: Wipf and Stock, 2006.

Nicole, Roger and J. Ramsey Michaels. *Inerrancy and Common Sense*. Grand Rapids: Baker, 1980.

Piper, John. *A Particular Glory: How the Christian Scriptures Reveal Their Complete Truthfulness*. Wheaton: Crossway, 2016.

Poythress, Vern. *Inerrancy and Worldview: Answering Modern Challenges to the Bible*. Wheaton: Crossway, 2012.

----------. *Inerrancy and the Gospels: A God-Centered Approach to the Challenges of Harmonization*. Wheaton: Crossway, 2012.

Stonehouse, N. B. and Paul Woolley, eds. *The Infallible Word: A Symposium by the Members of the Faculty of Westminster Theological Seminary.* Phillipsburg: Presbyterian and Reformed, 1967.

Thomas, Robert, ed. *Three Views on the Origins of the Synoptic Gospels.* Louisville: Kregel, 2002.

Walton, John and D. Brent Sandy. *The Lost World of Scripture: Ancient Literary Culture and Biblical Authority.* Downers Grove: InterVarsity Academic, 2013.

Warfield, B. B. *The Inspiration and Authority of the Bible.* Phillipsburg: Presbyterian and Reformed, 1980.

Williams, James. *God's Word in Our Hands: The Bible Preserved for Us.* Ambassador International, 2016.

Woodbridge, John and D. A. Carson, eds. *Scripture and Truth.* Grand Rapids: Baker, 1992.

----------. *Hermeneutics, Authority, and Canon.* Eugene: Wipf and Stock, 2009.

Christian Critiques of Fundamentalist Biblicism and Non-Fundamentalist Bibliology and Apologetics

Allert, Craig. *A High View of Scripture?: The Authority of the Bible and the Formation of the New Testament Canon.* Grand Rapids: Baker Academic, 2007.

Bacote, Vincent, et al., eds. *Evangelicals And Scripture: Tradition, Authority, and Hermeneutics.* Downers Grove: InterVarsity, 2004.

Bovell, Carlos. *Inerrancy and the Spiritual Formation of Younger Evangelicals.* Eugene: Wipf and Stock, 2007.

----------. *Interdisciplinary Perspectives on the Authority of Scripture: Historical, Biblical, and Theoretical Perspectives.* Eugene: Wipf and Stock, 2011.

----------. *Rehabilitating Inerrancy in a Culture of Fear.* Eugene: Wipf and Stock, 2012.

Barr, James. *Holy Scripture: Canon, Authority, Criticism.* Louisville: Westminster John Knox, 1983.

----------. *The Bible and the Modern World.* SMC Classics, 1973.

----------. *The Scope and Authority of the Bible.* SMC Classics, 2002.

Brown, William, ed. *Engaging Biblical Authority: Perspectives on the Bible as Scripture.* Louisville: Westminster John Knox, 2007.

Bruce, F. F. *The New Testament Documents: Are They Reliable?* Grand Rapids: Eerdmans, 2003.

Dunn, James. *The Living Word.* Minneapolis: Fortress Press, 2003.

Enns, Peter. *Inspiration and Incarnation: Evangelicals and the Problem of the Old Testament.* Grand Rapids: Baker Academic, 2005.

----------. *The Bible Tells Me So: Why Defending Scripture Has Made Us Unable to Read It.* New York: HarperOne, 2014.

----------. *How the Bible Actually Works.* New York: HarperOne, 2019.

Fretheim, Terence and Karlfried Froehlich. *The Bible as the Word of God: In a Postmodern Age.* Eugene: Wipf and Stock 1998.

Hauerwas, Stanley. *Unleashing the Scripture: Freedom the Bible from Captivity to America.* Nashville: Abingdon, 1993.

Hays, Christopher, and Ansberry, Christopher, eds. *Evangelical Faith and the Challenge of Historical Criticism.* Grand Rapids: Baker Academic, 2013.

Keener, Craig. *Miracles: The Credibility of the New Testament Accounts.* Grand Rapids: Baker Academic, 2011.

Licona, Michael. *Why Are There Differences in the Gospels?: What We Can Learn from Ancient Biography.* New York: Oxford University Press, 2016.

Merrick, J. and Stephen Garrett, eds., *Five Views on Biblical Inerrancy*. Grand Rapids: Zondervan, 2013.

Padgett, Alan, and Patrick Keifert, eds. *But is it All True?: The Bible and the Question of Truth*. Grand Rapids: Eerdmans, 2006.

Rogers, Jack, and Donald McKim. *The Authority and Interpretation of the Bible: An Historical Approach*. New York: Harper and Row, 1979.

Schlimm, Matthew. *This Strange and Sacred Scripture: Wrestling with the Old Testament and Its Oddities*. Grand Rapids: Baker Academic, 2015.

Smith, Christian. *The Bible Made Impossible: Why Biblicism is Not a Truly Evangelical Reading of Scripture*. Grand Rapids: Brazos Press, 2012.

Sparks, Kenton. *Sacred Word, Broken Word*. Grand Rapids: Eerdmans, 2012.

----------. *God's Word in Human Words: An Evangelical Appropriation of Critical Biblical Scholarship*. Grand Rapids: Baker Academic, 2008.

Stark, Thom. *The Human Faces of God: What Scripture Reveals When It Gets God Wrong (And Why Inerrancy Tries to Hide It)*. Eugene: Wipf and Stock, 2011.

Witherington, Ben. *The Living Word: Rethinking the Theology of the Bible*. Waco: Baylor University Press, 2009.

Secular Critiques of the Bible

Ehrman, Bart. *Lost Scriptures: Books that Did Not Make it Into the New Testament*. New York: Oxford University Press, 2005.

----------. *Misquoting Jesus: The Story Behind Who Changed the Bible and Why*. New York: HarperOne, 2007.

----------. *Jesus, Interrupted: Revealing the Hidden Contradictions in the Bible (And Why We Don't Know About Them)*. New York: HarperOne, 2010.

----------. *Forged*. New York: HarperOne, 2011.

----------. *Forgery and Counterforgery*. New York: Oxford University Press, 2012.

Helms, Randel. *Gospel Fictions*. Amhurst: Prometheus, 1988.

Price, Robert. *Inerrant the Wind: The Evangelical Crisis of Biblical Authority*. New York: Prometheus, 2008.

Satlow, Michael. *How the Bible Became Holy*. New Haven: Yale University Press, 2014.

Translation and Translations

Carson, D. A. *The Inclusive Language Debate*. Grand Rapids: Baker, 1998.

Fee, Gordon and Mark Strauss. *How to Choose a Translation for All Its Worth: A Guide to Understanding and Using Bible Version*. Grand Rapids: Zondervan, 2007.

Metzger, Bruce. *The Bible in Translation: Ancient and English Versions*. Grand Rapids: Baker, 2001.

Porter, Stanley, and Mark Boda, eds. *Translating the New Testament: Text, Translation, Theology*. Grand Rapids: Eerdmans, 2009.

Ryken, Leland. *The Legacy of the King James Bible: Celebrating 400 Years of the Most Influential English Translation*. Wheaton: Crossway, 2011.

White, James. *The King James Only Controversy: Can You Trust Modern Translations?*. Minneapolis: Bethany House, 2009.

Reference

Oxford Encyclopedias of the Bible

Yale Anchor Bible Dictionaries

New Interpreter's Bible Dictionaries

[Other sections of syllabus redacted because of irrelevance]

VIII.   Course Schedule

All faculty have the right to alter the schedule at any time.

Once/week schedule

	Topic	Assignments
1.	Introductions and Syllabus Review;	Read "The Bible" and "Versions of the Bible"
2.	"Bible" or "Bibles"?; "Intro to Intro to the Bible"	(*Origin*) Read handout: Hübner, "Intro to Intro" and "Thinking Critically about the First Testament Writings"
3.	"The Bible," "Bible Versions"	Read *Engaging*, ch 1-3
4.	Thinking Critically about First Testament Writings	
5.	Introducing the First Testament and the	Read *Engaging*, ch 4
6.	Pentateuch The Prophets The Writings	Read Van Der Toorn, ch 1-2
7.	Books or Scrolls?	Read Van Der Toorn, ch 4-5
8.	Writing and Authorship in the Ancient World	Read Norton, "Texts and Manuscripts of the Old Testament" (*Origin*)
9.	Who were the scribes, and what did they	Read Beckwith, "The Canon of the Old Testament"
10.	do? The Text of the First Testament	(*Origin*) Read McDonald, "Appendix A" and "B" (*The Formation*)
11.	First Testament canons	**Complete Take-Home Test 1**
12.	Receive Take-Home Test 1	
13.	*No class (finish take-home test)*	Read *Engaging*, ch 5-6
14.		Read handouts: Geisler, *Systematic Theology*, 351-354; Jones, "Notes on the LXX"
15.	**Hand-in Take Home Test 1**	Read *Engaging*, ch 7-8
16.	The Intertestamental period and NT World The Septuagint (Jones Handout) The Gospels and Acts (Geisler handout)	
17.	Paul and the Pauline Tradition	Read Comfort, "The Text of the NT" and Fisher,
18.	General Letters and Revelation	"The Canon of the NT" (*Origin*) Read handout: McDonald, "Appendix C" and "D" (*The Formation*)
19.	The Text of the Second Testament	
20.	The Canon of the Second Testament	**Complete Take-Home Test 2**
21.	*No class (finish take-home test)*	Read Fisher and Ryken, "The Bible as Literature"
22.		(*Origin*) Read Walker and Elliot, "Bible Languages" and "Bible Translation" (*Origin*)
23.	**Hand in Take-Home Test 2**	Read Comfort, "History of the English Bible (*Origin*)
24.	The Bible as Literature Bible Languages and Translation	
25.	The English Bible	Read handout: Goldingay, "Introduction" (*Models*
26.	The KJV and "KJV Onlyism"	*for Scripture*); Hübner, "Higher ed institution statements"
27.	Textual Differences in KJV and Modern	**Complete Take-Home Test 3**
28.	Translations An Introduction to Bibliology	
29.	**Exam Week (Hand-in Take Home Test 3)**	
30.		

IX. **Other Resources**

None.

Appendix G:

Syllabus for CHR331

Theologia Principia I: God and Creation

I.   General Information

Instructor:	Jamin Hübner	Email:	jhubner@jwc.edu
Office Hours:	Mon-Thurs, 1:30-4:30pm	Office	TBD
Mobile Phone:	[]		
Semester:	Fall 2017	Schedule: M/Wed, 10-11:15am
Credits:	3	Location: Evans Hall

II.   Course Description

An introduction to the task and method of theology, theology proper, theological anthropology, perspectives of sin and death, and of creation and their various implications.

III.   Course Objectives and Learning Outcomes

The students who successfully complete this course will—whenever engaging in theological discussions or doing theology in a variety of contexts—be able to competently:

1. Identify and understand the various methods of theology.
2. Recognize the various types of theology.
3. Identify and distinguish the "attributes of God," the relationship between divinity and the universe, theological anthropologies, views of sin and the fall, and other issues central to "God and creation."

These course objectives and outcomes require critical thinking and biblical studies, which are two of JWC's institutional objectives. They also fulfill the program goals of Christian Studies, such as to "explain and summarize the nature and contents of the New and Old Testament Scriptures, including an understanding the origin of the Bible," and "be able to apply...biblical principles to contemporary situations," and the program goals of the Christian Studies Program, such as obtaining a "thorough grounding in biblical...studies, and the development of interpretive skills.

IV.   Course Professor

Dr. Jamin Hübner is an entrepreneur, musician, and theologian from South Dakota. He is a graduate of Dordt College (BA Theology), Reformed Theological Seminary (MA Religion) and the University of South Africa (ThD Systematic

Theology), and a student at Southern New Hampshire University (MS Economics) and currently serves as the Director of Institutional Effectiveness, founding Chair of Christian Studies, and part-time Professor of Economics at John Witherspoon College.

V.   Prerequisites

None. (However, it is recommended that students take CHR101 beforehand if possible).

VI.   Required Texts/Resources

Books

Bird, Michael. *Evangelical Theology: A Biblical and Systematic Introduction.* Grand Rapids: Zondervan, 2013.

Migliore, Daniel. *Faith Seeking Understanding: An Introduction to Christian Theology.* Grand Rapids: Eerdmans, 2014.

Oden, Thomas. *Classical Christianity: A Systematic Theology.* New York: HarperOne, 1992.

Essays and Chapters (some are available for download on Populi or will be handed out)

Davis, Ellen and Richard Hays, eds. "Nine Theses on the Interpretation of Scripture." In *The Art of Reading Scripture.* Grand Rapids: Eerdmans, 2003.

Goldingay, John. *Models for Scripture.* "Introduction." Toronto: Clements, 2004.

Wright, N.T. *Scripture and the Authority of God.* "Prologue" and Selections. New York: HarperOne, 2013.

VII.   Optional Texts/Resources

Recommend Works on Theological Methodology

Bartholomew, Craig, et al. eds. *Scripture and Hermeneutics Series.* 8 Vols. Grand Rapids: Zondervan.

Fowl, Stephen. *Engaging Scripture: A Model for Theological Interpretation.* Eugene: Wipf and Stock, 2008.

Franke, John. *The Character of Theology.* Grand Rapids: Baker, 2005.

Goldingay, John. *Models for Scripture.* Toronto: Clements, 2004.

-----------. *Models for Interpretation of Scripture.* Toronto: Clements, 2004.

Grenz, Stanley. *Renewing the Center.* Grand Rapids: Baker, 2000.

-----------. *Who Needs Theology?: An Invitation to the Study of God.* Downers Grove: InterVarsity, 1996.

Hays, Richard and Ellen Davis, eds. *The Art of Reading Scripture.* Grand Rapids: Eerdmans, 2003.

Helmer, Kristine. *Theology and the End of Doctrine.* Louisville: Westminster John Knox, 2014.

Kaufman, Gordon. *In the Face of Mystery: A Constructive Theology.* Cambridge: Harvard University Press, 1993.

Lindbeck, George. *The Nature of Doctrine.* Louisville: Westminster John Knox, 2009.

Louth, Andrew. *Discerning the Mystery.* Gloucestershire: Clarendon Press, 1990.

Marshall, I. Howard. *Beyond the Bible*. Grand Rapids: Baker Academic, 2004.

McFague, Sallie. *Models of God*. Minneapolis: Fortress Press, 1987.

----------, *Metaphorical Theology*. Minneapolis: Fortress Press, 1982.

McCormick, Bruce, and Kimlyn Bender, eds. *Theology as Conversation*. Grand Rapids: Eerdmans, 2009.

Meadors, Gary, ed. *Four Views on Moving Beyond the Bible to Theology*. Grand Rapids: Zondervan, 2009.

Muller, Richard. *The Study of Theology*. Grand Rapids: Zondervan, 2001.

Olson, Roger. *The Essentials of Christian Thought*. Grand Rapids, Zondervan, 2017.

Pui-lan, Kwok, et al. eds. *Teaching Global Theologies: Power and Praxis*. Waco: Baylor University Press, 2015.

Ray, Kathleen, ed. *Theology That Matters*. Minneapolis: Fortress Press, 2006.

Solle, Dorothy. *Thinking About God: An Introduction to Theology*. Eugene: Wipf and Stock, 2016.

Scheinder, Laurel, and Stephen Ray. Jr. *Awake the Moment: An Introduction to Theology*. Louisville: Westminster John Knox, 2016.

Tracy, David. *Blessed Rage for Order*. Chicago: University of Chicago Press, 1975.

----------. *The Analogical Imagination: Christian Theology and the Culture of Pluralism*. New York: Herder and Herder, 1998.

Vanhoozer, Kevin. *First Theology*. Downers Grove: InterVarsity, 2002.

----------. *The Drama of Doctrine*. Louisville: Westminster John Knox, 2005.

Van Til, Cornelius. Ed. William Edgar. *An Introduction to Systematic Theology*. Phillipsburg: Presbyterian and Reformed, 2007.

Veeneman, Mary. *Introducing Theological Method: A Survey of Contemporary Theologians and Approaches*. Grand Rapids: Baker Academic, 2017.

Wright, N. T. *Scripture and the Authority of God*. New York: HarperOne, 2013.

----------, and Michael Bird. *The New Testament in Its World*. Grand Rapids: Zondervan Academic, 2019.

Recommended Works on Theology Proper and Creation

Bavinck, Herman. *Reformed Dogmatics*, vol. 2, *God and Creation*. Trans. John Vriend. Grand Rapids: Baker, 2008.

Bray, Gerald. *The Doctrine of God*. Downers Grove: InterVarsity, 1993.

de Chardin, Teilhard. *The Future of Man*. New York: Double Day, 2004.

Crosby, Donald, and Jerome Stone, eds. *The Routledge Handbook to Religious Naturalism*. New York: Routledge, 2018.

Erickson, Millard. *Who's Tampering With the Trinity?*. Grand Rapids: Kregel Academic, 2009.

Holmes, Stephen. *The Quest for the Doctrine of the Trinity*. Downers Grove: InterVarsity, 2012.

Jenson, Robert. *Theology as Revisionary Metaphysics: Essays on God and Creation*. Eugene: Cascade, 2014.

Jowers, Dennis, ed. *Four Views on Divine Providence*. Grand Rapids: Zondervan, 2011.

Kaufman, Gordon. *In the Face of Mystery: A Constructive Theology*. Cambridge: Harvard University Press, 1993.

MacDonald, Neil. *Metaphysics and the God of Israel: Systematic Theology of the Old and New Testaments*. Grand Rapids: Baker Academic, 2007.

Moltmann, Jürgen. *God and Creation*. Minneapolis: Fortress Press, 1993.

McFague, Sallie. *The Body of God*. Minneapolis: Fortress Press, 1993.

Placher, William. *The Domestication of Transcendence.* Louisville: Westminster John Knox, 1996.

Primavesi, Anne. *Sacred Gaia.* New York: Routledge, 2000.

Tanner, Kathryn. *God and Creation in Christian Theology.* Minneapolis: Fortress Press, 2005.

Torrance, T. F. *The Christian Doctrine of God, One Being Three Persons.* New York: T&T Clark, 2001.

----------. *Space, Time, and Incarnation.* New York: Oxford University Press, 1969.

Recommended Systematic Theologies[1]

Bavinck, Herman. *Our Reasonable Faith.* Trans. Henry Zylstra. Grand Rapids: Eerdmans, 1956.

Goldingay, John. *Biblical Theology: The God of the Christian Scriptures.* Downers Grove: InterVarsity, 2016.

Grenz, Stanley. *Theology for the Community of God.* Grand Rapids: Eerdmans, 2000.

Hodgson, Peter. *Winds of the Spirit: A Constructive Christian Theology.* Louisville: Westminster John Knox, 1994.

Migliore, Daniel. *Faith Seeking Understanding: An Introduction to Christian Theology.* Grand Rapids: Eerdmans, 2014.

Oden, Thomas. *Classical Christianity: A Systematic Theology.* New York: HarperOne, 1992.

Placher, William, ed. *Essentials of Christian Theology.* Nashville: Westminster John Knox, 2003.

"Classic" Systematic Theologies

Aquinas, Thomas. *Summa Theologica.* 5 Vols. Notre Dame: Christian Classics, 1981.

----------, ed., Peter Kreeft. *The Summa of the Summa.* San Francisco: Ignatius Press, 1990.

Bonaventure. *Breviloquium.* New York: Franciscan Institute, 2005.

Calvin, John. *Institutes of the Christian Religion.* Trans. Ford Battles. Ed. John McNeill. 2 Vols. Louisville: Westminster John Knox, 2006.

----------. *The Institutes of the Christian Religion* [1541 French text]. Trans. Robert White. Banner of Truth, 2014.

Lactantius. *Divine Institutes.* Trans. Anthony Bowen and Peter Garnsey. Liverpool: Liverpool University, 2004.

Lombard, Peter. 4 Vols. *The Sentences.* Trans. Giulo Silano. Toronto: PIMS.

Melanchthon, Philip. *Loci Communes.* Trans. Charles Hill. Eugene: Wipf and Stock, 2007.

Origen. *On First Principles.* Trans. G. W. Butterworth. Notre Dame: Christian Classics, 2013.

Schleiermacher, Friedrich. *The Christian Faith* (two vols). Trans. by Terrence Tice, Katherine Kelsey, and Edwina Lawler. Louisville: Westminster John Knox Press, 2016, orig. 1821.

---

[1] Note: "Systematic Theologies" in this bibliography also include symposiums/essay compilations, select theological introductions, and select anthologies/theological series'.

Revisionist/Constructionist Theologies

Hodgson, Peter. *Winds of the Spirit: A Constructive Christian Theology*. Louisville: Westminster John Knox, 1994.

Kaufman, Gordon. *In the Face of Mystery: A Constructive Theology*. Cambridge: Harvard University Press, 1993.

McFague, Sallie. *Models of God*. Minneapolis: Fortress Press, 1987.

Scheinder, Laurel. *Awake the Moment: An Introduction to Theology*. Louisville: Westminster John Knox, 2019.

Episcopal Systematic Theologies

Gilkey, Langdon. *Message and Existence: Introduction to Christian Theology*. New York: Seabury, 1981.

Markham, Ian. *Understanding Christian Doctrine*. 2nd ed. London: Wiley-Blackwell, 2017.

Roman Catholic Systematic Theologies

Balthsar, Hans Urs von. *The Glory of the Lord*. 7 Vols. San Francisco: Ignatius Press.

----------. *Theo-Drama*. 7 Vols. San Francisco: Ignatius Press.

----------. *Theo-Logic*. 3 Vols. San Francisco: Ignatius Press.

Beeck, Frans. *God Encountered: A Contemporary Catholic Systematic Theology*. 4 Vols. Collegeville: Liturgical Press.

Fiorenza, Francis and John Galvin, eds. *Systematic Theology: Roman Catholic Perspectives*. Minneapolis: Augsburg Fortress Press. 2011.

Gratsch, Edward J., ed. *Principles of Catholic Theology*. Staten Island: Alba House, 1981.

Laurance, John. *Introduction to Theology*. New York: Pearson. 2006.

Levering, *Engaging the Doctrine of Creation*. Grand Rapids: Baker Academic, 2017.

----------. *Engaging the Doctrine of Revelation*. Grand Rapids: Baker Academic, 2017

----------. *Engaging the Doctrine of the Holy Spirit*. Grand Rapids: Baker Academic, 2014.

Meuller, J. J. *Theological Foundations*. Winona: Anselm Academic, 2011.

Ott, Ludwig. *The Fundamentals of Catholic Dogma*. Rockford: Tan Books and Publishers, 1974.

Rahner, Karl. *Foundations of the Christian Faith*. The Crossroad Publishing Company, 1982.

Ratzinger, Joseph. *Principles of Catholic Theology*. San Francisco: Ignatius Press, 1987.

Sonderegger, Katherine. *Systematic Theology*, 3 vols. Minneapolis: Fortress Press, 2015—.

Towey, Anthony. *An Introduction to Christian Theology*. New York: Bloomsbury T&T Clark, 2013.

Eastern Orthodox Systematic Theologies

Pomazansky, Michael. *Orthodox Dogmatic Theology*. Trans. Seraphim Rose. Platina: Saint Herman Press, 2009.

Damascus, John. *An Exact Exposition of the Orthodox Faith*. Trans. E.W. Watson and L. Pullan. From *Nicene and Post-Nicene Fathers*, Second Series, Vol. 9. Ed. Philip Schaff and Henry Wace. Buffalo, NY: Christian Literature Publishing Co., 1899.

Ware, Timothy. *The Orthodox Church.* New York: Penguin Books, 1993.

Anglican Systematic Theologies

Bray, Gerald. *Gove is Love.* Wheaton: Crossway, 2012.

Brown, David. *God and Mystery in Words.* New York: Oxford University Press, 2008.

-----------. *God and Grace of Body.* New York: Oxford University Press, 2007.

-----------. *God and Enchantment of Place.* New York: Oxford University Press, 2006.

-----------. *Tradition and Imagination.* New York: Oxford University Press, 2004.

-----------. *Discipleship and Imagination.* New York: Oxford University Press, 2004.

Coakley, Sarah. *God, Sexuality, and the Self.* 3 vols. New York: Cambridge University Press. 2013

Ford, David. *The Modern Theologians: An Introduction to Christian Theology Since 1918.* Oxford: Wiley-Blackwell, 2005.

McGrath, Alistair. *Christian Theology.* Oxford: Wiley-Blackwell, 2010.

Mcquarrie, John. *Principles of Christian Theology.* New York: Pearson, 1977.

Packer, J. I. *Concise Theology.* Carol Stream: Tyndale House, 2001.

Thomas, Owen, and Ellen Wondra. *Introduction to Theology.* New York: Morehouse, 2002.

Thiselton, Anthony. *Systematic Theology.* Grand Rapids: Eerdmans, 2015.

Reformed/Puritan Systematic Theologies

à Brakel, Wilhelmus. *The Christian's Reasonable Service.* Trans. Joel Beeke. 4 Vols. Grand Rapids: Reformation Heritage Books, 1999.

Barret, Matthew, ed. *Reformation Theology: A Systematic Summary.* Wheaton: Crossway, 2017.

Barth, Karl. *Church Dogmatics.* 14 Vols. Peabody: Hendrickson, 2010.

Bavinck, Herman. *Reformed Dogmatics.* 4 Vols. Trans. John Vriend. Grand Rapids: Baker, 2008.

-----------. *Our Reasonable Faith.* Trans. Henry Zylstra. Grand Rapids: Eerdmans, 1956.

Beeke, Joel, and Mark Jones. *A Puritan Theology.* Grand Rapids: Reformation Heritage Books, 2012.

-----------, and Paul Smalley. *A Reformed Systematic Theology.* Wheaton: Crossway, 2019-.

Berkhof, Hendrikus. *Christian Faith.* Trans. Sierd Woudstra. Grand Rapids: Eerdmans, 1979.

Berkhof, Louis. *Systematic Theology.* Grand Rapids: Eerdmans, 1996.

Berkouwer, Gerrit C. *Studies in Dogmatics* (series). Grand Rapids: Eerdmans, 1952-1955.

Boettner, Loraine. *Studies in Theology.* Phillipsburg: Presbyterian and Reformed, 1974.

Boice, James. *Foundations of the Christian Faith.* Downers Grove: InterVarsity, 1986.

Dabney, Robert. *Systematic Theology.* Carlisle: Banner of Truth, 1985.

Brunner, Emil. *Dogmatics.* Philadelphia: Westminster Press, 1950-79.

Frame, John. *Systematic Theology.* Phillipsburg: Presbyterian and Reformed, 2013.

-----------. *Theology of Lordship* (series). 4 Vols. Phillipsburg: Presbyterian and Reformed, 1987-2010.

Gamble, Richard. *The Whole Counsel of God*. 3 Vols. Phillipsburg: Presbyterian and Reformed. 2009—.

Gerrish, Brian. *Christian Faith: Dogmatics in Outline*. Louisville: Westminster John Knox, 2015.

Heppe, Heinrich. *Reformed Dogmatics*. Grand Rapids: Baker Book House, 1978.

Hoeksema, Herman. *Reformed Dogmatics*. 2 Vols. Jenison: Reformed Free Publishing Association, 2005.

Hodge, Archibald A. *Outlines of Theology*. New York: R. Carter & Brothers, 1860.

Hodge, Charles. *Systematic Theology*. 3 Vols. Peabody: Hendrickson, 1999.

Horton, Michael. *The Christian Faith*. Grand Rapids: Zondervan, 2011.

-----------. *Pilgrim Theology*. Grand Rapids: Zondervan, 2013.

Kelly, Douglas. *Systematic Theology*. 3 Vols. Fearn: Mentor. 2008—.

Kuyper, Abraham. *Principles of Sacred Theology*. Grand Rapids: Eerdmans, 1954.

Moltmann, Jürgen. *God and Creation*. Minneapolis: Fortress Press, 1993.

-----------. *The Church in the Power of the Spirit*. Minneapolis: Fortress Press, 1993.

-----------. *The Crucified God*. Minneapolis: Fortress Press, 1993.

-----------. *The Trinity and the Kingdom*. Minneapolis: Fortress Press, 1993.

-----------. *Theology of Hope*. Minneapolis: Fortress Press, 1993.

-----------. *The Way Jesus Christ*. Minneapolis: Fortress Press, 1995.

Reymond, Robert. *A New Systematic Theology of the Christian Faith*. Nashville: Thomas Nelson. 1998.

Shedd, William. *Dogmatic Theology*. Phillipsburg: Presbyterian and Reformed, 2003.

Smith, Morton. *Systematic Theology*. Taylors: Greenville Seminary Press, 1994.

Turretin, Francis. *Institutes of Elenctic Theology*. Trans. George Giger. 3 Vols. Phillipsburg: Presbyterian and Reformed. 1997.

Vos, Geerhardus. Ed. Richard Gaffin. *Reformed Dogmatics*. 5 Vols. Bellingham: Lexham Press. 2014-2015.

Webber, Otto. *Foundations of Dogmatics*. Grand Rapids: Eerdmans, 1981–1983.

Zaspel, Fred. *The Theology of B.B. Warfield: A Systematic Summary*. Wheaton: Crossway, 2010.

Lutheran Systematic Theologies

Braaten, Carl. *Principles of Lutheran Theology*. Minneapolis: Augsburg Fortress Press, 2006.

Forell, George W. *The Protestant Faith*. Philadelphia: Fortress Press, 1975.

Gerhard, Johann. *Theological Commonplaces*. 17 Vols. St. Louis: Concordia Publishing. 2007—.

Hanson, Bradley. *Introduction to Christian Theology*. Minneapolis: Fortress Press, 1997.

Jacobs, Henry. *A Summary of the Christian Faith*. Watseka: Just and Sinner Publications, 2014.

Jenson, Robert. *Systematic Theology*. 2 Vols. New York: Oxford University Press. 2001.

----------. *Theology in Outline: Can These Bones Live?* New York: Oxford University Press, 2016.

Koehler, Edward. *A Summary of Christian Doctrine*. St. Louis: Concordia Publishing, 2006.

Kolb, Robert. *The Christian Faith*. Concordia Publishing, 1993.

Mueller, John. *Christian Dogmatics*. St. Louis: Concordia Publishing, 2003.

Pannenberg, Wolfhart. *Systematic Theology.* 4 Vols. Grand Rapids: Eerdmans, 2010.

Peters, Ted. *God—the World's Future: Systematic Theology for a New Era.* Minneapolis: Fortress Press, 2015.

Pieper, F. *Christian Dogmatics.* 4 Vols. St. Louis: Concordia Publishing. 2003.

Schwartz, Hans. *Creation.* Grand Rapids: Eerdmans, 2002.

----------. *The Human Being.* Grand Rapids: Eerdmans, 2013.

----------. *Christology.* Grand Rapids: Eerdmans, 1998.

----------. *Eschatology.* Grand Rapids: Eerdmans, 2000.

----------. *Theology in a Global Context.* Grand Rapids: Eerdmans, 2005.

----------. *The Christian Faith: A Creedal Account.* Grand Rapids: Baker Academic, 2014.

Weidner, Revere. *An Introduction to Dogmatic Theology.* Watseka: Just and Sinner Publications, 2014.

----------. *Ecclesiologia.* Watseka: Just and Sinner Publications, 2014.

----------. *Theologia.* Watseka: Just and Sinner Publications, 2014.

Voigt, A. Ed. Jordan Cooper. *Biblical Dogmatics: A Study of Evangelical Lutheran Theology.* 3 Vols. Watseka: Just and Sinner Publications, 2013.

Broadly Protestant, Reformed, and/or "Evangelical" Systematic Theologies

Barth, Karl. *Evangelical Theology.* Grand Rapids: Eerdmans, 1992.

Becker, Matthew. *Fundamental Theology: A Protestant Perspective.* New York: Bloomsbury T&T Clark, 2015.

Bird, Michael. *Evangelical Theology.* Grand Rapids: Zondervan, 2013.

Bloesch, Donald. *Essentials of Evangelical Theology.* Abridged in 1 Volume. Peabody: Hendrickson, 2006.

Burrows, Millar. *An Outline of Biblical Theology.* Philadelphia: Westminster Press, 1946.

Garrett, James Leo. *Systematic Theology: Biblical, Historical, and Evangelical.* 2 Vols. 4th ed. Eugene: Wipf and Stock, 2014.

Guthrie, Shirley. *Christian Doctrine.* Louisville: Westminster John Knox, 1994.

Hall, Douglas John. *Thinking the Faith.* Minneapolis: Fortress Press. 1989.

----------. *Professing the Faith.* Minneapolis: Fortress Press. 1993.

----------. *Confessing the Faith.* Minneapolis: Fortress Press. 1996.

Jewett, Paul. *God, Creation, and Revelation.* Grand Rapids: Eerdmans, 1991.

Jones, Beth. *Practicing Christian Doctrine: An Introduction to Thinking and Living Theologically.* Grand Rapids: Baker Academic, 2014.

Migliore, Daniel. *Faith Seeking Understanding: An Introduction to Christian Theology.* Grand Rapids: Eerdmans, 2014.

McClendon, James. *Systematic Theology.* 3 Vols. Waco: Baylor University Press, 2012.

Olson, Roger. *The Christian Belief Mosaic.* Downers Grove: InterVarsity, 2016.

Placher, William, ed. *Essentials of Christian Theology.* Nashville: Westminster John Knox, 2003.

Plantinga, Richard, Thomas Thompson and Matthew Lundberg. *An Introduction to Christian Theology.* New York: Cambridge University Press, 2010.

Torrance, T. F. *The Trinitarian Faith.* New York: T&T Clark, 2000.

Thielicke, Helmut. *The Evangelical Faith.* 3 Vols. Trans. Geoffrey W. Bromiley. Grand Rapids: Eerdmans.

Thistelton, Anthony. *Systematic Theology.* Grand Rapids: Eerdmans, 2015.

Wilfried, Härle. *Outline of Christian Doctrine.* Trans. Nicholas Sagovsky and Ruth Yule. Grand Rapids: Eerdmans, 2015.

Von Zahn, Theodore. *The Christian Faith.* 2 Vols. New York: Hodder and Stoughton, 1913.

Fundamentalist Baptist/Evangelical Systematic Theologies

Akin, Daniel, ed.. *A Theology for the Church.* Nashville: Broadman and Holman, 2014.

Bob Venture, ed. *Systematic Theology.* Vestavia Hills: Solid Ground Christian Books.

Bankroft, Emery, and Ronald Mayers. *Elemental Theology.* Grand Rapids: Kregel Academic, 1996.

Buswell, J. Oliver. *Systematic Theology of the Christian Religion.* Grand Rapids: Zondervan, 1962.

Culver, Robert. *Systematic Theology.* Fearn: Mentor, 2005.

Demarest, Bruce and Gordon Lewis. *Integrative Theology.* Grand Rapids: Zondervan, 2014.

Erickson, Millard. *Christian Theology.* Grand Rapids: Baker Academic, 2013.

-----------. *Introducing Christian Doctrine.* Grand Rapids: Baker Academic, 2001.

Geisler, Norman. *Systematic Theology.* Minneapolis: Bethany House, 2011.

Grudem, Wayne. *Bible Doctrine.* Grand Rapids: Zondervan, 2000.

-----------.*Systematic Theology.* Grand Rapids: Zondervan, 1999.

Gulley, Norman. *Systematic Theology.* 3 Vols. Grand Rapids: Berrian Springs, 2003-2012.

Lindsell, Harold and Charles J. Woodbridge. *A Handbook of Christian Truth.* Westwood: F.H. Revell Co., 1953.

Strong, Augustus. *Systematic Theology.* Philadelphia: American Baptist Publication Society. 1907.

Dispensational Fundamentalist Baptist/Evangelical Systematic Theologies

Baker, Charles. *A Dispensational Theology.* Grand Rapids: Grace Publications, 1971.

Chafer, Lewis. *Systematic Theology.* Grand Rapids: Kregel Academic, 1993.

Enns, Paul. *Moody Handbook of Theology.* Chicago: Moody Press, 2008.

Lightner, Robert. *Evangelical Theology.* Grand Rapids: Baker, 1986.

MacArthur, John, and Richard Mayhue, eds. *Biblical Doctrine.* Wheaton: Crossway, 2017.

McCune, Rolland. *Systematic Theology Biblical Christianity.* Detroit: Detroit Baptist Theological Seminary, 2009.

Ryrie, Charles. *A Survey of Bible Doctrine.* Chicago: Moody Press, 1989.

-----------. *Basic Theology.* Chicago: Moody Press, 1999.

Swindoll, Chuck, and Roy Zuck, eds. *Understanding Christian Theology.* Nashville: Thomas Nelson, 2003.

Svigel, Michael and Nathan Holsteen. *Exploring Christian Theology.* 3 vols. Minneapolis: Bethany House, 2014-2015.

Torrey, R. A. *Fundamental Doctrines of the Christian Faith.* New York: George Doran, 1918.

Thiessen, Henry. *Lectures in Systematic Theology.* Grand Rapid: Eerdmans, 2006.

Pentecostal/Charismatic Systematic Theologies

Horton, Stanley. *Systematic Theology*. Springfield: Gospel Publishing House, 1994.

Menzies, William and Stanley Horton. *Bible Doctrines: A Pentecostal Perspective*. Springfield: Logion Press, 1993.

Kärkkäinen, VeliMatti. *Christology*. Grand Rapids: Baker Academic, 2003.

-----------. *Ecclesiology*. Downers Grove: InterVarsity, 2002.

-----------. *Pneumatology*. Grand Rapids: Baker Academic, 2002.

-----------. *The Doctrine of God*. Grand Rapids: Baker Academic, 2004.

Williams, Ernest S. *Systematic Theology*. Springfield: Gospel Publishing House, 1953.

Williams, J. *Renewal Theology*. 3 Vols. Grand Rapids: Zondervan, 1996.

Yong, Amos, and Jonathan Anderson. *Renewing Christian Theology*. Waco: Baylor University Press, 2014.

Wesleyan/Nazarene Systematic Theologies

Wiley, H. *Systematic Theology*. 3 Vols. Kansas City: Beacon Hill Press. 1940-1943.

Carter, Charles, ed. *A Contemporary Wesleyan Theology: Biblical, Systematic, and Practical*. 3 vols. Grand Rapids: Zondervan, 1983.

Dunning, H. *Grace, Faith, and Holiness*. Kansas City: Beacon Hill Press, 1988.

Grider, J. *A Wesleyan-Holiness Theology*. Kansas City: Beacon Hill Press, 1994.

Greathouse, William and H. Dunning. *An Introduction to Wesleyan Theology*. Kansas City: Beacon Hill Press, 1989.

Purkiser, W.T. Richard S. Taylor, Willard H. Taylor. *God, Man, and Salvation*. Kansas City: Beacon Hill Press, 1977.

Wynkoop, Mildred. *Foundations of Wesleyan-Arminian Theology*. Kansas City: Beacon Hill Press, 1972.

Methodist Systematic Theologies

Buchanan, Charles. *The Gospel for the New Age*. Nashville: Cokesbury Press, 1925.

Oden, Thomas. *Systematic Theology*. 3 Vols. New York: HarperOne. 2006.

Ogden, Schubert. *Understanding the Christian Faith*. Eugene: Wipf and Stock, 2010.

DeWolf, L. Harold. *A Theology of the Living Church*. New York: Harper, 1960.

Gonzalez, Justo. *An Introduction to Christian Theology*. Nashville: Abingdon Press, 2002.

Lawson, John. *Introduction to Christian Doctrine*. Wilmore: Asbury Pub. Co., 1980.

Pardington, George. *Outlines Studies in Christian Doctrine*. Harrisburg: Christian Alliance Publishing Co., 1926.

Miley, John. *Systematic Theology*. New York: Hunt and Eaton, 1892-1894.

Other Notable Systematic Theologies

Evans, James and Stephen Ray. *We Have Been Believers: An African American Systematic Theology*. Minneapolis: Fortress Press, 2012.

Finney, Charles. Ed. L. Parkhurst. *Systematic Theology*. Minneapolis: Bethany House, 1994. (1878)

Inbody, Tyron. *The Faith of the Christian Church: An Introduction to Theology*. Grand Rapids: Eerdmans, 2005.

Lacugna, Catherine. *Freeing Theology: Essentials of Theology in Feminist Perspective*. San Francisco: Harper San Francisco, 1993.

Largen, Kristin. *Finding God Among Our Neighbors: An InterFaith Systematic Theology*. Minneapolis: Fortress Press, 2013.

Tillich, Paul. *Systematic Theology*. 3 Vols. Chicago: University of Chicago Press. 1951-1963.

Global Systematic Theologies
Kärkkäinen, VeliMatti. *Christ and Reconciliation*. Grand Rapids: Eerdmans, 2013.
----------. *Trinity and Revelation*. Grand Rapids: Eerdmans, 2014.
----------. *Creation and Humanity*. Grand Rapids: Eerdmans, 2015.
----------. *Spirit and Salvation*. Grand Rapids: Eerdmans, 2016.
----------. *Hope and Community*. Grand Rapids: Eerdmans, 2017.

On Global Theology
Bevans, Stephen. *An Introduction to Theology in Global Perspective*. Marynoll: Orbisbooks, 2009.
Tennet, Timothy. *Theology in the Context of World Christianity*. Grand Rapids: Zondervan, 2013.

[Other sections of syllabus redacted because of irrelevance]

VIII. JWC Course Schedule

30-Session Format (Gathers Twice Per Week)

	Topic	Assignments
1.	Introductions, Syllabus Review	Read Bird, 1.1-1.4
2.	Intro to Theology I: What is Theology?	Read Migliore ch 1
3.	Intro to Theology II: What is Theology?	Read Bird 1.5-1.8
4.	How to Do Theology I: Sources, Approach	Read Migliore ch 3
5.	How to Do Theology II: The Bible and Theology	Goldingay, ch 1 ("Introduction: Scripture's Varied Forms"); Wright, *Scripture and Authority of God* (Intro); Hays and Ellen, "Nine Theses."
6.	How to Do Theology III: The Bible and Theology II	Read Oden ch 8
7.	How to Do Theology IV	**Study for Test 1**
8.	**Test 1**	Read Bird 2.1-2.2
9.	The Trinity I	Read Migliore ch 4a; Oden ch 5
10.	The Trinity II	Read Bird 2.3
11.	The Nature of God I	Read Migliore ch 4b; Oden ch 1
12.	The Nature of God II	Read Oden ch 2-3
13.	The Nature of God III	**Study for Test 2**
14.	**Test 2**	Read Bird 2.4
15.	Creation I	Read Migliore ch 5
16.	Creation II	Read Oden ch 6
17.	Creation III	Read Bird 2.5
18.	Revelation I	Read Migliore ch 2
19.	Revelation II	Read Oden ch 4
20.	Revelation III	Read Bird 2.6
21.	God's Purpose and Plan I	Read Migliore ch 4c
22.	God's Purpose and Plan II	Read Oden ch 7
23.	God's Purpose and Plan III	**Study for Test 3**
24.	**Test 3**	Read Bird 7.1-7.3; Migliore ch 7a
25.	Theological Anthropology	Read Bird 7.4; Migliore ch 7b
26.	Sin, Death and Evil I	Read Bird 7.5; Migliore ch 6
27.	Sin, Death and Evil II	Reading Break
28.	Reading Break (no class)	**Study for Test 4**

29.	Exam Week: Test 4
30.	

Appendix H:

Syllabus for CHR207

Introduction to Christian Apologetics

I.   **General Information**

Instructor:	Jamin Hübner	Email:	jhubner@jwc.edu
Office Hours:	Mon-Thurs, 1:30-4:30pm	Office	JWC Annex
Mobile Phone:	[...]		
Semester:	Spring 2018	Schedule: Tues/Th, 8:30-9:45am	
Credits:	3	Location: Evans Hall, Caritas	

II.   **Course Description**

A survey of both apologetic methodologies and various arguments used to support the credibility of the Christian world-and-life view.

III.   **Course Objectives and Learning Outcomes**

The students who successfully complete this course will—whenever encountering ideas or arguments in the various situations of life—be able to competently:

1. Identify and understand the nature of Christian beliefs and truth claims.
2. Identify and understand the nature of popular objections to the Christian faith.
3. Recognize the various methodologies of Christian apologetics.
4. Identify and distinguish poor arguments from good arguments for/against Christianity.
5. Recognize the key debates surrounding the controversial claims of Christianity.

These course objectives and outcomes require critical thinking, which is one of JWC's institutional objectives.

IV.   **Course Professor**

Dr. Jamin Hübner is a entrepreneur, musician, and theologian from South Dakota. He is a graduate of Dordt College (BA Theology), Reformed Theological Seminary (MA Religion) and the University of South Africa (ThD Systematic Theology), and the Southern New Hampshire University (MS Economics) and currently serves as the Director of Institutional Effectiveness, founding Chair of

Christian Studies, and part-time Professor of Economics at John Witherspoon College.

V. Prerequisites

None.

VI. Required Texts/Resources

Cowan, Stephen B., ed. *Five Views on Apologetics*. Grand Rapids: Zondervan, 2000. "Introduction."
(**Note**: *this chapter will be provided to you by the professor; no need to purchase the book!*)
McGrath, Alister. *Mere Apologetics*. Grand Rapids: Baker, 2012.
Grenz, Stanley. *A Primer on Postmodernism*. Grand Rapids: Eerdmans, 1996.
Wilkins, Steve, and Mark Sanford. *Hidden Worldviews*. Downers Grove: InterVarsity, 2009.

VII. Optional Texts/Resources

Apologetics in History
Dulles, Avery. *A History of Apologetics*. San Francisco: Ignatius, 2005.
Edgar, William and Oliphint, K. Scott, eds. *Christian Apologetics Past and Present: A Primary Source Reader*. 2 Vols. Wheaton, IL: Crossway, 2009 and 2011.

Apologetic Methodology and Introductions
Beilby, James. *Thinking About Christian Apologetics*. Downers Grove: InterVarsity, 2011.
Clark, David K. *Dialogical Apologetics: A Person-Centered Approach to Christian Defense*. Grand Rapids: Baker, 1993.
Cowan, Steven B, ed. *Five Views on Apologetics*. Counterpoints Series, edited by Stanley N. Gundry. Grand Rapids: Zondervan, 2000.
Davison, Andrew. *Imaginative Apologetics: Theology, Philosophy and the Catholic Tradition*. Grand Rapids: Baker Academic, 2012.
Frame, John. *Apologetics: A Justification of Christian Belief*. Phillipsburg: Presbyterian and Reformed. 2015.
Koukl, Gregory. *Tactics: A Game Plan for Discussing Your Christian Convictions*. Grand Rapids: Zondervan, 2009.
McGrath, Alister. *Mere Apologetics*. Grand Rapids: Baker, 2012.
Ramm, Bernard. *Varieties of Apologetics*. Grand Rapids: Baker, 1961.
Sinkinson, Chris. *Christian Confidence: An Introduction to Defending the Faith*. Downers Grove: InterVarsity, 2012.
Sire, James W. *A Little Primer on Humble Apologetics*. Downers Grove: InterVarsity, 1996.
Stackhouse, John G. *Humble Apologetics: Defending the Faith Today*. Oxford: Oxford University Press, 2002.

Historical Jesus and Christian Origins
Bauckham, Richard. *Jesus and the Eye Witnesses: The Gospels as Eyewitness Testimony*. 2nd ed. Grand Rapids: Eerdmans, 2017.
--------. *The Jewish World Around the New Testament*. Grand Rapids: Baker Academic, 2010.

---------. *The Christian World Around the New Testament*. Grand Rapids: Baker Academic, 2017.

Bird, Michael. *The Gospel of the Lord: How the Early Church Wrote the Gospels*. Grand Rapids: Eerdmans, 2014.

---------. *Jesus the Eternal Son: Answering Adoptionist Christology*. Grand Rapids: Eerdmans, 2017.

-------- and James Crossley. *How Did Christianity Begin?: A Believer and Non-Believer Examine the Evidence*. Grand Rapids: Baker Academic, 2008.

Boyd, Greg, and Paul Eddy. *The Jesus Legend*. Grand Rapids: Baker Academic, 2007.

Dunn, James. *Christianity in the Making*, 3 volumes: *Jesus Remembered* (2003); *Beginning From Jerusalem* (2008); *Neither Jew Nor Greek* (2015). Grand Rapids: Eerdmans.

Evans, Craig A. *Fabricating Jesus: How Modern Scholars Distort the Gospels*. Downers Grove, IL: InterVarsity, 2006.

Hurtado, Larry. *Destroyed of the Gods. Early Christian Distinctiveness in the Roman World*. Waco: Baylor University Press, 2016.

------. *The Lord Jesus Christ: Devotion to Jesus in Early Christianity*. Grand Rapids: Eerdmans, 2005.

Licona, Michael. *The Resurrection of Jesus*. Downers Grove: InterVarsity, 2010.

Keener, Craig. *The Historical Jesus of the Gospels*. Grand Rapids: Eerdmans, 2012.

Wright, N. T. *Christian Origins and the Question of God*: *The New Testament and the People of God* (1992); *Jesus and the Victory of God* (1996); *The Resurrection and the Son of God* (2003); *Paul and the Faithfulness of God* (2013). Minneapolis: Fortress Press.

------ and Michael Bird. *The New Testament in Its World*. Grand Rapids: Zondervan Academic, 2019.

World Religions and Pluralism

Hexham, Irving. *Understanding World Religions: An Interdisciplinary Approach*. Grand Rapids: Zondervan, 2011.

Metzger, Paul. *Connecting Christ: How to Discuss Jesus in a World of Diverse Paths*. Nashville: Thomas Nelson, 2012.

Much, Terry, Netland, Harold, and McDermott, Gerald, eds. *Handbook of Religion: A Christian Engagement with Traditions, Teachings, and Practices*. Grand Rapids: Baker Academic, 2014.

Newbigin, Leslie. *The Gospel in a Pluralist Society*. Grand Rapids: Eerdmans, 1989.

Placher, William. *Unapologetic Theology: A Christian Voice in a Pluralistic Conversation*. Louisville: Westminster John Knox Press, 1989.

Strange, Daniel. *Their Rock is Not Like Our Rock: A Theology of Religions*. Grand Rapids: Zondervan, 2015.

Tennet, Timothy C. *Christianity at the Religious Roundtable: Evangelicalism in Conversation With Hinduism, Buddhism, and Islam*. Grand Rapids: Baker, 2001.

Kärkkäinen, Veli-Matti. *An Introduction to the Theology of Religions*. Downers Grove: InterVarsity Press, 2003.

Post-Modernity and Christianity

Greer, Robert. *Mapping Postmodernity: A Survey of Christian Options*. Downers Grove: InterVarsity, 2003.

Grenz, Stanley. *A Primer on Postmodernism*. Grand Rapids: Eerdmans, 1996.

Middleton, J. Richard and Walsh, Brian. *Truth is Stranger Than it Used to Be*. Downers Grove: InterVarsity, 1995.

Newbigin, Leslie. *Proper Confidence: Faith, Doubt, and Certainty in Christian Discipleship.* Grand Rapids: Eerdmans, 1995.

Penner, Myron. *The End of Apologetics: Christian Witness in a Postmodern Context.* Grand Rapids: Baker Academic, 2013.

Penner, Myron, ed. *Christianity and the Postmodern Turn: Six Views.* Grand Rapids: Brazos Press, 2005.

Phillips, Timothy and Okholm, Dennis, eds. *Christian Apologetics in the Postmodern World.* Downers Grove: InterVarsity, 1995.

Raschke, Carl. *The Next Reformation: Why Evangelicals Must Embrace Postmodernity.* Grand Rapids: Baker Academic, 2004.

Smith, James. *Who's Afraid of Postmodernism?: Taking Derrida, Lyotard, and Foucault to Church.* Grand Rapids: Baker Academic, 2006.

--------. *Who's Afraid of Relativism?* Grand Rapids: Baker Academic, 2014.

Classical Apologetics

Craig, William Lane. *Reasonable Faith: Christian Truth and Apologetics.* Wheaton: Crossway, 1994.

--------. *On Guard.* Colorado Springs: David C. Cook, 2010.

Sproul, R. C. *Defending Your Faith: An Introduction to Apologetics.* Wheaton: Crossway, 2003.

Sproul, R. C. Gerstner, John, and Lindsey, Arthur. *Classical Apologetics: A Rational Defense of the Christian Faith and a Critique of Presuppositional Apologetics.* Grand Rapids: Zondervan, 1984.

Presuppositional Apologetics

Bahnsen, Greg. *Van Til's Apologetic.* Philadelphia: Presbyterian & Reformed 2003.

--------. *Presuppositional Apologetics.* Nacogdoches: Covenant Media Press, 2011.

--------. *Always Ready.* Nacogdoches: Covenant Media Press, 1996.

Hübner, Jamin. ed. *The Portable Presuppositionalist.* 3rd ed. Rapid City: Hills Publishing Group, 2014.

Frame, John. *Apologetics: A Justification of Christian Belief.* Wheaton: Crossway, 2015.

Oliphint, K. Scott. *Covenantal Apologetics.* Wheaton: Crossway, 2013.

Van Til, Cornelius. *Defense of the Faith.* Ed. by K. Scott Oliphint. Philadelphia: Presbyterian & Reformed, 2008.

--------. *Christian Apologetics.* Ed. William Edgar. Philadelphia: Presbyterian & Reformed 2003.

Cumulative Cases for Christianity (Large and Small)

Groothuis, Douglas. *Christian Apologetics.* Downers Grove: InterVarsity, 2011.

Beckwith, Francis, Moreland, J. P., Craig, William, eds. *To Everyone an Answer.* Downers Grove: InterVarsity, 2004.

Keller, Timothy. *The Reason for God: Belief in an Age of Skepticism.* New York: Dutton/Penguin, 2008.

Moreland, J. P., Sweis, Khaldoun, and Meister, Chad, eds. *Debating Christian Theism.* New York: Oxford University Press, 2013.

Lewis, C. S. *Mere Christianity.* New York: Macmillan, 1943.

Moreland, J. P. and Craig, William Lane. *Philosophical Foundations for a Christian Worldview.* Downers Grove: InterVarsity, 2017.

Strobel, Lee. *A Case for a Creator.* Grand Rapids: Zondervan, 2004.

--------. *The Case for Christ.* Nashville: Thomas Nelson, 2013.

--------. *The Case for Grace*. Grand Rapids: Zondervan, 2015.

--------. *The Case for Faith*. Grand Rapids: Zondervan, 2014.

--------. *The Case for the Resurrection*. Grand Rapids: Zondervan, 2010.

--------. *The Case for Christianity Answer Book*. Nashville: Thomas Nelson, 2014.

Existence of God and Atheism

Andrews, Edgar. *Who Made God?: Searching for a Theory of Everything*. Carlisle: EP Books, 2012.

Berlinski, David. *The Devil's Delusion: Atheism and Its Scientific Pretentions*. New York: Basic Books, 2009.

Dembski, William A. *The Design Inference: Eliminating Chance Through Small Probabilities*. Cambridge: Cambridge University Press, 1998.

Evans, C. Stephen. *Natural Signs and Knowledge of God: A New Look at Theistic Arguments*. New York: Oxford University Press, 2012.

Gonzalez, Guillermo and Richards, Jay W. *The Privileged Planet*. Washington, D. C.: Regnery, 2004.

Hart, David. *Atheist Delusions: The Christian Revolution and Its Fashionable Enemies*. New Haven: Yale University Press, 2010.

-------. *The Experience of God*. New Haven: Yale University Press, 2014.

McGrath, Alister E. *Intellectuals Don't Need God and Other Modern Myths: Building Bridges to Faith Through Apologetics*. Grand Rapids: Zondervan, 1993.

Meyer, Stephen. *The Return of the God Hypothesis*. New York: HarperOne, 2020.

Schumacher, Lydia. *Theological Philosophy: Rethinking the Rationality of Christian Faith*. New York: Routledge, 2018.

Smith, Christian. *Atheist Overreach*. New York: Oxford University Press, 2018.

Reliability of the Old Testament

Berman, Joshua. *Inconsistency in the Torah: Ancient Literary Convention and the Limits of Source Criticism*. New York: Oxford University Press, 2017.

Block, Daniel. *Israel: Ancient Kingdom or Late Invention?* Nashville: Broadman and Holman, 2008.

Dever, William. *Beyond Texts: An Archeological Portrait of Ancient Israel and Judah*. Atlanta: SBL Press, 2017.

Friedman, Richard Elliott. *The Exodus*. New York: HarperOne, 2017.

Hess, Richard. *Israelite Religions: An Archeological and Biblical Survey*. Grand Rapids: Baker Academic, 2007.

--------, and Bill Arnold, eds. *Ancient Israel's History: An Introduction to Issues and Sources*. Grand Rapids: Baker Academic, 2014.

Hoffmeier, James. *Ancient Israel in Sinai: The Evidence for the Authenticity of the Wilderness Tradition*. New York: Oxford University Press, 2011.

Kitchen, K. A. *On the Reliability of the Old Testament*. Grand Rapids: Eerdmans, 2003.

Reliability of the New Testament

Bird, Michael. *The Gospel of the Lord: How the Early Church Wrote the Story of Jesus*. Grand Rapids: Eerdmans, 2014.

Blomberg, Craig. *The Historical Reliability of the New Testament: Countering the Challenges to Evangelical Christian Belief*. Nashville: B & H, 2016.

Keener, Craig. *Miracles: The Credibility of the New Testament Accounts*. Grand Rapids: Baker Academic, 2011.

----------. *Christobiography: Memory, History, and the Reliability of the Gospels.* Grand Rapids: Eerdmans, 2019.

Licona, Michael. *Why Are There Differences in the Gospels?: What We Can Learn from Ancient Biography.* New York: Oxford University Press, 2016.

David K. Pettegrew, William R. Caraher, and Thomas W. Davis, eds. *The Oxford Handbook of Early Christian Archaeology.* New York: Oxford University Press, 2019.

Wallace, Daniel. *Revisiting the Corruption of the New Testament.* Grand Rapids: Kregel, 2010.

Mormonism, Watchtower Society/Jehovah's Witnesses

Gruss, Edmond. *Jehovah's Witnesses: Their Claims, Doctrinal Changes, and Prophetic Speculation. What Does the Record Show?* Xulon Press, 2001.

Johnson, Eric, and McKeever, Bill. *Mormonism 101.* Grand Rapids: Baker, 2015.

Rhodes, Ron. *Reasoning from the Scriptures with Jehovah's Witnesses.* Eugene: Harvest House Publishers, 2009.

Problem of Evil and Suffering

Adams, Marilyn McCord, *Horrendous Evils and the Goodness of God. Cornell Studies in the Philosophy of Religion.* Ithaca, NY: Cornell University Press, 2000.

Blocher, Henri. *Evil and the Cross.* Trans., David G. Preston. Downers Grove: InterVarsity, 1994.

Feinberg, John. *The Many Faces of Evil: Theological Systems and the Problem of Evil.* Rev ed. Wheaton: Crossway, 2004. Originally published by Zondervan, 1994.

Hart, David. *The Doors of the Sea.* Grand Rapids: Eerdmans, 2011.

Hick, John. *Evil and the God of Love.* New York: Harper & Row, 1966.

Lewis, C. S. *The Problem of Pain.* New York: Macmillan, 1962.

Markham, Ian. *Understanding Christian Doctrine.* 2nd ed. London: Wiley-Blackwell, 2017.

Murray, Michael. *Nature Red in Tooth and Claw: Theism and the Problem of Animal Suffering.* New York: Oxford, 2011.

Soelle, Dorothy. *The Silent Cry.* Minneapolis: Fortress Press, 2001.

Sollereder, Bethany. *God, Evolution, and Animal Suffering: Theodicy Without a Fall.* New York: Routledge, 2018.

Stackhouse, John. *Can God Be Trusted? Faith and the Challenge of Evil.* New York: Oxford, 1998.

Swinburne, Richard. *Providence and the Problem of Evil.* New York: Oxford, 1998.

van Inwagen, Peter. *The Problem of Evil.* New York: Oxford University Press, 2008.

Wolterstorff, Nicholas. *Lament For a Son.* Grand Rapids: Eerdmans, 1987.

Wright, N. T. *Evil and the Justice of God.* Downers Grove, IL: InterVarsity, 2006.

[Other sections of syllabus redacted because of irrelevance]

VIII.   Course Schedule

All faculty have the right to alter the schedule at any time.

30-Session Format (Gathers Twice Per Week)

Topic	Assignments
Introduction; apologetics in scripture	Read McGrath ch 1

2.	What is apologetics?	Read Cowan, *Five Views* (Intro)
3.	Apologetics in history; methodology	Read McGrath ch 2
4.	Apologetics in contemporary culture	Read McGrath ch 3
5.	Theological Basis of apologetics	Read McGrath ch 4
6.	Importance of Audience	Read McGrath ch 5
7.	Reasonableness of Christianity	Read McGrath ch 6a
8.	Pointers to Faith I	Read McGrath ch 6b
9.	Pointers to Faith II	Read McGrath ch 7
10.	Gateways for Apologetics	Read McGrath ch 8-9
11.	Questions and Developing Approaches	**Study for Test 1**
12.	**Test 1**	Read *Hidden Worldviews*, ch 1-2
13.	Intro and Individualism	Read *Hidden Worldviews*, ch 3
14.	Consumerism	Read *Hidden Worldviews*, ch 4
15.	Nationalism	Read *Hidden Worldviews*, ch 5
16.	Moral Relativism	Read *Hidden Worldviews*, ch 6
17.	Scientific Naturalism	Read *Hidden Worldviews*, ch 7
18.	New Age	Read *Hidden Worldviews*, ch 8
19.	Postmodern Tribalism	Read *Hidden Worldviews*, ch 9
20.	Salvation by Therapy	Read *Hidden Worldviews*, ch 10-11
21.	Developing a Christian Worldview	**Study for Test 2**
22.	**Test 2**	Read Grenz, ch 1-2
23.	Post-modern Ethos	Read Grenz ch 3
24.	Post-modern ~~world~~ view	Read Grenz ch 4
25.	Modernism	Read Grenz ch 5
26.	Prelude to Postmodernism	Read Grenz ch 6
27.	Philosophers of Postmodernism	Read Grenz ch 7
28.	The Gospel and the Postmodern Context	
29.	**Exam Week: Test 3**	
30.		

BONUS Post-Script Appendix:

Healthy Heretic's Dairy-Free Pumpkin Pie

Ingredients[1]:
1. Unbaked pre-made (or homemade) pie crust
2. 3 large local organic eggs
3. ¾ cup of regular Silk™ or So Delicious™ coconut milk
4. ¾ cup of Silk™ or Oatley™ oat milk
5. Half-cup of organic cane sugar
6. Pinch of Himalayan sea salt (fine ground)
7. Pinch on the butt
8. 2 teaspoons of organic pumpkin pie spice
9. Earth Balance® European Style Buttery Spread (it's soy-free!)

Directions:
1. Use fork to liberally (like a flaming liberal) poke holes in crust to avoid bubbling.
2. Pre-bake crust in buttered pan at 400° F until light brown.
3. Now think about what you've just done.
4. Take out and let cool as you continue on to step…
5. Mix milk(s) and eggs in mixing bowl, preferably a nice one that you would normally (or at least on a not-bad day) enjoy mixing with—but don't mix *yourself* in (or into) the bowl, because you're not an ingredient, no matter how high and mighty you and your comrades may think of yourself. And

---

[1] The text that hereby follows is neither verbally inspired nor inerrant, whether in the original recipe autographs or in any family of authorized manuscript tradition. (And I am *quite* aware of the French chef's debate on the *vorlage*). As you will learn through experience, however, it is more than adequate—and borderline heavenly in the results. A word of caution is, still, nevertheless, advised: if in reading this text, you are tempted in any way to legitimize systematic violence, political loyalties that empower tyrannical dictators, or hatred against Jews, Palestinians, gays, spiders, dog-owners, anarchists, queer-folk, or anyone else, do not attempt to bake, now or later.

don't mix *your partner, spouse, or pet* in the bowl either, as tempting as it may be.

6. Add and mix other ingredients with a mini-wire-whisk, or a fork, but probably not a ball-whisk, because they actually don't work as good as one initially imagines them to work.

7. Carefully pour pumpkin mix onto the pie crust—and with a genuine smile, because you know just how happy you will be when eating this marvelous pie.

8. Convection bake (best in an electric oven) at 400° for 15 minutes, then 350° for the next 25-35 minutes. Double check using previously-obtained knowledge and intuitions (shake-jiggle test, fork-pull test, general observation, atomic-test, etc.) to ensure it's done. If you have no previous knowledge of knowing about how pies should feel, appear, perform, and emanate, then you're obviously on your own, and I'm truly sorry if it's come to this.

9. Remove from oven (with oven mitts, *not* softball mitts) and let cool for an hour.

10. Refrigerate for at least 8-12 hours.

11. Remove from fridge and prepare to slice.

12. Slice with pizza cutter or sharp knife as desired. (The 8-slice path is really just a social construct; it's not unethical to slice differently—keeping 1 Cor 10:23 in mind.)

13. After serving on appropriately-sized plates (again, 1 Cor 10:23), add two unrighteously-sized globs of So-Delicious™ Coco-Whip. (This is the best part, and yes, it is considerably superior to all other forms of dairy whips in taste, texture, and health. You'll thank me later!)

14. Eat while reading the forbidden books listed in the bibliographies of this forbidden book, next to a real fire. Consider drinking with coffee, tea, or single-malt scotch.

People are born soft and supple,
Dead, they are stiff and hard
Plants are born tender and pliant,
Dead, they are brittle and dry.

Thus, whoever is stiff and inflexible
Is a disciple of death.
Whoever is soft and yielding
Is a disciple of life.

The hard and stiff will be broken.
The soft and supple will prevail.

—LAO-TZU

Made in the USA
Columbia, SC
03 February 2020